Greening the Financial Sector

Doris Köhn
Editor

Greening the Financial Sector

How to Mainstream Environmental Finance in Developing Countries

Springer

Editor
Doris Köhn
Senior Vice President
Africa and Middle East
Palmengartenstr. 5-9
KfW Entwicklungsbank
60325 Frankfurt am Main
Germany
info@kfw-entwicklungsbank.de

ISBN 978-3-642-43180-7 ISBN 978-3-642-05087-9 (eBook)
DOI 10.1007/978-3-642-05087-9
Springer Heidelberg Dordrecht London New York

Softcover reprint of the hardcover 1st edition 2012

Printed on acid-free paper

Springer is part of Springer Science+Business Media (www.springer.com)

Foreword

In light of a growing number of extreme weather events in developing countries, it is becoming more and more evident that the most vulnerable people at the 'base of the pyramid' will also suffer most from climate change. Climate change is expected to put development successes in jeopardy and makes sustainable poverty alleviation more difficult. Hence, a strategy for adaptation to and mitigation of climate change is indispensable for sustainable development and poverty reduction in emerging and developing markets.

Ecological sustainability is also reflected in the Millennium Development Goals: Achieving MDG 7 aims at environmental protection as well as sustainable use of natural resources. I am deeply convinced that ecological sustainability is a major requirement for development and a crucial contribution to the fulfilment of the MDGs. The German Ministry for Economic Cooperation and Development (BMZ) has therefore introduced a 'climate check' to consider climate protection and adaptation aspects in strategies and programmes of German development cooperation. As industrial nations are important drivers of climate change, they bear a historic responsibility. However, global environmental problems cannot be solved without contributions from emerging and developing markets. Sustainable and globally effective solutions can only be achieved through extensive international cooperation and contributions by all stakeholders. Against this background, my ministry is committed to mainstreaming environmental finance in development finance.

In 2009 Germany allocated EUR 1 billion for climate protection and adaptation measures in developing countries. At the Copenhagen Summit the German government agreed to provide an additional EUR 420 million annually as part of the EU's fast-start climate funding until 2012.

Despite all these efforts, the public sector alone will not be able to handle an order of this magnitude and should, therefore, form strategic alliances with the private sector. Public and private finance should complement each other in order to provide an intelligent mix of financial instruments. In this context, the target is to raise an amount of USD 100 billion per year by 2020 for climate protection and adaptation measures from public and private sources.

How can these ambitious goals be achieved? I am convinced that the financial sector in developing and transition countries has an important role to play in this process. Environmental finance markets will need to be established and existing environmental finance instruments will need to be mainstreamed to ensure climate protection. Green finance is one of the answers to obtain the necessary financial resources required. Investing in energy efficiency, for instance, has had encouraging effects both in financial and ecological terms. The financial sector has the potential not only to complement scarce public resources, but also the know-how to combine public and private funds in an intelligent way. It is also important to me to note that financial markets are not only vital for the development of the overall economy – sometimes not a very popular argument in these times – but can also be important agents of sustainable development. In this sense financial systems development has been and will remain a very important development challenge as well. So why not try to address both challenges at the same time? Green finance tries to do exactly that.

KfW has already been very active in promoting environmental finance through the financial sector, particularly in the field of energy efficiency and renewable energy. I am grateful that these efforts have helped to mainstream green finance products into the "regular" product mix of financial institutions in our partner countries. After setting up a number of green finance projects in late 2008, KfW dedicated its annual financial sector symposium to environmental finance. At this high profile event, public and private sector representatives came together and discussed, inter alia, how to convince financial institutions that financing investments in climate protection is a promising new field of business. I appreciate that the KfW symposium on greening the financial sector has generated a number of contributions from international experts. I am glad that all these have been bundled together in this book which I am sure will be highly valuable for knowledge sharing and forming effective alliances and networks.

I would like to thank KfW for all its efforts to support the financial sectors in developing and transition countries to fight the impact of climate change. This engagement has contributed effectively to the efforts from public sources, and I hope it will do so in the future. Tapping the potential of the financial sector has become even more important in the light of public budget constraints after the financial crisis and is a powerful tool to address problems like climate change in a sustainable way.

July 2011

Dirk Niebel
German Federal Minister for
Economic Cooperation and Development

Preface

This book is part of a publication series initiated by KfW on selected topics in the field of financial systems development, which is one of the core competencies of KfW Development Bank. This edition will focus on environmental finance. It will cover a broad range of issues including programmes to promote energy efficiency and renewable energies as well as innovative approaches such as weather insurance.

Why is this topic important? Given the manifold deficits of financial sectors in developing and transition countries, one might be tempted to believe that embarking on "green" finance is not a priority for financial systems development.

However, I don't share this view. Environmental finance can and should serve as an interface to other sub-sectors of financial sector promotion such as microfinance, housing finance or agricultural finance. For example, existing clients of financial institutions include small and medium-sized enterprises and households, and these are often suffering from high energy prices or have no access to sustainable energy supply. At the same time, these clients are vulnerable to extreme weather events, and often hit hardest by the impact of climate change. There are many other examples which show that the financial sector has an enormous potential to support "green" investments.

However, in order to tap this potential on a sustainable basis, it is important to have a sound understanding which role financial institutions can and should play. Likewise, financial institutions need to understand the demand side of environmental finance markets and the framework conditions in order to be able to design adequate financial products.

For many years, KfW has been financing "green" investments in Germany. In particular, KfW started its promotion of energy efficiency in housing in the early 1990's. KfW has significantly contributed to set the standards for "Low Energy Houses" in Germany. Support is provided if the refurbished or new home meets KfW Efficiency House standards, which set limits based on the energy consumption and heat loss values. Higher energy efficiency is rewarded by better conditions.

Likewise, KfW Entwicklungsbank has embarked on financing energy efficiency and renewable energy investments through the financial sector in developing and transition countries. The total active portfolio in environmental finance sums up to EUR 789 million (as of end 2010), of which EUR 651 million have been committed in 17 countries and EUR 138 million in regional and global funds devoted to environmental finance.

But finance is not enough! We continuously encourage our partner governments to ensure conducive framework conditions for environmental investments such as cost-covering energy tariffs, appropriate legal terms and law enforcement.

Without such a sound environment, neither financial institutions nor their potential clients are likely to get involved in these promising markets.

So I think we are well placed – and this is our clear objective – to share our competence as an environment bank as part of our long-standing co-operation with our partners in developing and transition countries.

I am happy that a number of internationally renowned experts have contributed to this book, besides two contributions from KfW. May this book contribute to share knowledge and provide new insights for the different stakeholders.

As this publication is also available online, my special wish is that it contributes to a fruitful learning process around the globe and to familiarize financial institutions in KfW's partner countries with the financing potential for "green" investments. Banks need to be convinced that this product is a profitable business line in order to get involved in a sustainable way. My sincere hope is that this book can contribute to this vision.

I would like to thank the authors for their efforts in preparing and revising the papers and not least my colleagues who made this publication possible, especially Matthias Adler and Beate Königsberger.

July 2011

Doris Köhn
KfW Entwicklungsbank
Senior Vice President Private and Financial Sector
and Africa and Middle East Regions

Table of Contents

Abbreviations

ADB	Asian Development Bank
ADEME	Agencie de l'Environnment et de la Maîtrise de l'Energie (French Environment and Energy Management Agency)
Ag DSM	Agricultural Demand Side Management
ANME	Agence Nationale pour la Maîtrise de l'Énergie
AREED	Africa Renewable Energy Enterprise Development
BEA	Berlin Energy Agency
BEE	India Bureau of Energy Efficiency
BEEF	Bulgaria Energy Efficiency Fund
BfAI	Bundesagentur für Aussenwirtschaft
BIO	Belgian Investment Company for Developing Countries
BNDES	Brazilian National Development Bank
BRL	Brazilian Real
C/I	Commercial/industrial
CABEI	Central American Bank for Economic Integration
CAREC	Central American Renewable Energy and Cleaner Production Facility
CBP	Cooperative Bank of Palawan
CCX	Chicago Climate Exchange
CDF	Cash Deposit Fund
CDM PD	CDM Project Designer
CDM	Clean Development Mechanism
CEA	Cambridge Energy Alliance
CEB	Ceylon Electricity Board
CEEF	Commercializing Energy Efficiency Finance
CER	Certified Emission Reduction
CFI	Commercial Finance Institution
CFL	Compact Fluorescent Light
CFU	Carbon Finance Unit, The World Bank
CIA	Central Intelligence Agency
CLO	Collateralized Loan Obligation
CME	Chicago Mercantile Exchange
COP	Conference of the Parties
CSB	Cseka Sporitelna Bank
CT	Clean Technology
DBP	Development Bank of the Philippines

DCA	Development Credit Authority
DEDE	Department of Alternative Energy Development and Efficiency
DFI	Development Finance Institution
DFID	Department for International Development
DIGH	Dutch International Guarantees for Housing
DPR	Detailed Project Report
DSM	Demand Side Management
DWM	Developing World Markets
EBRD	European Bank for Reconstruction and Development
EE	Energy Efficiency
EERE	Energy Efficiency and Small-Scale Renewable Energy
EF	Environmental Finance
EFG	Environmental Finance Group
ENCON	Energy Conservation Fund (Thailand)
ENSO	El Niño Southern Oscillation
ERPA	Emission Reduction Purchase Agreement
ESA	End-user Agreement
ESCO	Energy Service Company
ESKOM	Electricity Supply Commission (South Africa)
ETS	Emission Trading System
EU ETS	European Union Emissions Trading Scheme
FI	Financial Institution
Finnfund	Finnish Fund for Industrial Cooperation, Ltd
FLL	Facility Liability Limit
FMO	Netherlands Development Finance Company
GDP	Gross Domestic Product
GEF	Global Environment Facility
GFA	Guarantee Facility Agreements
GHG	Greenhouse Gas
GIRIF	Global Index Reinsurance Facility
GVEP	Global Energy Village Partnership
GW	Gigawatt
GWh	Gigawatt hours
HEECP	Hungary Energy Efficiency Co-financing Program
HEEFF	Housing Energy Efficiency Financing Facility
I&T Broker	Information and Technology Broker
IADB	Inter-American Development Bank
IBRD	International Bank for Reconstruction and Development
ICLEI	International Council for Local Energy Initiatives
IDB	Inter-American Development Bank
IEA	International Energy Agency

IFC	International Finance Corporation
IIED	International Institute for Environment and Development
IPCC	International Panel for Climate Change
IPP	Independent Power Producers
IREDA	Indian Renewable Energy Development Agency
ITL	International Transaction Log
KfW	KfW Bankengruppe
kW	Kilowatt
kWh	Kilowatt Hour
LECO	Lanka Electricity Company
LLDC	Least Developed Country
LNG	Liquefied Natural Gas
LPG	Liquefied Petroleum Gas
LRF	Loss Reserve Fund
MDG	Millennium Development Goals
MEDREP	Mediterranean Renewable Energies Programme
MFI	Microfinance Institution
MIF	Multilateral Investment Fund
MSME	Micro, Small and Medium Enterprise
MW	Megawatt
NAFINSA	Mexican National Development Bank
NOAA	National Oceanographic and Atmospheric Administration, United States
O & M	Operations and Maintenance
OECD	Organization for Economic Cooperation and Development
OTC	Over-the-counter
PCD	Project Cash Deposit
POA	Programmes of Activities
PPP	Public Private Partnership
PROSOL	Programme Solaire (Solar Program)
PSOD	Private Sector Operations Department (of ADB)
PV	Photo-voltaic
R&D	Research and Development
RE	Renewable Energy
REC	Rural Electric Cooperatives
REEEP	Renewable Energy and Energy Efficiency Partnership
RFP	Request for Proposal
RFQ	Request for Qualification
ROI	Return on Investment
SEA	Sustainable Energy Authority
SEB	State Electric Board
SEEDS	Sarvodaya Economic Enterprise Development Services

SELCO	Solar Electric Light Company (India)
SEWA	Self Employed Women's Association (India)
SHS	Solar Home Systems
SIDBI	Small Industries Development Bank of India
SME	Small and Medium Enterprises
SMEs	Small and Medium Enterprises
SSPC	Shell Solar Philippines Corp.
SST	Sea surface temperature
STB	Societé Tunisienne de Banque (Tunisian National Bank)
STEG	Societé Tunisienne de l'Electricité et de Gaz (Tunisian Electricity and Gas Company)
SWH	Solar Water Heater
TA	Technical Assistance
TGLL	Transaction Guarantee Liability Limit
TREDF	Triodos Renewable Energy for Development Fund
UNDP	United Nations Development Program
UNECE	United Nations Economic Commission for Europe
UNEP	United Nations Environment Program
UNFCCC	United Nations Framework Convention on Climate Change
USAID	United States Agency for International Development
USD	US Dollar
VAT	Value Added Tax
VSD	Variable Speed Drives
WB	World Bank
WEC	World Energy Council
Wp	Watt peak
WRI	World Resource Institute
ZAR	South African Rand

CHAPTER 1

Mainstreaming Environmental Finance into Financial Markets – Relevance, Potential and Obstacles

Peter Lindlein[*]

Abstract

Mainstreaming environmental finance widens the utilisation of existing instruments and extends them to environmentally beneficial activities. The objective is to serve clients in ways that make environmental finance a normal set of retail products. The sheer number of households and MSMEs (micro, small and medium enterprises) give providers the weight and opportunity to address environmental concerns. Financial institutions have a key role in environmental finance in ways that ensure sustainable development (Millennium Development Goal 7).

Households, MSMEs and municipalities have an enormous range of technically viable environmental investments. But the actual demand is still much below the potential. This is because the material and/or financial benefits of environmental activities have been limited. 'Greenbacks' have been more important than 'green thought'. However, this market is growing along with higher energy prices, and will grow further if the emphasis on subsidy is shifted from fossil energy to sustainable energy.

The current demand for environmental investment is limited. But many potential investments are on the frontier of viability. To increase their viability, they usually require longer maturities and a high sensitivity to the structure and the conditions of capital cost financing.

The trend of green financial products has not yet penetrated emerging markets and developing countries. Most banks are in the early stages of integrating environmental factors into their internal procedures, offering only a few financial products in this field, because they believe other opportunities earn higher returns. Environmental finance faces a three-dimensional gap between needs and supply: instruments, funds and conditions. These, and the insufficient knowledge, lack of institutional capacity, and opportunity and start-up costs, constitute the challenges for financial institutions entering the field of environmental finance. But success-

[*] Chief Executive Officer, iCee GmbH.

D. Köhn (ed.), *Greening the Financial Sector: How to Mainstream Environmental Finance in Developing Countries*, DOI 10.1007/978-3-642-05087-9_1,

ful cases prove that there are significant advantages from approaches that at the same time address the demand for environmental finance and benefit both the financial institution and the borrower.

Increasing the range for such win-win situations will require substantial support from the international community, not only in the form of access to funds, but also in becoming more proactive by including environmental aspects in banks internal sustainability strategies. It will take enormous efforts for financial institutions and their international partners to capitalise on the fact that energy is money. Moreover, environmental protection means business – and money and business are bankable.

1 The Relevance of Environmental Finance

Environment – from renewable energy to resource efficiency, and from clean production to climate change: these concerns have risen to the top ranks of the global agenda of politics, business and finance. Massive problems predicted by some experts for decades are materializing. High fuel prices, shortages of electricity, massive environmental risks in emerging economies and man-made climate change have moved from the debating table to reality. After decades of controversial discussions these issues are emerging as facts, becoming mainstream topics of thought and policy. What was an opportunity has now become a necessity: the financial sector has to develop its approaches and instruments in order to make environmental finance a mainstream priority, responding to a challenge that is both local and global.

This is of special importance to developing countries and emerging economies. It seems obvious that their paths and patterns of growth cannot simply follow the stages of the industrialized countries. Both have to leap over into a stage of sustainable development. To 'Ensure Environmental Sustainability' is a Millennium Development Goal (MDG Target 7). Thus, environment is not something that is supplementary – it is an essential dimension of development, and environmental finance will have to be one of its crucial instruments.

There is a strong case for 'environmental finance', a term used for a wide range of activities and instruments at various levels. These have in common that the activities financed are supposed to contribute to the common good, which is 'environment'. From a financial sector perspective, this includes the direct financing of projects, (public) financial (dis-)incentive schemes, bilateral and multilateral projects and programmes, and global schemes such as carbon markets and global funds.[1] 'Environmental finance' in reality is multidimensional, encompassing objectives, techniques, sponsors and regions, to name a few.

1 The increasing importance of environmental finance is underlined by the fact that 12 such funds were founded in 2007 alone, offering funds for various environmental activities and investment levels: Global Climate Change Alliance of the European Commission

The following remarks refer only to simplified, stylized facts of that diverse universe, including providing basic energy to the poorest in least developed countries (LLDCs) in a sustainable way, improving building insulation in Eastern Europe, providing energy efficient and waste reducing equipment for micro, small and medium enterprises (MSMEs) in emerging markets, and building renewable energy plants for local supply everywhere. Furthermore, 'environment' may not even be the major purpose and benefit of such an activity, but only one important aspect. Therefore we must avoid tunnel vision, instead addressing a very wide range of activities, while exploring the relevance and potential of environmental finance through the financial sector.

Environmental finance through the financial sector? What does this term mean? It refers to any kind financial service (equity, credit, guarantees and insurance) on the demand side, consisting of producers, service companies, smaller municipalities and households for environmentally-relevant activities within the normal product line and client range of a financial institution. Mainstreaming environmental finance into the financial sector primarily means widening the use of existing institutions and instruments and extending them to the environmentally-beneficial activities of their existing and potential clients, making environmental finance a regular retail product. This may be done in combination with public incentive schemes and special funds.

Where does mainstream environmental finance fit in the spectrum of the financial sector? Toward one end is large-scale project finance, and toward the other is retail finance. From the clients' perspective, environmental finance probably resembles large-scale project finance. This would seem to be the case because households and MSMEs face major expenditures in the form of long-term investments, often with low annual costs but with returns and therefore benefits over long periods of time. But from the perspective of financial institutions these clients and their activities fall into another size category requiring an approach that is appropriate for a mass market of smaller activities. These consist of MSME finance and household finance, which may not always result in sufficient cash flow for income generation or cost reduction to cover debt service. For ecological, economic and social reasons, environmental finance cannot be restricted to large projects:

(GCCA), International Window of the Environmental Transformation Fund of the United Kingdom, German International Climate Initiative, German Life Web Initiative, Spanish-UNDP Spanish MDG Fund, NORAD Rainforest Initiative, Japanese Cool Earth Partnership, Australian Global Initiative on Forests and Climate, World Bank Forest Carbon Partnership Fund (FCPF), World Bank Clean Technology Fund (CTF), GEF-IFC Earth Fund, World Bank Strategic Climate Fund (SCF) and Pilot Program for Climate Resilience (PPCR) and Kyoto Protocol Adaptation Fund. Source: Geer, Timothy (WWF International). *The New Financing Architecture for the Environment – and some associated issues*, Presentation in Manila, June 2008.

- Along with renewable energy, energy and resource efficiency are topics for MSMEs as well as for households. Any approach that ignores the enormous possibilities for reducing energy consumption and greenhouse gas emissions of MSMEs and households would be incomplete. It would miss the potential to decouple economic development from the growth of energy consumption.
- Large renewable energy projects are very important due to their size and economies of scale. However, as millions of poor people have no direct access to the services and benefits of networks linked to these large projects, decentralised solutions are in order – and they require finance. Environmental finance through the financial sector can offer a shortcut to reach the poor, support decentralized solutions and directly improve the living conditions of the poor. For example, financial institutions can provide funds that can help the poor to use decentralized energy solutions, instead of waiting for years to be connected to the grid.
- Furthermore, the financial sector can channel funds to international and global schemes at the project level in the real sector, where change must occur. A strategic element could include important segments of the private sector as a step on the road to commercialisation and massification of environmental investment throughout the economy.

Working through the financial sector may also create strong impacts on the living conditions of the marginalised, making environmental finance an instrument of poverty alleviation. For example, this approach can contribute to opening up other energy resources for the poor in grids with limited electricity capacity.

Thus, both approaches – classic large-scale project finance and environmental finance through the financial sector – are complementary. Each contributes to the goals of environmental finance, making full use of practical solutions. Small projects and environmental finance through the financial sector can be simple and quick. Local financial institutions are close to the clientele: they know their track records and understand their concerns – and the possibilities to structure financial services accordingly.

The sheer number of households and MSMEs, their close relevance to environmental issues, and the opportunity to address their concerns directly give financial institutions a strategic role in environmental finance and in the massification required for sustainable development (MDG 7). Furthermore, without the inclusion of the target group of MSMEs and households, efforts to develop an open, rule-based, predictable and non-discriminatory financial system (MDG 8) would lack an essential pillar. Mainstreaming environmental finance into financial markets will improve income and living conditions. In poor countries this can help to a) reduce poverty (MDG 1); b) improve education (MDG 3) through improved school facilities and lighting at home; and c) improve health (MDG 4 and 6) through energy efficiency and infrastructure improvement through reduced pollution and better air quality. Clearly, financing investments and the corresponding development of the financial sector are closely relevant to both the achievement of the MDG goals and to harmonizing economic development with environmental sustainability.

Engaging in environmental finance at the base of the economic and social pyramid could offer benefits for financial institutions:

- Financial institutions would engage in a burgeoning field that is becoming ever more important in both real and financial aspects. Thus, finance could secure its share of the growing 'green' market.
- Environmental finance can be good business, as can financial services that serve the poor. Like MSME finance, household finance and environmental finance offer an opportunity for business development, attracting new clients and strengthening relationships with present customers. This formula could strengthen the dynamics of the market.
- Financial institutions would find not only an opportunity for cross-selling and portfolio building. In addition, risk would be reduced as energy efficiency can improve clients' financial situations.

Clearly, there are benefits not only to individual financial institutions, but also to financial systems development. Mainstreaming environmental finance could extend the scope and size of the financial sector and deepen it by increasing the numbers of clients, providing better coverage, and offering newer products and longer maturities. Environmental finance could extend MSME promotion, offering this target group finance to strengthen their capacities in the fields of environment and energy, moving them a step further from survival towards sustainability.

To summarise, there is a substantial case for mainstreaming environmental finance into financial markets, but to a great extent environmental finance remains within the realm of potential. Why has this massive potential not been tapped further? One answer can be found in the real sector, which together with the financial sector, constitutes the economy. The next section, provides an overview of the demand for environmental financial products, after which the current state of the supply side and related challenges are presented.

2 Overview of the Demand Side of Environmental Finance Markets

A precondition for demand for environmental finance is an investment decision in the real sector, i.e. the demand for environmental products and equipment, which is the topic of the next sub-sections. Later, the way in which this real demand is transformed into demand for financial products will be closely examined.

2.1 Types of Potential Investment Demand for Environmental Activities

The typical potential clients of environmental finance include households, MSMEs in all sectors of the economy, and smaller municipalities. The following table gives an overview of their activities categorised by environmental areas:

Table 1. Clients and Types of Environmental Activities

Clients/ EF Type	Households	MSMEs	Municipalities	Remark
Renewable Energy	Solar Water Heating; Solar-Photovoltaic; Biogas	Biomass; Small Hydro; Wind; Solar Water Heating	Small Hydro; Biomass (waste to energy); Wind; Solar PV	M(SME)/municipalities power suppliers in energy generation M(SME) and co-generation (e.g. biomass)
Energy Efficiency	Lighting; Domestic Appliances; Eco-efficient Housing (Retrofitting, Insulation)	Industrial Energy Efficiency; Eco-efficient Buildings	EE Public Lighting; Public Buildings; Power Distribution Network	Households, by number almost all, by amount mainly the present better-off consumers, i.e. medium and high income households; Potential for loss reduction through improvement of electricity distribution network
Clean Production		Resource Efficiency incl. Recycling; End of Pipe Approaches, Ie.g., Sewage Plants		Reduction of Pollution and Pollution Treatment
Climate Insurance		Small Farmers		
Environ-mental Supply Chain		Equipment Production; Service Companies		Local supply can be a bottleneck; you can import the equipment, but the service for implementation and maintenance may be difficult to procure; important to build up production and service capacities and networks

This illustrates that there is an enormous range of investments in environmental finance which are technically and economically viable. The following figure gives examples of typical investment costs in relation to financial risk and classifies them into categories:[2]

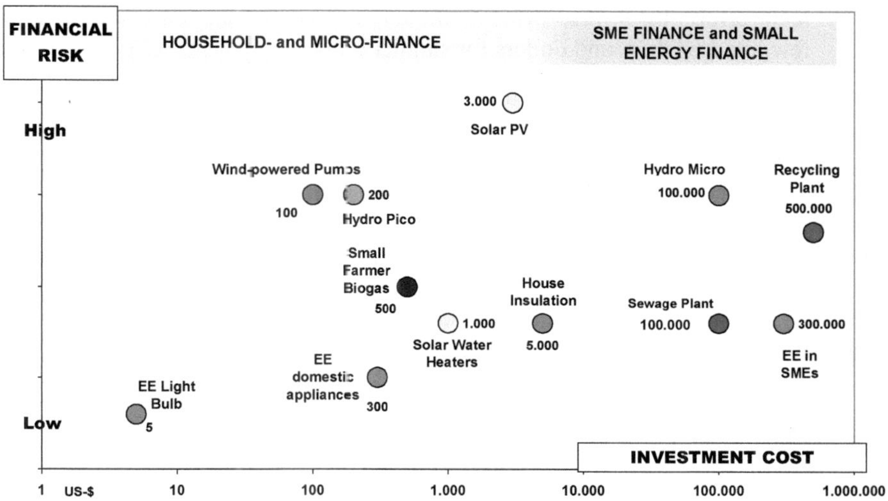

Fig. 1. Examples of Investment Cost and Financial Risk of EE and RE Investments

The figure includes activities having an investment cost of up to USD 1 million. The upper limit encompasses the great majority of loan amounts financial institutions in emerging markets and developing countries provide in their regular business with their clients.[3]

- For just a few dollars, households could improve energy efficiency by using compact fluorescent light bulbs for a few dollars; for a few hundred dollars, they could improve energy efficiency by employing modern domestic electrical appliances. Solar water heaters placed on roofs would cost a few hundred dollars and houses could be insulated for a few thousand. Improved public lighting would cost several hundred thousand dollars for smaller municipalities.

---

[2] Adapted from: Lindlein, Peter and Wolfgang Mostert. *Financing Renewable Energy*. KfW Frankfurt, 2005.

[3] However, in some emerging economies with larger banks and more advanced financial systems, projects with an investment cost of USD 5 million or more, such as smaller cogeneration plants, may be addressed by environmental finance through the financial sector; this closes the gap to typical structured project finance, which starts at about USD 10 million.

- Renewable energy approaches range from USD 100 for Pico Hydro Units to over a few thousand dollars for Solar Photo-Voltaic Systems to USD 100,000 for Micro Hydro.
- Recycling plants and sewerage treatment, both with a very wide range of investment cost, are examples of resource efficiency and pollution abatement efforts by SMEs. Typical amounts for smaller units are several of a few hundred thousand dollars for smaller units.

The determination of what is actually economically and financially viable, and also expressed as demand, depends to a large extent on the framework conditions and energy prices in the respective country.

To grasp the size of the challenge, renewable energy projects alone are calculated by the IEA to be about USD 7 billion per year for all sizes of projects. This sum would enable renewable energy to comprise a significant portion of the energy consumption of developing countries. Donor assistance provides less than 20%, leaving a huge financing gap. Market-based mechanisms are required to leverage much greater amounts, beyond what donors could supply.

2.2 Reasons for Low Actual Investment Demand

In general, the actual demand for environmental finance is far below the potential, despite the fact that the more advanced developing countries have often established their own policies for energy efficiency, renewable energies and pollution control. Some observers attribute this gap to a lack of awareness of and interest in the client target groups. They simply follow a "business as usual" rationale, which is similar for households and MSMEs:

- Poor people and small companies are first aware of a lack of access to goods and services, including modern energy forms and a lack of access to the grid. To engage these people, environmental activities must offer actual material benefits. Their rationale for engagement may take into consideration the environmental activities that affect them, but with little regard for the environmental effects of their own activities on the rest of society.
- Even if there are clear benefits, municipalities, MSMEs and households have limited funds to spend, and environmental activities are ranked low on the priority list. In their stressed situation, 'greenbacks' are much more important than 'green thought'. Financial institutions can provide funds to increase this limit, but clearly, there are limitations in the access to finance for both investors and for financial institutions.
- Another aspect is the time horizon. There is a strong preference for short-term and intermediate returns. The long pay-back periods of energy efficiency or renewable energy are not sufficiently attractive. To be sustainable in the long run, this barrier has to be overcome.

These rationales motivate decision makers to take different approaches to some of the main areas of environmental activities:

- **Energy Efficiency:** Here low demand is mainly a result of low and subsidized energy prices. Electricity prices in the range of USD 5–7 cts/KWh in countries such as Bolivia, Egypt, India and South Africa preclude material energy savings. The efficiency potential in households and in commerce is targeted only when a clear financial benefit is foreseeable. Rising electricity prices in Brazil, China and other countries will stimulate this demand.
- **Renewable Energy:** For most households and MSMEs, energy means access to the electricity grid. Individual household solutions are perceived as second best. They will never be connected to the grid controlled by the better off, causing an image problem for renewable energy solutions. In general, MSMEs have a more practical attitude in this matter and judge the potential solutions based on benefit and cost criteria. Commercial renewable energy approaches face a series of problems when linking to the grid is required, due to unfavourable framework conditions (i.e., regulations and prices). As renewable energy for a firm's own consumption does not face this bottleneck, investment in co-generation has flourished.
- **Cleaner Production:** In the case of pollution control and abatement in MSMEs, the common good benefits to the environment play a very minor role in determining individual decisions. Investment occurs only if environmental regulations are strictly enforced or a clear financial benefit is likely.

The present global change in energy prices and its local impacts make permanent energy subsidies impossible. The impacts of heavy pollution in urban areas that affect daily life are moving decision makers to alter their priority lists. Accordingly, thinking is starting to change and stronger action in all areas may follow.

However, many potential investors, especially households, are now facing a practical problem: the lack of systematic, solid, up-to-date information on the different technical and economic solutions and their availability and actual cost in a specific region. Although one may easily assume that the internet has improved the availability of data, many countries continue to lack reliable, practical information. This is related to the dearth of experience and data that might guide practical investment. In many countries, there are no showcases for environmental solutions within the reach of the decision-making public; uncertainty and high transaction costs hamper progress and experimentation. But when buying a solar water heater (SWH) is as simple as buying a car, as in China with its network of SWH-producers and suppliers, transaction costs decline and investment decisions are made by millions of consumers.

How can potential clients' awareness and propensity to invest be raised? The drivers behind the growth in 'green' financial products in Europe and the US are knowledge, awareness and regulation. People and companies in emerging markets and developing countries, each with different framework conditions, have different incentives and information. Their decision-making is not necessarily influenced by a common good but rather by individual benefits. Awareness campaigns should move beyond pleas for green consciousness. They should demonstrate potential individual benefits and practical ways of achieving them, offering reliable, clear, relevant and complete information. These goals can be promoted through case studies, the dissemination of practical knowledge and hands-on approaches. The solar service centres in Germany, for example, combine such strategies.

As the actual demand lies below the potential in these markets, so does the local production of the corresponding equipment and goods. Also, providers of installation and maintenance of environmental equipment are hard to find in many developing countries, especially outside the larger cities.

Giving clear information on the ways and benefits of environmental activities is easier said than done when prices are used to calculate the benefits. Market forces have limited predictability. In addition, the state and regulating bodies intervene in pricing through taxes, subsidies and regulations. Moreover, this is not always done in a reliable, predicable way that provides sufficient information for decisions regarding environmental activities which require a long-term perspective.

Combined, these factors contribute to high transaction costs and elevated risk and uncertainty for environmental actions in the perception of decision makers at all levels; this perception, in turn, inhibits decisions to allocate funds for environmental investment.

At present, the actual demand for environmental finance in emerging markets and developing countries is much lower than the potential, but there are already some sectoral and regional hotspots:

- Energy efficiency has already gained momentum in the industrial sector and in households; this is especially the case in Eastern Europe, which suffers from an outdated industrial base, poor housing conditions and large energy efficiency problems.
- Renewable energy creates significant demand as financial viability increases, as in the cases of wind and small hydro energy. Demand is also generated where considerable public support brings green solutions to the frontier of bankability, as in India and the Philippines.
- The present demand for cleaner production and pollution abatement is strong only when financial incentives (e.g., pollution fees) are instituted or when environmental standards, including the risk of disruption of operation, are legally enforced.[4] Especially in reference to financial incentives and standards enforcement, "it is no coincidence that sustainability per-

[4] An econometric study completed in 2000 in China (Wang, Hua. *Endogenous enforcement and effectiveness of China's pollution levy system.* Policy Research Working Paper WP 2336) shows that industrial plants respond strongly to pollution levies and enforcements either by abating pollution or end-of-pipe treatment for pollution.

formance is linked to the political system"[5] and that in some Latin American democracies this field is more active than in other regions.

Furthermore, there are strong drivers that increase demand. These include rising energy prices and pressing environmental problems, along with other aspects of globalisation. Trade agreements and growing environmental requirements from foreign buyers will force entrepreneurs in Asia to be more active as international investors, who will set environmental standards for their affiliates. Pressure from NGOs will grow as a result of their publicizing the consequences of environmental negligence and as technical solutions become more affordable.

2.3 The Crucial Double Role of Subsidies

Properly set, subsidies could create a cushion against the financial imperfections of the environmental investment market and help to create the personal incentives that are necessary for optimal investment decisions.[6]

However, despite liberalization of the energy sector in many countries, the prevailing framework conditions and subsidy schemes continue to expand environmental investment, which is to some extent the result of subsidized prices for fossil fuels. Global subsidies for energy (net of taxes) are estimated at USD 280 billion per year (about 0.6% of global gross domestic product), of which 94% are for fossil energy.[7] Although the weighted average of consumer subsidies is rather low, consumers in some countries pay energy prices that are considerably lower than the average, especially for electricity: 20–40% lower, as depicted in Fig. 2. These are average rates; some consumers may enjoy even higher subsidies and lower tariffs.

Such state interventions are an element of social policy (e.g., India[8]) or they are intended to promote industrial investment (e.g., South Africa). But low energy prices are hardly an incentive to search for alternative generation or energy efficiency solutions. In fact, subsidies contribute to the low demand for environmental activities in these countries.

---

5 Jennifer Morgan, sustainable business manager at WWF-UK., In Mike Scott. *Local conditions dictate the development of services*. Financial Times, Sustainable Banking, Special Report, 3 June 2008.

6 For details see Session 2.

7 In most OECD countries, gross energy subsidies are heavily outweighed by taxes. But Russia and Iran have annual energy subsidies of about USD 40 billion, and six other countries – China, Saudi Arabia, India, Indonesia, Ukraine and Egypt – provide subsidies in excess of USD 10 billion per year each. All figures are net of taxes for each fuel source. Morgan, Trevor. *Energy Subsidies: Their Magnitude, How they Affect Energy Investment and Greenhouse Gas Emissions, and Prospects for Reform*. UNFCCC Secretariat/Financial and Technical Support Programme. June 2007.

8 See Stern, Nicolas. *The Economics of Climate Change: The Stern Review*. Report to the Cabinet Office, HM Treasury. Cambridge: Cambridge University Press, 2006, p.279.

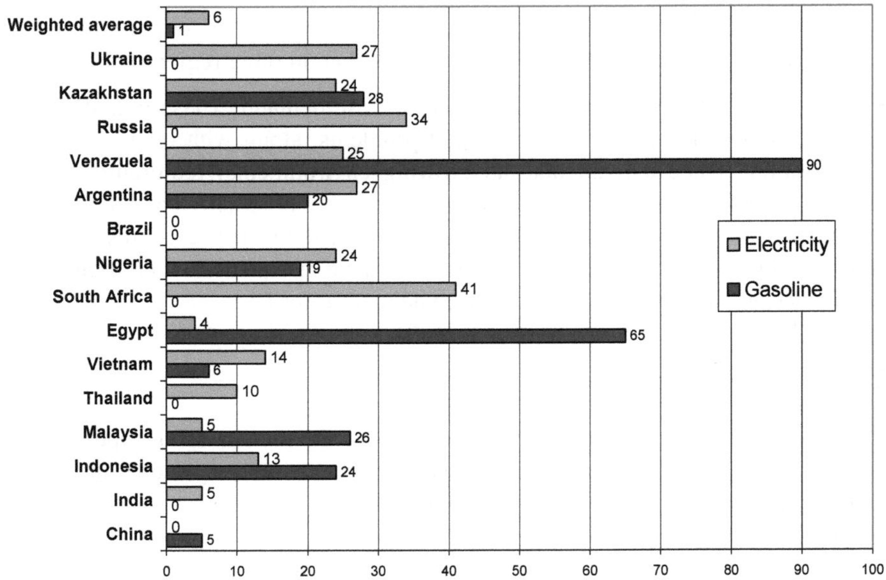

Fig. 2. Consumption subsidy as percentage of reference price in Non-OECD countries, 2005
Source: Morgan, Trevor. *Energy Subsidies.* 2007 based on figures from IEA.

With increasing real global prices for primary energy, the use of subsidies to keep prices at such low levels will at some point become unsustainable. Some countries listed in Figure 2 have already reacted and have increased energy prices substantially. Such actions will terminate a disincentive for environmental activities.

To reverse the subsidy balance in favour of sustainable energy and environmental solutions, and create an incentive for them, would help to secure the future instead of clinging to the past. But environmental subsidies are still rather limited: *The Stern Report* estimates that annual government support for deployment of renewable energy is currently on the order of USD 10 billion worldwide.[9] However, many industrial countries and some developing nations have adopted subsidy incentive schemes to compensate for the higher costs of renewable energy investments. Different subsidy instruments are used, as the following examples illustrate:

- Germany had a scheme to promote renewable energy with higher feed-in tariffs to the grid and through the recovery of investment cost. This resulted in subsidies of about EUR 6 cts/kwh for the investors, which was more than twice the wholesale price at that time. This approach contributed substantially to the relative success of renewable energy, but at significant cost for all customers who had to finance the subsidy through a higher cost of electricity.

---

[9] Figure without biofuels. See Stern, Nicolas. *The Economics of Climate Change*, p.367.

- For some years China has halved the value added tax and income tax for wind and biogas.
- Ghana reduced the import tariff for compact fluorescent lamps (CFL) to replace incandescent lamps.
- Brazil had a successful scheme to promote its biofuel industry: farmers received subsidies to grow sugar-cane. The fuel price was also subsidised to make biofuel cheaper than petrol, and alcohol-powered cars had a lower VAT rate.
- India offers financing for renewable energy at favourable conditions through the Indian Renewable Energy Development Agency (IREDA).

In a proper context, targeted smart subsidies can enhance environmental investment. Lessons learnt suggest that they should address not only direct investment and operating costs, but should also include training and educational subsidies to build local expertise, user awareness, appropriate technology adaptation, quality standards and entrepreneurial activities.[10] Smart subsidies build nascent markets without undermining incentives for clients or commercial firms. These subsidies should be based on the classic criteria for the design and evaluation of a subsidy, such as to reach a focus on the target group, achieve impact and output at the least cost subsidy and the means to finance it. In the case of environmental activities, this means:[11]

- A clearly defined target group is required; ideally this would be the decision makers for environmental activities.
- Subsidies should support least-cost options. The subsidy must be big enough to make a real difference for the decision maker, but subsidies are limited. Thus the targets for such subsidies should be the 'low-hanging fruits', i.e. renewable energy activities that are close to financial viability.
- Subsidies should encourage commercial participation by the private sector to leverage their impact.
- Subsidies should have a built-in phase-out date to maintain an incentive for producers to become financially viable.

All subsidies affect the bankability of environmental activities. Some do this through capital cost compensation schemes that lower the amount of subsidy; others affect bankability by increasing the returns of the activity. Of special importance for the financial sector are subsidies included within the financing terms. Such subsidies can take the form of lower interest rates or include risk-sharing and technical assistance at below market costs. The pricing of interest rate subsidies is ideally deter-

---

[10] See Rijal, Kamal. *Energy Subsidies in Developing Countries: Can we make it for those whom it is intended?* Joint UNEP and UNECE Expert Meeting on Energy Subsidies, 2007.

[11] Pros and cons on subsidies and details on the adequate approaches are discussed by Wolfgang Mostert in this volume. See also UNEP/IEA. *Reforming Energy Subsidies*, 2002.

mined by the crucial line between the commercial market rate for average risks and the creation of adequate financial access for environmental activities, given the distortions in capital markets. Experience has proven that loans for special purposes with interest rates below the market rate are highly prone to misuse.

2.4 Characteristics of the Demand for Environmental Finance

Due to the relative amount of the cost and the limited funds available, the demand for environmental investment is almost automatically transformed into demand for environmental finance. The drivers of the diverse universe of environmental activities create a rather wide range of demand characteristics for environmental finance:

- **Different client groups** create demand for environmental finance; these range from poor households to MSMEs to small municipalities. The types of investment demanded range from improvement in personal living conditions to commercial activities to public investment. Motives include individual benefits in the form of improved living conditions, cost savings, long-term profitability and pollution abatement triggered by legal requirements. Medium-sized companies and municipalities may be motivated by social responsibility.
- **Existing and new clients:** Energy efficiency and cogeneration activities as well as pollution abatement investments are usually undertaken by companies/households offering a financial track record and a base for collateral. However, renewable energy projects often are greenfield activities initiated by new companies and developers.
- **Partial cost base and different levels of cash-flow generation:** The environmental aspect may be only one element of an investment activity, either being built-in (e.g. efficiency) or as one element of a major investment. Thus it may represent only part of the total cost, or it could come on top of other substantial costs. Not all the environmental activities create a direct cash flow.
- **Type of finance and own funds:** The type of finance they demand includes forms of mezzanine finance and risk instruments. The required loan amounts come in all sizes, often with limited own funds.
- **Time horizon:** The longer the payback period of the activity and/or the relation of investment cost to the disposable income, the longer are the maturities that are required.

Thus, demand for environmental finance arises from many different client segments of financial institutions, each requiring different financial products. Many of these activities are on the frontier of viability or bankability. What they have in common is a tendency to require longer maturities and a high sensitivity to the structure and the conditions of capital cost financing. This translates into a strong preference for interest rates in the lower range of the market. A classification of these demand characteristics is presented in the following table:

Table 2. Characteristics of the Demand for Environmental Finance

Clients/ Factor	Households	Micro-enterprises	SMEs	Small Municipalities
Kind of activities	• Renewable Energy • Energy Efficiency	• Renewable Energy • Energy & Resource Efficiency • Pollution Abatement	• Renewable Energy • Energy & Resource Efficiency • Pollution Abatement • Climate Insurance • Supply for Energy and Environment Investment and Operation	• Renewable Energy • Energy Efficiency • Pollution Abatement
Motivation	• Personal Benefit	• Personal/ Commercial Benefit	• Commercial Benefit • Legal Requirement • (Corporate Social Responsibility)	• Budget • Social Responsibility • Legal Requirement
Types of financial products	• Loans • Insurance	• Loans • Insurance • Guarantees	• Equity • Loans • Leasing • Guarantees • Insurance	• Loans • Guarantees • Insurance
Amounts (Loans) in USD	10 – 10,000	100 – 100,000	100,000 – 1,000,000	1,000,000 +
Maturities (Loans)	Medium – Long	Medium – Long	Long	Long
Collateral Base	• Personal Property	• Property • Cash Flow	• Property • Cash Flow	• Budget • Cash Flow

How and to what extent this demand could be met by the supply of the financial sector is explored in the next section.

3 Overview of the Supply Side of Environmental Finance Markets

3.1 Markets, Actors and Products

Analysis of the mainstreaming of environmental finance into regular product lines has to consider two aspects: the development of normal business practice and the approach and practice of environmental finance.

The revolution of financial markets and the progress many financial institutions have made in the last decade(s) are impressive. But despite globalisation, the scope of products offered by commercial financial institutions varies enormously, depending on the maturity, outreach and the degree of a country's financial sector development. Limited access to common financial instruments and products constrains the demand for environmental finance. Mainstreaming environmental finance has to consider the condition and shortcomings of this sector and its institutions, as the table below illustrates.[12]

Table 3. Typology of Commercial Financial Markets

Classification of Financial Markets	Availability of Financing Instruments	Availability of Risk-Mitigation Instruments	Typical Constraints	Examples
Advanced Emerging Financial Markets	Advanced	Limited	Limited access to mezzanine finance	India, Thailand, Philippines, Mexico, South Africa, China
Emerging Financial Markets	Regular	None – minimal	Limited access to long-term finance; equity, leasing and risk instruments difficult to access	Former CIS, Argentina
Basic Financial Systems	Very Basic	None	Very limited product range; only short- and mid-term loans	Mongolia, Nepal

[12] For a detailed country ranking of the maturity of financial markets see *The Financial Development Report 2008* by the World Economic Forum, especially Pillar 7: Capital availability and access, p.13.

In some emerging markets and many developing countries there is still a gap in the supply of mainstream products. In some cases, MSMEs and poor households have no access at all to formal financial institutions. These countries may also lack the base upon which environmental finance for this target group could be offered.

The acceptance that financial institutions offer towards environment and sustainability is a process marked by several stages of development:[13]

- Defensive banking: Non-active, delaying or opposing environmental aspects as criteria, because they are perceived to undermine business with good clients not interested in green finance, to produce insufficient contributions to profitability goals, and/or to increase the overall risk exposure of the bank, as environmental finance has to compete with traditional products.
- Reactive banking: Inclusion of environmental aspects in internal activities; reduction of credit risk by integrating environmental issues in credit risk assessment processes.
- Competitive sustainability advantage: Proactive, full integration of the external side, offering environmentally-friendly finance, continuously looking for win–win solutions.
- Responsible competitiveness: The bank does not look for the highest short-term financial rate of return, but for the highest sustainable rate of return, while being profitable in the long run. This means that the bank finances environmental projects at somewhat higher risk, lower rates of return and longer payback periods in comparison to standard short-term funding, in order to strengthen its strategic position based on a long-term perspective.

Interest in sustainability varies according to local characteristics. The actual progress that financial institutions make in these stages of integration of environmental aspects into policy and action differs by region and the maturity of the financial sector:

- In Asia, many banks perceive the environmental legal risk of their clients as rather low, and they are not very active in this field. They pay much more attention to renewable energy finance, which is strongly supported by governments and offers attractive opportunities for banks.[14]
- In Eastern Europe, banks' attitudes mirror the approach of society: there are firm regulations, but weak enforcement. Equally important for potential

[13] See for example: Jeucken, MHA and JJ Bouma. *The Changing Environment of Banks*; African Institute of Corporate Citizenship (AICC) – Sustainability Banking in Africa, Johannesburg, 2004.

[14] IFC. Banking *on Sustainability. Financing Environmental and Social Opportunities in Emerging Markets*, Washington 2007, Chapter 1.

borrowers is the fact that the large banks tend to be linked to large financial industrial groups or to powerful regional governments and concentrate their lending on group members. Thus there are some isolated examples of near-commercial loans in the environmental sectors.[15] Energy-efficiency is gaining attention.

- In Latin America – despite having award-winning banks in this field – many financial institutions still have to integrate environmental dimensions into their internal systems. The attitudes of such banks have been described as a central bottleneck for environmental activities.[16]
- In Africa the financial services sector has responded far more slowly to the challenges and opportunities that environment presents. Private sector financial institutions are particularly behind in this respect. The African banking sector's understanding of environmental risk is limited and there is little recognition of the potential offered.[17]

This does not mean that the bigger banks in emerging markets do not have environmental finance products on their list.[18] But the massive trend of green financial products and services found in Europe, where dozens of banks offer products like green mortgages,[19] clean car loans, climate credit cards or eco-deposits, has not yet penetrated emerging markets and developing countries. Most of the banks in emerging markets are in the early stages of integrating environmental aspects into their internal procedures and offer only a few financial services and products in this field.

Thus in many developing countries there are no products tailored for or targeted to environmental finance, which is still in its early stages of complex and lengthy case-by-case financing. The only option for households and MSMEs is to use the banks' customary financial products, which are designed for other purposes and therefore do not have appropriate conditions for environmental activi-

---

[15] OECD. *Financing Water and Environment Infrastructure. The Case of Eastern Europe, the Caucasus and Central Asia*, OECD 2006, p.70ff.

[16] See the evaluation of clean production financing programs: Pratt, Lawrence and others. *Analisis de Mecanismos para el Financiamiento de la Produccion mas Limpia en la Pequeña y Mediana Empresa Latinoamericana*. FOMIN/BID, July 2003.

[17] African Institute of Corporate Citizenship (AICC). *Sustainability Banking in Africa*. Johannesburg 2004, p.15ff.

[18] 38% of respondents of a survey of 26 financial institutions in 14 Central and Eastern European (CEE) countries provide at least one environmental financial product. Source: UNEPFI. *Finance & Sustainability in Central & Eastern Europe*. 2004.

[19] E.g. for green mortgages: if the buildings meet higher energy efficiency standards, it is assumed that future energy costs are lower, thus leaving a higher disposable income for debt service. This increase in debt-service capacity could be used either to increase the loan amount or to reduce the risk premium.

ties. This means that regular household loans would be used to finance solar-water heater or housing energy efficiency measures, which would be carried out on an ad hoc basis due to the limited funds and terms available.

However, this gap in commercial financial markets is not completely shut. The gap is narrowed by non-commercial financial institutions, consisting of parastatal development banks and special institutions, (green) microfinance institutions and NGOs. They offer financial products which are relevant or even targeted for environmental finance. Non-banking financial companies, like the Indian Renewable Energy Development Agency (IREDA), offers terms up to 15 years, and many microfinance institutions have become established parts of the financial market. The special institutions offer medium- to long-term loans for selected environmental purposes, such as specific renewable energy technologies. Green microfinance institutions provide financial services to the poor for the acquisition of sustainable small energy solutions like wind pumps. However, their products and outreach appear rather limited.

Environmental activities may imply special risks, such as renewable energy that has a fuel risk. Risk instruments are needed to reduce such risks for the project sponsor and the financial institutions. Renewable energy may depend on wind and rainfall; small farmers who are affected directly by climate change may benefit from weather insurance. However, the commercial insurance market is in its early stages in many developing countries. These countries are unable to cope with this challenge without support. International insurance companies such as the Allianz Group are trying to extend their outreach to renewable energy. However they are hampered by a lack of creditworthy local insurers, restrictive local insurance regulations and limited distribution channels.[20]

A lack of data is one of the biggest problems facing local insurance industries in developing countries today. This has implications for environmental investment in these countries, because operating histories are difficult to model accurately, in turn making it difficult to project future loss and price risk in an economic and sustainable manner. Linked to this issue are the low insured values associated with small scale projects, which make it difficult for underwriters to achieve an underwriting profit even on loss-free accounts. However, promising pilot schemes such as those of ICICI Lombard in India have sold weather insurance to more than 250,000 farmers across India.[21] Institutions such as Opportunity International Bank of Malawi (OIBM) and the Malawi Rural Finance Corporation (MRFC), with significant start-up support from donors, are now offering packaged loan and index-based microinsurance products to groups of farmers.

---

[20] Marsh Ltd. *Survey of Insurance Availability for Renewable Energy Projects.* March 2006.

[21] ICICI Lombard offers weather insurance for mustard crops; Source: Moneycontrol.com, Published on 1 September 2008.

International structures like the carbon market are important sources of environmental finance. Impressive developments include more than 3,000 projects in 68 countries that were targeted to reduce 2,500 million tons of carbon dioxide – equivalent to a market volume exceeding USD 60 billion in 2007. Another positive development is the emergence of secondary markets trading financial products, such as monetisation of future carbon receivables and carbon delivery guarantees.[22] However, these schemes are complex, burdened with very lengthy, costly procedures with an unpredictable result. The project design document has to be approved by government at the national level, then validated by a Designated Operation Entity before it can be approved by the CDM Executive Board and registered. The cost for this process is estimated at USD 100,000, which makes it clear that smaller environmental activities can benefit only when they are bundled. This bundling approach is also necessary for medium-sized projects, as investors indicate that without these CDM funds their approval cannot be assured. Thus contrary to politicians' intentions, carbon credits take the character of a cherry on top of a cake. Nevertheless, the financial sectors in emerging markets are responding to these schemes, and some international banks are trying to promote CDM markets in the poorest countries.[23]

3.2 Problems in the Supply of Finance for Environmental Activities

The green wave in financial services in Europe and the US is a rather recent phenomenon. For many years the popular perception was that banking is relatively neutral in regard to environmental aspects. The influence that its clients exercise over natural resources was not considered. So it is not surprising that in emerging markets and developing countries, neither corporate environmental responsibility nor opportunities for environmental finance have received the consideration they deserve. Despite some progress, the problems listed in a survey of Latin American banks several years ago seem to characterise many financial institutions:[24]

- "The majority of managers in Latin America are still not taking environmental risk into consideration in their credit screening processes. Efforts are limited to checking legislation and environmental assessment in project financing, but not in mainstream loans to companies."

---

22 State and Trends of the Carbon Market 2008.

23 Banco Sumitomo Mitsui Brasileiro in Brazil increased its portfolio of carbon credits in 2007 by 1.5 million credits, generated from 15 small- and medium-sized projects, including biomass power generation, small hydro projects and methane technology. One of the bank's innovations has been to set up a payment bond issuance to guarantee the payments to be made by Japanese companies buying credits. Standard Bank currently has five projects in Africa. Source: Hartley, Fiona: *Benefits of trading trickling southwards*, in: Financial Times – Sustainable Banking, Special Report, 3 June 2008.

24 Pacheco Capella, Alberto. *Sustainable Finance: An assessment of environmental risks and opportunities in Latin America.* Lund 2002.

- "A vast majority of managers are not aware of the opportunities of the 'green' market, due to a lack of information."
- "Legislation governing banking and the environment is either lax or non-existent. Legislation and stakeholders are necessary to create a sustainable shift in banking in the region."

The lack of awareness and attention explains why understanding and sectoral knowledge remain limited in financial institutions. This includes the extent to which environmental activities mean good banking business. This implies that risks may be overestimated while the benefits of these activities are underestimated. However, it is not easy to build the required expertise because financial institutions in these countries face the same information problems in evaluating risks as do their clients. In this situation environmental finance is considered unattractive because the perceived risk is not adequately covered by appropriate instruments or higher returns.

This leads to possibly the most important cause of the low supply of environmental finance, which is easily forgotten in the discussion of pure environmental finance: financial institutions in developing countries seem to have sufficient alternative opportunities to earn higher returns at lower risks than with other products and clients. So even if environmental finance means business, it is not attractive enough to be put on the priority list, mirroring the situation on the demand side. However, this situation changes completely when the environmental component is linked to cross-selling high return products. Examples include household loans with an energy efficiency element, a housing loan with an additional amount for an energy-efficient housing component, company loans for modernisation or extension including an additional amount to meet a pollution regulation.

There is still a lack of priority for pure environmental finance. This should not be surprising given the experience in Europe and the US, where green financial products have responded to trends in society and in the real economy, which were seen as efforts to expand mature financial markets. But even there, green financial products have fallen short of industry expectations.[25] The real challenge in this area is not simply the introduction of new niche 'green' labelled products, but rather the integration of environmental incentives into mainstream commerce. This leads to the main challenge and problem: what has really flourished in the Western world is the financing of environmental activities which are financially attractive to both the borrower and the financial institution. This is mainly due to conducive framework conditions and incentive schemes, creating a triple win for the investor, the financier and for society.

---

25 UNEPFI. *Green Financial Products and Services.* August 2007.

Despite all the promising and successful examples of environmental finance in emerging markets,[26] the mainstream financial sector in developing countries is characterized in this respect by a three-dimensional gap in environmental finance between the needs and the supply:

- Available financial instruments, especially for the larger activities in the segment, which require some risk instruments, and for financial instruments linked to the supply of technical solutions like leasing.
- Amount of funds: Environmental activities are often afterthoughts to the common financial concerns of households and MSMEs. Adding the environmental dimension requires additional funds, exhausting debtors' credit limits assigned by financial institutions. Furthermore, these additional amounts and/or the new financial products require additional refinance, which may be a problem for the financial institution.
- Term structure may be an even more important consideration. A number of environmental investments require medium or long-term maturities. Financial institutions may be reluctant to provide longer maturities. Many banks still have a serious maturity mismatch between mid- to long-term lending requirements, and they suffer a shortage of access to corresponding refinancing.

4 Challenges for Financial Institutions

Where the price signals given either by the market or the state are strong, environmental initiatives flourish, and advanced financial markets responded to this demand. Globalization is developing rapidly with mergers in the financial sector, which will deepen markets, open refinancing channels and increase lending capacity. Especially in the case of environmental finance, global banks may standardize their policies across their international networks.

Market forces in the real sectors and increases in energy prices will be two additional strong drivers that will increase the demand for environmental activities, especially for energy efficiency. Financial institutions will not wait for ideal framework conditions, but rather will start to analyze current bankable demand and do their homework in order to increase their business in this field.

According to an IFC study, the global potential for lending to energy efficiency projects alone is USD 80 billion per year. [27] The huge demand of environmental investment will require financing, giving financial institutions a fundamental role

---

[26] To cite individual examples would be arbitrary, but a look at the awards and shortlists of the Financial Times Sustainability Banking Awards in recent years offers valuable insight.

[27] *Banking on Sustainability. Financing Environmental and Social Opportunities in Emerging Markets*. Washington 2007, p.60.

in sustainable development. In Europe and the US, state-of-the-art engagement practices by commercial banks respond to this challenge along two main tracks:

- By addressing the environmental credit risk of borrowers, banks improve their risk management and express their social responsibility. They signal that industries should improve environmental management practices. They identify opportunities for investment and finance with their clients. In this respect they may deal with environmental problem cases and turn them around into new business.
- 'Environmental finance' is focusing on greater investments in environmentally sound companies, environmental investments, infrastructure and clean energy.[28]

Thus, financial institutions have to deal strategically and comprehensively with the risk elements and the opportunities of environmental finance.

To move from defensive banking to proactive banking, financial institutions must overcome internal challenges. A recent study identified the following barriers to financing in environmental activities:[29]

- Insufficient knowledge: It is hard to get relevant and reliable information about the opportunities and benefits of investing in these areas of business in emerging markets. But the lack of knowledge also reflects the fact that many banks have not undertaken systematic initiatives in this field.
- Lack of institutional capacity: Scarce generic information, limited practical experience, and lack of training contribute to the failure of many loan officers' inability to assess potential investment opportunities that include innovative environmental applications. This is a special challenge in rural areas.
- Matching financial conditions: Longer payback periods require longer loan terms. This may severely limit financing possibilities, because many financial institutions in developing countries do not have adequate access to long-term refinancing and have a limited capacity for term transformation.
- Opportunity costs due to lower returns: Many of these environmental activities are relatively small in size and have high transaction costs, like financing of SWH. Others cannot generate a direct financial benefit at all, although they are necessary for the client. These include pollution abatement for commercial enterprises, so that they can continue in business under new regulations, which may strain their debt service capacity. For the lending

---

28 Emtairah, Tareq; Hansson, Lars; Hao, Guo. *Environmental challenges and opportunities for banks in China: the case of the Industrial and Commercial Bank of China*, in Greener Management International. March 2007.

29 IFC. *Banking on Sustainability. Financing Environmental and Social Opportunities in Emerging Markets*, Washington 2007, p.56.

institution, the returns generated from such transactions are smaller than those of other, less risky ventures, demonstrating that there is opportunity cost in environmental finance.

- Set-up cost: Integrating environmental concerns into a financial institution and developing environmental products require substantial resources.

It is simple to claim that "these issues can be resolved by gaining access to financial resources and technical assistance from the international development community and investors."[30] Despite all the sectoral barriers there are opportunities, especially in agro-business, energy efficiency and renewable energy. Ecotourism has also been discovered by banks that have participated in workshops on sustainable finance.[31]

There are clearly lessons from successful cases. These include Banco Real (Brazil), Nedbank (South Africa) and Industrial Development Bank of Turkey (TSKB).[32] However, each institution must develop its own approach and make its own commitment:[33]

- The first step is to be aware of the requirements and potential of environmental business. These must be identified and assessed systematically under prevailing market conditions and in consideration of the drivers which will change them soon. Financial institutions should undertake market research and analyses of the environmentally-related requirements and preferences of various customer segments. It is important to identify and focus on the win-win situations that reduce opportunity cost over time. This approach results in a sustainable and operational strategy.

- The next step is to implement the required changes, starting by highlighting the implications for corporate governance and integrating environmental risk into the portfolio and its management. Comprehensive integration requires hiring, supporting and training specialised managers or consultants, and allocating resources to develop a knowledge management framework.

---

30 IFC. *Banking on Sustainability. Financing Environmental and Social Opportunities in Emerging Markets*, Washington 2007, p.56.

31 Annex: Research Methodology and Survey Results to Banking on Sustainability. *Financing Environmental and Social Opportunities in Emerging Markets*, Washington 2007.

32 See the winners of the Regional Sustainable Banking Awards of the IFC and the Financial Times in recent years.

33 See the IFC Study, and also the 'Practitioner's Ideas for Innovation Tomorrow' (p.67) and the 'Paths to Sustainability Banking' (p.75) in African Institute of Corporate Citizenship (AICC). *Sustainability Banking in Africa*, Johannesburg 2004 and UNEP Finance Initiative. *Green Financial Products and Services – Current Trends and Future Opportunities in North America.*

- Then clients and partners should be identified by a) communicating these changes externally, starting with existing clients; b) participating in thematic trade fairs and arranging workshops for branches of industry; c) networking and forming alliances, cooperating with suppliers and dealers of environmental equipment and services, and learning from successful examples which are now becoming more numerous in emerging financial markets, as in the cases of Banco Real in Brazil and the Industrial and Commercial Bank in China; and d) through the identification of public-private-partnerships.
- Adjust/expand the line of financial products in scope and depth, possibly in cooperation with other financial sector institutions, e.g. to find long-term refinance, adequate guarantees and insurance. Financial institutions should attempt to understand and design green products in the same way that conventional banking products are treated. This is particularly important when considering key product-enhancing features, such as flexibility, user-friendliness and ease of personnel management.
- Financial institutions can attempt to overcome perception barriers and stimulate demand for green products and services through creative, educational marketing campaigns.
- The institutions must devise systems to monitor and verify all of these aspects.

Steps to address the challenges of environmental finance should go beyond the mere risk aspects within the different areas of a bank. These steps are listed in Table 4.

There are substantial potential benefits for banks to use these tools and incentives, as confirmed by a recent survey of 120 financial institutions in 43 countries:[34]

- Include environmental aspects in loan assessments, risk management and financing products. These procedures diversify and strengthen the portfolio and help indirectly to reduce the risk of non-performing loans (74% of the respondents).
- Work to enter a market with a huge growth potential that will attract new clients (35%) and increase business with existing clients through cross-selling with environmental financial products. These strategies can foster revenue growth (9%).
- With these types of activities, early entrants in particular can enjoy higher visibility in the market, contributing to increased business and brand value (39%).

[34] IFC. *Banking on Sustainability. Financing Environmental and Social Opportunities in Emerging Markets*. Washington, 2007, p.12ff.

Table 4. Internal Bank Activities that can Mainstream Environmental Finance

Internal Resources	Activity and Value Added
Human Resources	• Provide skills training to account officers that focuses on sustainability as a marketing tool to win business from priority market segments • Provide incentives and rewards for staff that achieve triple bottom line investments (financially, socially and environmentally high performing) • Use the institution's sustainability track record to recruit high calibre business school graduates
Risk/Credit Review	• Carry out environmental and social risk assessments of investments • Assist loan officers in the differential risk pricing of loans
Syndicates	• Secure lead management of syndicates for complex projects • Bring additional co-financing to complex sectors; participation by additional banks may rely on the sound environmental and social due diligence of the lead institution
Marketing and Corporate Relations	• Work with account officers and priority clients to identify needs as a basis for client sustainability • Develop marketing materials and communications tools to approach target markets • Develop communications tools to mainstream sustainability internally • Manage SRI communications and develop communications materials in approaching additional non-clients and stakeholders (NGOs, raters, analysts, etc.)
Retail Relationship Manager	• Identify smaller-cap client base with sustainability needs • Lead sector-wide marketing to the client base (e.g. seminars on process efficiency or on identifying export market opportunities for sustainable companies)
Treasury	• Issue green payables (e.g., earmarked green deposits; eco-bonds) based on the institution's sustainable portfolio • Secure access to international funds
Environment and Sustainability	• Provide strategic overviews • Provide central environmental and social advisory functions

Source: Extracted from IFC. Beyond Risk, table 'Mainstreaming sustainability', p.54.

Thus, there is a long catalogue of tasks to meet the challenges. Many smaller and medium-sized financial institutions may need substantial support to adapt. This is similar to the situation of microfinance more than a decade ago, which has proved that many bankable activities can create new markets. These new markets can be exploited with the proper financial techniques and support, although matching longer maturities – a very important aspect of environmental finance – still may require external support.

5 Perspectives and the Role of Donor Support in Environmental Finance

With increasing environmental problems, demand for environmental investment will rise. There are already signs of a new boom in green investment in the industrial countries. And reality also bites in the emerging economies: the recent blackouts in South Africa and massive environmental problems in the emerging economies make it clear that the demand for environmental finance will increase globally and locally. The global rush for energy and resources will include renewable energy and affect searches for environmental solutions such as resource efficiency. More renewable energy technologies, such as photovoltaic technology, will move towards commercial viability. This will happen at all levels and project sizes. The financial sectors in emerging markets and developing countries will have to make efforts to cope with this demand. Financial institutions will have to acquire new capacities and extend their financial capabilities.

Cooperation at an international level will be crucial. Donors and global (semi-) commercial funds will be required, as they can provide the capital for environmental finance at matching maturities. Donors' objectives and instruments should include support for access to commercial finance by making equity and long-term debt finance available in sufficient quantities and on competitive terms for investments in EF projects. Priority activities and instruments should focus on the gaps in the financial sector in the countries concerned. This may include:[35]

- Supporting the private industrial sector, including MSMEs, equipment producers, vendors, service companies, by providing enterprise development support, seed capital, debt finance, mezzanine finance (e.g., Central American Renewable Energy and Cleaner Production Facility/CAREC) and equity (e.g., IFC Renewable Energy and Energy Efficiency Fund/REEF; ADB Clean Energy Private Equity Investment Fund; KfW environmental credit lines for BMI Apex Bank in El Salvador, and for ProCredit Bank Ukraine);

[35] For details on lessons of these and similar projects, factors of success and future approaches, see the chapter in this publication by John MacLean.

- Supporting the Specialized Financial Institutions for RE, microfinance and funds (e.g. KfW credit lines for the India Renewable Energy Development Agency/IREDA), energy efficiency (Bulgaria Energy Efficiency Fund) and microfinance (Grameen Shakti in Bangladesh financing household solar PVs and biogas systems);

- Creating new financial vehicles such as revolving funds, credit lines and contingent business loans;

- Reducing (commercial) risks through financial guarantees (such as IFC Guarantee Facilities for Energy Efficiency e.g. "Gas fired heating for households" by Raiffeisen Leasing in Hungary with a loss reserve guarantee) and insurance schemes (such as the Global Index Reinsurance Facility/GIRIF supported by IFC and KfW).

Most of these approaches are not new. Donors and DFIs have used such schemes in many cases. Where inferior results were achieved, neither the market and framework conditions nor the financial institutions were fully prepared to cope at that time. Although there have been many successful programmes designed and implemented by certain financial institutions, their structural impact on the financial sector often has been limited. However, with adequate framework conditions, commercial financial institutions have learned from the experiences of successfully promoted financial institutions. These include IREDA in India, where domestic banks such as IDBI, ICICI and IFCI among others, subsequently developed their own environmental finance business.

Market conditions for environmental activities are changing on a global scale, as is the willingness of banks to cooperate and work systematically in this endeavor. At the beginning this may seem to be a difficult task, because it affects their ongoing business and may hamper the operation of otherwise easy business with good clients. It is not by chance that 86% of the financial institutions participating in the abovementioned IFC survey expressed an interest in receiving further technical assistance in this field. This includes staff training, access to industrial risk briefings, and practical tools such as software for environmental assessment.

On the sectoral level, donors could support countries in obtaining access to the various (semi-) commercial international environmental funding sources. The dialogue with governments should address framework conditions (energy tariffs and taxes, market regulations) and offer support for their adjustment. To be convincing, this will require more than just good arguments. Although the budget priority lists are changing, this (financial) challenge imposes an additional burden for the developing countries. Additional funds will be required to guide the adjustment process and cushion the social blow. Dialogue with banks should focus on a transfer of hands-on experience that stresses that environmental finance can indeed be good business.

6 Conclusions

The global market is growing with higher energy prices. There is increasing awareness of the priorities for environmental investment on one side. There is also a large set of technical solutions offered by a growing specialized environmental industry. The main fuel of industrialisation – oil – may run dry during our lifetimes, and has already become much more expensive. This will make many renewable energy and energy efficiency activities financially viable and increase the demand for finance.

There is an opportunity and a priority for mainstreaming environmental finance. The cooperation of the financial sector is essential for this approach. It should offer the target group adequate finance to meet its needs in environment and energy, and to directly improve their living conditions so that they can face their challenges and make the step from survival to sustainability. But such environmental activities will occur only if there is a clear financial benefit for both the financial institution and the borrower. Increasing the range for such win-win situations will require substantial support from the international community for the financial sector. This support has to be not only in the form of access to adequate funds; in addition, support is required to help financial institutions overcome their defensive attitudes and become more proactive. This requires financial institutions to include environmental aspects in their own sustainability strategies. It will take enormous efforts for them and their international partners to capitalise on the fact that energy is money and environmental protection means business – and money and business are bankable.

References

African Institute of Corporate Citizenship (AICC) (2004) Sustainability Banking in Africa. Johannesburg.

Corporation of London and DEFRA: Financing the Future. The London Principles. The Role of UK Financial Services in Sustainable Development. London.

Emtairah, T., Hansson, L., Hao, G. (2007) Environmental Challenges and Opportunities for Banks in China: The Case of Industrial and Commercial Bank of China. In: Greener Management International, March 2007.

Financial Times (2008) Sustainable Banking. Special Report, 3 June 2008.

International Energy Agency (IEA) (2008) World Energy Outlook 2008. Paris.

International Finance Corporation (IFC) (2004) Beyond Risk, Sustainability and the Emerging Markets Financial Sector. Washington.

IFC (2007) Banking on Sustainability. Financing Environmental and Social Opportunities in Emerging Markets. Washington.

Jeucken, M.H.A., Bouma, J.J. (2001) The Changing Environment of Banks. In: The 2001 Symposium of the International Research Network for Quality, Environment and Corporate Social Responsibility, 22 June 2001 Nijmegen. Shipley: ERP Environment.

Lindlein, P., Mostert, W. (2005) Financing Renewable Energy. Frankfurt: KfW.

MARSH Ltd. (2006) Survey of Insurance Availability for Renewable Energy Projects. UNEP, March 2006.

OECD (2006) Financing Water and Environment Infrastructure. The Case of Eastern Europe, the Caucasus and Central Asia. OECD.

Pacheco Capella, A. (2002) Sustainable Finance: An Assessment of Environmental Risks and Opportunities in Latin America. Lund.

Pearce, B. (2002) Financing the Future: The London Principles of Sustainable Finance.

Pratt, L., Rojas, E. (2001) Programa ambiental en bancos latinoamericanos: Una Evaluacion, Centro Latinoamericano de Competitividad. INCAE Costa Rica.

Pratt, L. et al. (2003) Analisis de Mecanismos para el Financiamiento de la Produccion mas Limpia en la Pequeña y Mediana Empresa Latinoamericana. FOMIN/BID, July 2003.

Rijal, K. (2007) Energy Subsidies in Developing Countries: Can We Make It for Those Whom It Is Intended? Joint UNEP and UNECE Expert Meeting on Energy Subsidies.

Schmidheiny, S., Zorraquín, F. (1996) Financing Change: The Financial Community, Eco-efficiency and Sustainable Development.

Stern, N. (2006) The Economics of Climate Change: The Stern Review. Report to the Cabinet Office, HM Treasury. Cambridge: Cambridge University Press.

Taylor, R.P. (2008) Financing Energy Efficiency: Lessons from Brazil, China, India, and Beyond. Washington: World Bank.

UNEP/IEA (2002) Reforming Energy Subsidies.

UNEPFI (2004) Finance and Sustainability in Central and Eastern Europe.

UNEP Finance Initiative (2007) Green Financial Products and Services – Current Trends and Future Opportunities in North America. A Report of the North American Task Force (NATF) of the United Nations Environment Programme Finance Initiative. August 2007.

World Economic Forum (2008) The Financial Development Report. Geneva.

CHAPTER 2

Mainstreaming Framework Conditions for Environmental Finance – The Role of the Public Sector

*Wolfgang Mostert**

Abstract

The term "environmental finance" in this paper refers to standard financing products of commercial banks for investments in clean technology. Investments in EE&RE products represent the main potential market for these. Whereas the existence of a potentially large market for investments in EE&RE is beyond doubt, its realization needs unlocking. In unlocking the market potential, the public sector has two roles to perform: (i) to introduce a set of incentive instruments to create a large-scale and long-term demand; and (ii) to coordinate the activities of actors (supply-side actions). Concerted CT deployment programs comprise an integrated package of environmental finance, together with "demand pull" and "technical supply-side" measures to create demand for investments. As incentive to include environmental finance in their product portfolios, banks may require the inclusion of a "bank engagement program", comprising measures that reduce their risks, their costs of transaction and their costs of capacity building, during the market upstart phase. Successful programs are complex. Yet a large number of instruments exist to customize solutions to local conditions, and the know-how to design and implement integrated packages is becoming increasingly well-established.

1 Demand for CT: A Condition for Environmental Finance

For the purposes of this paper, "environmental finance" is defined as "standardized financing products for clean technology (CT)[1] offered by financial institutions as

* Director, W. Mostert Associates.

[1] The term "clean technology" (CT), as shorthand for "environmental technology," refers to technologies that have a lower consumption of materials and fuels and release fewer emissions into the air, water, and soil than conventional technologies. They comprise: (i) technologies in energy efficiency and in renewable energy systems, (ii) production technologies for saving water and raw material, and (iii) technologies in investments for reducing end-of-pipe pollution that recover materials for reuse.

D. Köhn (ed.), *Greening the Financial Sector: How to Mainstream Environmental Finance in Developing Countries*, DOI 10.1007/978-3-642-05087-9_2,

part of their own business strategy".[2] Thus, the subject concerns the mainstreaming of finance for the mass market of small scale investments in CT made by small businesses, households and public institutions. Because energy efficiency (EE) and renewable energy (RE) technologies represent the bulk of the CT market, this paper examines only EE&RE technologies. Framework conditions in emerging and developing countries are the main focus, but for reference purposes examples from OECD countries are also included.

In order to mainstream environmental finance, the financial sector requires first and foremost a framework that creates the right market demand for its products. One can gain a good understanding of the ideal market conditions for environmental finance by looking at the characteristics of products that banks in emerging and developing economies are eager to finance: real estate, mobile phone vendors, cars and motorcycles. The most important are:

1. The annual demand for finance is large and "perpetual", giving banks good prospects for productivity.
2. Bank staff understand the products; hence, banks face low costs for internal training.

Thus, mainstreaming of environmental finance requires a framework that creates a large and long-term demand for standardised CT finance products. Large demand justifies upfront investments in internal capacity building and permits the development of standardised financial products; standardisation reduces transaction costs.

The framework conclusion is confirmed by statements from the financial community. At the "Renewables Conference" held in 2004 in Bonn, the financial community issued the following statement: "Strength, clarity, and stability are decisive characteristics of the policy that attracts capital to renewable energy: that policy must be specific enough to improve the bankability of projects and provide conditions for steady market growth in the renewables sector. An effective policy framework must be 'loud, long, and legal': (i) The signal to the market, through *incentive structures* or other means, needs to be 'loud' and clear to attract capital into the sector; (ii) *Rules and incentives need to be stable and sustained* for a duration that reflects the financing horizons of the projects; (iii) A legally-established regulatory framework based around *binding targets or implementation mechanisms* is needed to provide the basis for long-life capital-intensive investments."[3]

---

2 The term "environmental finance" refers to "commercial financial products that assists the deployment of CT-products"; these finance user investments in CT. However, investments in emission reductions that are enforced by Government regulations (e.g. waste water treatment facilities) fall outside the theme of environmental finance; they form part of general investments in production technology. Corporate investments in the supply chain for CT products and services are not covered by the narrow definition of environmental finance used in this paper.

3 Hamilton & Sonntag (2004).

Investments in EE&RE of relevance for environmental finance have long lifetimes and long payback periods. Environmental finance comprises primarily medium and long-term loans; these require longer-term certainty for the continuation of the conditions that motivate investment. This is why the finance community needs signals that are long and legal.

The finance community needs a loud signal because environmental finance is a new and, until recently, was a small niche field for the finance industry. To motivate the entry investments by the finance community into the development of an environmental finance portfolio, the medium to long-term market prospects for environmental finance products must be good.

2 Clean Technology: A Potential Market That Needs Unlocking

2.1 A Large Potential Market with a Long-Term Future

A short look at the characteristics of the CT market helps to understand the hesitancy of banks during the initial market development stages. Table 1 shows the British Government's estimates of carbon emissions in the industrial, public and household sectors in the UK.

Table 1. UK Carbon Emissions (2002) by Sector

	Number of entities	Annual carbon emissions	In percent of total
Energy intensive industry	2,400	25 Mtc	25,5%
Large non-energy intensive organisations	13,200	13 Mtc	13,3%
SMEs	909,000	10 Mtc	10,2%
Public sector		8 Mtc	8,1%
Households	21,000,000	42 Mtc	42,9%
		98 Mtc	100%

Source: HM Treasury (2005)

Roughly 25% of annual carbon emissions come from the 2,400 large energy intensive entities. EE and the use of RE are part of their core know-how in process technology and are financed as part of overall corporate finance; the financing of their investments is not, therefore, relevant to the topic of environmental finance addressed in this chapter. The market segment for environmental finance is made up of the relatively small-scale investments in EE&RE made by the 13,200 large non-energy intensive firms, the 909,000 SMEs, the 21 million households, the public sector and finally, the suppliers for these. The financial situation and specific EE&RE needs of the segments are very heterogeneous.

Cost-of-supply curves for CO_2 mitigation typically show a large cost-effective EE&RE potential. An example is the UK cost of abatement curve shown in the table overleaf.[4] The "*negative cost measures*" in the chart refer to investments in EE&RE which are cost-effective for private investors based on their financial return from energy savings without separate payments for achieved carbon reductions. In developing countries, "*positive cost measures*" are the target for CDM-projects and programs.

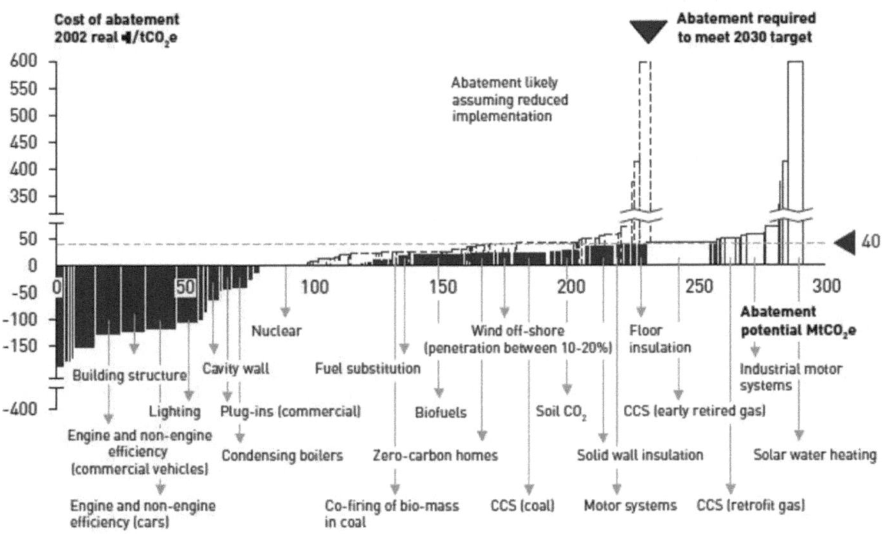

Fig. 1. 2030 UK cost curve for additional greenhouse gas reduction measures
Source: CBI (2007)

The combined message from Table 1 and Fig. 1 is that the cumulative market for environmental finance for EE&RE is potentially very large.

2.2 A Market Potential That Needs to Be Tapped

While EE&RE policy has become part of the mainstream in energy policy in most countries, at least since 2004, the potential market in individual countries still needs unlocking. Three major and interlocked obstacles to investments in cost-effective EE&RE measures are listed below:

[4] Copied from CBI (2007), see also Enkvist & Nauclèr & Rosander (2007).

1. **Competing options and needs.** During times of rapid economic growth, investments in cost savings ("defensive investments") are lower on the priority list of enterprises than investments in capacity expansion ("offensive investments"). During periods of low growth in demand for their products and services when companies turn their attention to cost saving measures, managers can find profitable efficiency improvements "everywhere": in staffing levels, purchase and stock policies, etc. Managers aim at minimizing overall inefficiency in the company, not just in a specific area such as EE. For investments outside the core activity (i.e. in support services and ancillary services), firms apply the 20/80 rule: that 80% of a potentially achievable result can be realised with 20% of the effort required to reach 100%. Households show a similar investment optimising attitude: when a new house is purchased, they invest in a new kitchen and/or in a new bathroom rather than in the EE-investments recommended in the energy certificate for the house. The first lead to visible improvements, the latter represent one financial investment opportunity amongst others.

2. **Asymmetric information about EE benefits.** Due to lack of required specialised technical knowledge, household consumers and small businessmen are unable to know whether a set of cost-saving measures proposed by a vendor or technician really results in the promised financial savings to the investor.

3. **CT technologies have *higher upfront investment costs* than conventional technology.** This is why terms for "environmental finance" that reduce the level of upfront equity finance to the legal minimum and give investors a positive operating cash flow from the first year after the investment are absolutely essential.

2.3 Generic Framework for Environmental Finance

Banks will engage in lending for clean technologies only if they are convinced that the government's promotion policy is durable. The credibility of that depends on the quality of the implemented framework.

Due to the interlocked nature of the obstacles to market development, effective frameworks to promote environment finance are complex, consisting of packages of complementary and mutually reinforcing instruments. To see what works and what does not, governments, therefore, monitor the outcomes of their support packages and look at international experiences for inspiration.

Best practice is always based on circumstance: concepts for market transformation through public initiatives cannot be copied successfully without significant adaptations to specific local conditions. Although framework conditions vary from one country to another, the contours of a framework for environment finance which is generally applicable can be established. The framework shown in Fig. 2 groups government interventions by three major categories of instruments: "demand pull", "technology push" and "finance push" instruments.

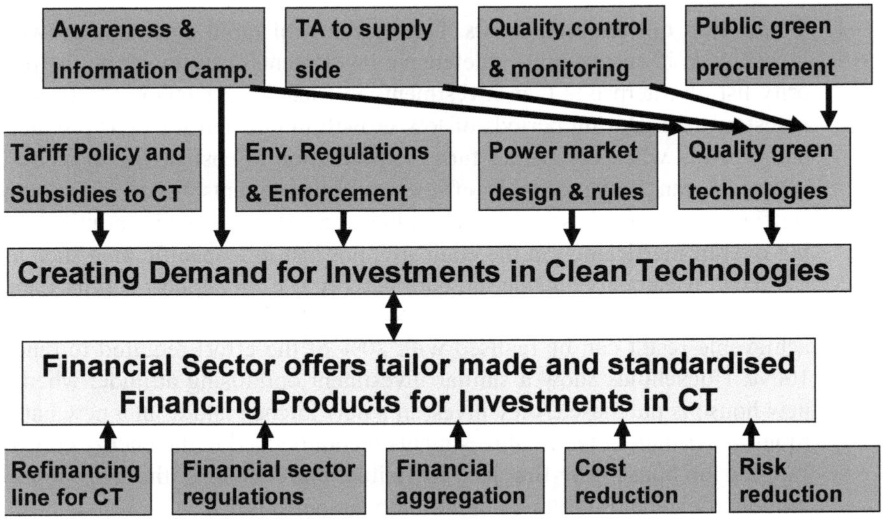

Fig. 2. Generic Public Framework for Environmental Finance

"Demand pull" instruments increase demand for CTs directly; they are used to overcome the motivation hurdle to investments posed by competing wants and needs. Instruments include pricing/tariff policies, information campaigns to create consumer awareness, environmental regulations and enforcement, and power markets that facilitate entry of generation using renewable energy.

"Technology push" (or technical supply side) instruments affect demand for CTs indirectly by strengthening the quantity and quality of CT products and services and reducing their costs. They include information to consumers about the CT-characteristics of products, technical assistance to actors in the supply chain, monitoring and quality control of supply, and public procurement policies favouring CT. The aim of some of these measures is to give consumers confidence in the products and advisory services, overcoming the problem of asymmetric information.

"Finance push instruments" (or bank engagement programs) aim to increase the supply of environmental finance: these are tailor-made products which reduce the hurdle of high upfront investment costs. Instruments comprise refinancing lines, financial sector regulations that facilitate environmental finance, assistance in establishing non-conventional financing channels, and measures to reduce bank transaction costs and lending risks.

Figure 2 shows a coherent national deployment strategy: three packages interact to create a market demand for clean technology. Banks look at the framework from a slightly different angle. For them, the essential aspects of the technical supply side and finance push measures are not that they assist in demand creation. Rather, banks are interested in how technical supply side measures can assist the development of standardised clean finance products and to what extent bank engagement programs reduce initial bank barriers to entry.

The following three chapters look at the framework as seen through the lenses of the financial community. As far as possible, each chapter structures the treatment of subjects to start with those that are the most important for banks.

3 Demand Pull Instruments: Signals That Are Loud, Long and Legal

3.1 Legal Signals: Fixing Policy Targets for EE&RE

Long-term government commitment to the development of a CT-market is expressed by lawmakers' adoption of a long-term policy for CT comprised of (i) quantified targets for the penetration of CT by a fixed date, (ii) an action program, (iii) long-term forecasts for the financial implications for the national budget, and (iv) specified budget allocations for the initial years.

Quantified targets without specified commitments and budgeted action plans have little chance of implementation. The risk of underperformance is high in EE&RE and CO2-mitigation policies, because they do not affect the population directly as, say, underperformance in health or education policies. Postponing the achievement of a target by a few years is, therefore, not an election losing exercise. The experience of Egypt's policy targets for RE during the last 20 years illustrates the situation in many OECD and developing countries. In 1986, Egypt adopted a penetration target for new RE equal to 3% of *final energy supply* in the year 2000. Ten years later, the *3%* target for RE was postponed to 2010 and shortly after 2000 redefined to refer to *3% of electricity supply* in 2010.

Because of such experiences, many clean technology advocates prefer to see *long-term quantitative targets enshrined in a law* rather than in the form of a cabinet decision, as the latter is easier to adjust. Turning a quantitative policy target into a legal obligation is happening for CO2-mitigation policies in Annex I countries[5] because of international treatises and conventions. In the EU, directives imposing CO2-emission reduction and RE penetration targets for 2020 are subtranslated into specific targets for each member country. But in the emerging and developing economies, the legal target approach is not likely to be adopted in the near future. In these countries, the financing community will be more impressed by the quality of the framework as a guide to credibility, rather than by the formal adoption in a law of a very long-term goal – such as the UK's 2050 target of an 80 percent reduction in carbon emissions!

---

[5] The industrialised countries and economies in transition listed in Annex I of the United Nations Framework Convention on Climate Change. Their responsibilities under the Convention include a binding commitment to reducing their GHG emissions relative to 1990 levels by the year 2012.

A more immediate priority, therefore, is to improve the quality of the policy making process which adopts the targets. A major reason for non-compliance with politically fixed targets for EE&RE market shares is that the target is fixed by government in a top-down, ad hoc manner with little reference to detailed economic cost-benefit calculations. A bottom-up approach to fix penetration targets for EE&RE is to set targets for individual sectors according to the economically viable EE&RE potential in each sector. The resulting *overall penetration target is more credible*, because it reflects the marginal cost-effectiveness of EE&RE and because the monitoring of outcomes at the sector level allows planners to react faster with changes in policy instruments when results do not live up to expectations.

3.2 Rational Policies for Energy Prices

A second, immediate priority is the introduction of rational pricing policies that are socially balanced. The elimination of subsidies to fossil fuels and electricity tariffs sends a louder and longer "legal" signal than the introduction of subsidies to EE&RE.

The typical situation in developing and emerging economies is summarized in Table 2.

Table 2. Pricing of Fossil Fuels and Electricity in Developing and Emerging Economies

	Gas and oil for power stations	**Liquefied Petroleum Gas and Kerosene**	**Electricity for HH**	**Transport fuels: diesel, gasoline**
Net exporters of energy	Subsidized	Subsidized	Lifelines tariffs	Subsidized
Net importers of energy	Full cost	Sales to households subsidized	Lifelines tariffs cross-subsidized by higher consumptions	Taxed

OECD countries usually adopt sensible pricing policies, directly promoting the deployment of CT through "green taxation" (taxes on fossil fuels, electricity, water, disposable containers and waste). Taxation policy may be inefficient – lobbyists can skew taxation in favour of specific interests, but overall, the price signals point in the right direction.

Many *fuel-importing developing countries* use taxes on fossil fuels to save foreign exchange and raise revenue for the state budget. Yet, also in these countries, household fuels are often subsidized to reduce the impact of increasing fuel prices on the financial situation of lower-income groups.

Developing countries that are net exporters of energy tend to give high subsidies to hydro-carbon fuels and to electricity, thereby undermining the creation of a market for EE&RE. In 2008, Egypt spend almost USD 11 billion on energy subsidies, equivalent to 5% of GDP, more than on the government budgets for education (USD 6 billion) and health care (USD 3 billion) combined.[6] Malaysia had one of the biggest fuel subsidy bills in the world, estimated at as much as 7% of GDP in 2008, before the government took the decision to increase prices by 40% in June 2008.[7]

Governments in developing countries are fully aware of the *damaging effect of high energy subsidies on the economy*: the price distortion leads to inefficient allocation of resources in the free market, while the financial burden on the public budget crowds out high value support to education, health and infrastructure. They also know that the *equity impact of energy subsidies is deficient:* since higher-income households consume more energy, wealthier households receive more subsidy support than poorer households. The exceptions are well-designed electricity lifeline tariffs for small levels of monthly electricity consumption that are cross-subsidized by higher-consuming households and subsidies to kerosene.

To replace energy subsidies with direct social income support is, therefore, in principle attractive to policymakers.[8] Nevertheless, many governments in developing countries believe that they cannot implement such schemes because (i) they cannot identify low-income households that are eligible for a social income subsidy as many live in the informal economy, and (ii) they do not have the local government capability to administer cash transfer schemes. Governments, who during 2008 approved increases in energy prices, therefore tried other avenues to reduce the burden on the poor: imposing price controls on more basic goods, subsidizing public transport and spending on infrastructure investments to create jobs. Yet, social survey methods to pinpoint the poor have been applied successfully in a number of countries and a number of innovative delivery channels are used to overcome the problem of weak local administrative capacity.

3.3 RE&EE Subsidies and Use of Regulation

The long-term credibility of a scheme to support the deployment of EE&RE depends on its cost-effectiveness. It depends on three aspects: (i) the quality of subsidy design, (ii) use of new loan instruments or (iii) use of regulation when this is feasible and more efficient.

Criteria for Identification and Optimisation of Subsidy Instruments

Although in principle subsidies are a scarce good, the cost-effectiveness of many national schemes in developed countries, compared to feasible alternatives, is sur-

---

6 Friedman (2008).

7 The Economist May 2008.

8 Many economies in transition managed the transformation from subsidized household energy prices to full cost prices by letting municipal administrations pay part of the monthly energy bills of low-income households directly to utilities.

prisingly low. Too many schemes over-compensate beneficiaries, have high free rider effects and distort markets unnecessarily. In less-rich developing countries, such RE&EE schemes would have a very short lifetime.

A variety of subsidy instruments are used to strengthen the demand for EE&RE.[9] The *primary objective* of making investments in CT commercially viable can be achieved by "any" subsidy. Optimisation, as illustrated in Figure 3, calls for taking into account a number of design criteria

- *Impact effectiveness:* the scheme must lead to a significant expansion of the market and to cost reductions in CT, and generate employment and foreign exchange earnings/savings.
- *Distributional efficiency:* planners do not want to over-compensate investors, create big distortions on the market (e.g. by giving RE-generators too many exemptions from the general rules of the power market) or set up a system that imposes high administrative costs on recipients and on the public administrator of the scheme.
- *Burden sharing efficiency:* the schemes should not impose a heavy burden on low-income households or on energy intensive industries that are subject to fierce foreign competition nor lead to unwanted redistribution of income between firms and social groups.

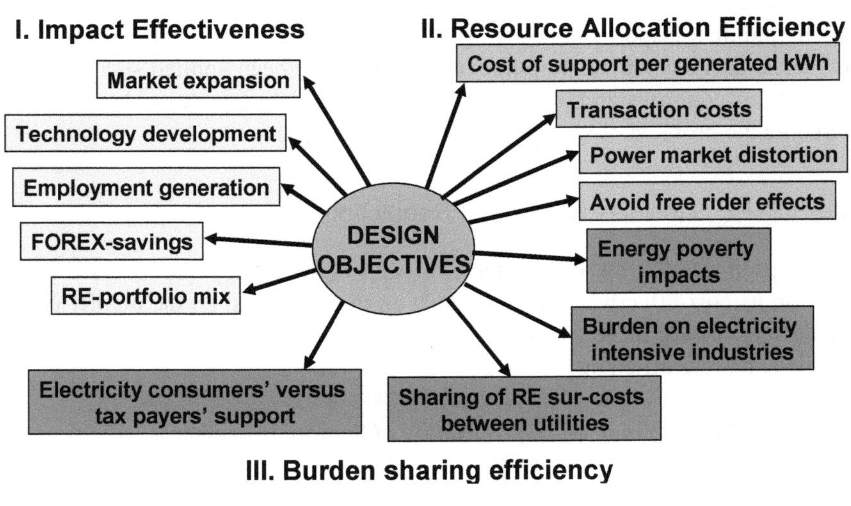

Fig. 3. Criteria for Optimisation of Subsidy Schemes to EE & RE

9 RE&EE subsidies have three sources of finance: (i) the state budget; (ii) consumers of conventional energy; and (iii) grant funds and soft loans from clean technology funds for international carbon finance. A subsidy can be given to (i) the cost of investment, (ii) to output, or (iii) to costs of operation. get-neutral. See Lindlein & Mostert (2005) for a presentation of subsidy instruments using the "financing source-subsidy target" matrix.

In countries worldwide, one can see a trend towards increasing sophistication of policy instruments for EE&RE.[10] Recent subsidy schemes in emerging and developing economies are remarkably well-designed. Inter alia, they include efforts to identify *budget neutral subsidies*; as such, they touch the core of the optimisation issue, which is subsidy affordability for the government:

The Ministry of Energy in Tunisia convinced the Tunisian Ministry of Finance of the benefits of introducing a per-system subsidy to solar water heaters. The decisive argument was that solar water heaters replace consumption of subsidized Liquefied Petroleum Gas (LPG) for water heating and that, according to calculations, the reduction in replaced subsidy payments to LPG was higher than the cost of the subsidies to solar water heaters.

- Egypt has a dual price system for its national natural gas production. Natural gas consumed in Egypt is priced at the "cost of production", exports of gas at the "price from export contracts". Output from grid-connected wind farms replaces power generation at natural gas-fired power plants, allowing Egypt to use saved gas consumption to increase its exports of gas (mainly in the form of LNG). The decision was taken to split the increase in gas revenue 50%/50% between the Ministry of Oil and a Renewable Energy Fund, which was created under the Ministry of Electricity. The REF pays a subsidy per kWh to wind farms, which they receive on top of the electricity tariff per kWh paid by the national transmission company.
- The *Sri Lanka Sustainable Energy Fund* is funded by a variety of sources, making its long-term viability a high probability.[11] The objective of the fund is to support investments in EE&RE; first and foremost investments in RE generation, which are paid technology-specific feed-in-tariffs by the national power company CEB.[12] The fund reimburses the power company for the difference between (a) the average cost per kWh of conventional generation in the system[13] and (b) the feed-in-tariffs. The strategic objective of the mechanism is dual: to secure sustainable funding for EE&RE investments, yet avoid political opposition from CEB due to costs imposed on CEB by an increased penetration of RE generation.

---

10 See IEA (2008) and OPTRES (2008).

11 See Sri Lanka Sustainable Energy Authority Act, No.35, 2007.

12 Technology-specific feed-in-tariffs pay different tariffs for different technologies, reflecting differences in their average costs of production per generated kWh. In order to allow a broader portfolio of investments to enter the market, higher-cost technologies (e.g. solar PV-systems) get a higher tariff than lower cost technologies (e.g. wind turbines).

13 The average cost of the tariffs paid to independent power producers (IPPs) using thermal power and the costs of the production generation plants owned by CEB, which are mainly medium-scale hydropower,.

Mixing Subsidies and Long-Term Loans

A separate optimisation issue is the balance and interaction between the subsidy instrument and the loan finance instrument. The barrier of high upfront costs of SME and household investments in EE&RE can be reduced by a combination of up-front grants and use-specific long-term loans on favourable terms. Together, these two instruments must bring the up-front cash payment down to the feasible minimum and reduce the annual cash payments during the amortisation period to a level which is below the payments for saved conventional energy.

Often loans are sufficient to overcome an initial purchase hurdle. Some demand side management programs, for example, give compact fluorescent lamps (CFLs) to households free of charge. A more efficient alternative are schemes where commercial banks lend funds to the electricity distribution utilities for purchasing CFLs that are distributed or sold to clients. Clients do not pay for the bulbs up-front; rather, the utility adds a loan amortisation surcharge to the monthly utility bill until the loan is fully repaid. In Sri Lanka, the electricity distribution companies CEB and LECO provided interest-free loans to customers to purchase up to three CFLs. The loans were repayable in 12 monthly instalments and were recovered through the electricity bill. An independent testing facility was established to authorise the different brands of CFLs.

3.4 Balance Between Market Based and Regulatory Instruments for Market Expansion

Governments have a large arsenal of instruments to draw from: catalogues of laws, regulations and policy instruments can be found on relevant websites.[14] Instruments for creating a higher demand for EE&RE technologies can be divided into two categories:

1. "Command and control instruments":
   - Regulations imposing use of EE&RE technologies
   - Norms and standards for EE in buildings, appliances and vehicles
   - "Voluntary agreements", negotiated agreements between industry associations and governments to attain specific targets for EE
2. "Market based instruments":
   - Incentives for action: economic and financial incentives for investing in EE
   - Information: EE labeling, information campaigns, demonstration projects

[14] See IEA's Energy Efficiency Policies and Measures Database http://www.iea.org/textbase/pm/index_effi.asp or American Council for an Energy-Efficient Economy's http://www.aceee.org/energy/state/ for measures in US states.

For every instrument, there exists an alternative. Energy efficient lamps, for example, can be promoted by a package of *market instruments,* e.g. promotion campaigns, grants and utility-based lending; or through use of *regulation,* for example interdicting sales of incandescent lamps. A third optimization issue concerns the balance between the use of grant/market instruments and the use of regulatory instruments. When should which be used?

Market-based instruments have a comparative advantage in "promoting good practice". They are most effective when incentives for action (investment grants, soft loans, loan guarantees, tax credits, and fossil fuel taxation) are combined with effective know-how building (information on the advantages of EE through labeling, demonstration projects, support to advisory offices, and promotion campaigns). The importance of government-financed *awareness*[15] and *information*[16] *campaigns* is well-established. Whereas information about CT characteristics, availability of advisory services and environmental finance is straightforward, still very little is known about how to design effective awareness campaigns that can change consumer behaviour and lifestyles towards "energy modesty".

Command and control instruments are used, above all, to address systemic causes of market failure; their comparative advantage is in preventing bad practices. Examples from EE are (i) norms for fuel efficiency in new cars, where progress in efficiency was undermined by consumer preferences for horse power, acceleration and advanced air conditioning (all promoted by marketing campaigns from car manufacturers); and (ii) norms for EE of apartment buildings, where EE faces market obstacles such as landlord-tenant differences of interest. Regulations imposing energy audits and compulsory investments in non-energy intensive industries, where energy is just one cost factor among many that compete for management attention, are an example of promoting good practice. For environmental finance the most important regulations are:

- Regulations for EE and RE in building codes;
- Regulations for labelling of appliances; and
- Regulations for the integration of rooftop photo-voltaic (PV) systems in power market transactions.

Building codes[17] impose standards for EE[18] in new construction.[19] EE standards are a good instrument in theory; in practice, they suffer from severe implementation

---

[15] To create interest in EE&RE, most effectively through information on the financial benefits of EE&RE.

[16] About technical options, available technical products, service companies and conditions for environmental finance.

[17] Building codes for EE exist in two forms. *Prescriptive codes* set separate performance levels for major envelope and equipment components, such as minimum thermal resistance of walls. Due to easier enforcement, they are the most common. *Overall performance-based codes* prescribe an annual energy consumption level per square meter of floor area or an

and enforcement problems. Only 40% of new buildings comply with building codes in the UK; this figure is as low as 20% in the Netherlands (depending on effectiveness of monitoring activity by the local municipality) and 5% in China. Since countries increasingly apply full-cost-of-supply tariffs for industrial and commercial customers, there is a potential market for standardised EE packages for industrial and commercial buildings. However, it is prudent to conclude that in most emerging and developing countries the situation is not ripe for the development of tailor-made environmental finance for standard EE-packages in residential building renovations. It is more cost-effective to focus on improving the enforcement mechanisms for the building code for new buildings: annual additions to the building stock in emerging economies are much higher than in developed economies due to the positive growth rates of their national populations and the fact that demand for building space increases with the growth in per capita income.

EE standards are also introduced for *major energy consuming appliances;* yet, the enforcement record here is also mixed. Thailand implemented energy efficiency standards for air conditioning and refrigerators as part of a DSM program. Although similar labelling programs were introduced for refrigerators and air-conditioning systems, significant energy savings were achieved only for refrigerators. In the case of air conditioning, where the number of manufacturers was very high in contrast to the number of refrigerator manufacturers, serious enforcement problems occurred. The air-conditioning market would have needed stricter enforcement and stronger market intervention strategies.

The components of a sustainable regulatory framework for investments in small-scale distributed (embedded) generation such as rooftop PV systems are well known:

- Compulsory rules imposed on distribution companies for grid connection;
- Feed-in-tariff for surplus (or total) sales of electricity from the PV-system to the distribution grid; and
- Rules for net metering.[20]

---

energy cost budget. They provide more scope and incentives for innovation, but require better trained building officials and inspectors. Building codes for RE require instalment of building integrated RE-systems (e.g. rooftop PV-systems, solar water heater systems) in new construction (covering a minimum percentage of the building's energy consumption) or provide for reservation of space for later instalment of RE systems in or on the building.

[18] "EE buildings" are buildings that achieve low levels of annual energy consumption through a mixture of (i) architectural design, (ii) use of highly-insulating materials including EE-glass and window frames, (iii) EE cooling & heating, ventilation and lighting systems, (iv) power supply from building integrated PV (BIPV) and (v) water saving measures.

[19] In the EU codes also apply for existing buildings in connection with major renovations.

[20] Net metering allows the building or home owner to sell to the grid any excess electricity generated by the PV installation; the customer's electric meter will run backward when the solar electric system produces more power than is needed to operate the home that

4 Technical Supply Chain: Standardisation Through Coordination

4.1 Linking Standardised EE&RE Products to Standardized Finance

A bank can introduce standardised finance products only for standardised CT products. Among relevant EE&RE products one can distinguish between "off-the-shelf" products for stand-alone applications and products that are integrated components of buildings or of industrial processes.

Examples of the first category are solar PV-panels, solar water heaters and, at the micro-scale: compact fluorescent lamps. Standardisation for these means building "guarantees" for quality through equipment specifications and standards for products, and through certification of qualified vendors and installers who participate in government-sponsored promotion campaigns.

EE-equipment for industrial processes and EE-retrofitting of industrial, public and private buildings are examples of the latter. Here, standardisation involves:

1. *Environmental/energy audits in industry* and *energy certificates for buildings*. Standardisation in this case is not in terms of content, but in terms of guaranteed quality: investment packages with CT benefits are identified by specialised experts and have a positive financial rate of return. Because audits present a package of individual measures, investors can ask banks to finance either some of the measures or the whole package.
2. *Model ESCO contracts for energy saving contracts and energy supply contracts.*[21] These are particularly important for promoting energy savings in the public sector and for creating sufficient national demand for the operation of ESCO-companies.

4.2 Capacity Building and Quality Control in the Technical Supply Chain

For the future of environmental finance, it is essential that consumers have faith in the quality of promoted products, in their installation and in the availability after-sales-service. Governments use two complementary instruments to promote quality in the supply chain: one is capacity building, the other is regulation.

---

time. A special utility-grade inverter converts the DC power from the PV modules into AC power that exactly matches the voltage and frequency of the electricity flowing in the utility line; the system must also meet the utility's safety and power-quality requirements. In the event of a power outage, safety switches in the inverter automatically disconnect the PV system from the line.

[21] ESCOs are companies that perform energy audits and invest in the identified package of EE-measures at the plant of the beneficiary. Beneficiaries have no net cash costs. The ESCO is paid out of a pre-defined share of the value of energy savings during operation until the "loan" is amortised.

A number of countries can boast good results with dedicated capacity building programs. Tunisia and Morocco, for example, implemented successful capacity building programs for "solateurs" (installers of water heater systems).

A necessary supplementary instrument used in public support programs for EE&RE is regulation: to have access to a subsidy, investors must get the work done by certified experts, vendors and installers who have participated in specialised training courses; often there is a list of qualified vendors and experts for investors to choose from. The system involves random checks of the quality of executed works and withdrawal of licenses for dealers and/or installers that do not perform. In this way, for example, Bangladesh, Sri Lanka, and Nepal managed to create country-wide dealer and retailer networks for solar PV-systems.

4.3 Increasing Supply by Lowering Costs of Entry for Service Providers

Governments use several tools to increase the number of companies providing CT products and services:

- Increase of the supply of qualified experts by introducing Master of Science courses at universities in EE&RE and by offering EE&RE courses at vocational training institutes
- Direct assistance for the creation of specialized companies, e.g. by organising training courses given by foreign specialists in the organisation and financing of ESCOs
- Public procurement of EE&RE services through mandated energy audits and investment programs for public buildings. This is important in particular to build sufficient national demand for the operation of energy service companies (ESCOs).
- Facilitating the rental of high-cost specialised equipment

For example; Sri Lanka eases the entry of new-comers in EE-consulting and engineering through the facilitation of an instrument bank[22] and calibration services, both are rented out on an ad-hoc short term basis by the Sustainable Energy Authority.

4.4 National and Local Governments as Organisers of Supply Chain Networks

Market transformation through public policy is by definition implemented through public-private-partnerships (PPPs). Several sophisticated and successful PPPs for

[22] Comprising flue gas analyzer, temperature data loggers, power analyzer, portable power meter, air flow meter, temperature, humidity & TDS meter.

the promotion of EE&RE have been implemented in OECD and in emerging and developing countries. In this section, the first example provided is of a program coordinated under the auspices of central government; the second is coordinated under the auspices of local government.

National Government as Facilitator of Financial and Technical Supply Networks

In 2005 Tunisia launched the Progamme Solaire, or PROSOL program, which uses a number of innovative instruments and broad collaboration between government agencies, the national power company, the financial sector and solar system installers to achieve its results. PROSOL is implemented jointly by:

- the Ministry of Industry and Energy,
- the national agency for EE, Agence Nationale pour la Maîtrise de l'Énergie (ANME),
- the national power company, Société Tunisienne de l'Electricité et de Gaz (STEG),
- the financial sector, and
- solar water heater dealers and installers.

Financial and technical assistance support provided by PROSOL is co-financed by the state, the Global Environment Facility (GEF), the United Nations Development Program (UNDP) and the Italian government.

PROSOL focused initially on the promotion of 200 and 300-litre solar water heating systems for residences aiming to install 500,000 m^2 by 2009. Financial support to solar water heaters (SWHs) comprises a direct subsidy as well as an investment rate subsidy. SWHs get a subsidy of 100 DT (EUR 59) per m^2 up to a total sum of TND 400, which amounts to 19% of the installed price of a 200 liter 2 m^2. SWH (price of TND 1100) and to 22–27% of the installed price for a 300 liter 4 m^2 system (TND 500–1800).[23] The purchase of a 2 m^2 SWH costing TND 1100 is financed by the subsidy of TND 200 and a consumer cash payment of TND 150; the remaining TND 750 is financed by a five-year bank loan with an interest rate of 7% instead of the usual 14%, and which is repaid through a surcharge on the monthly electricity bill.

The interest rate reduction is achieved partly by a USD 2 million GEF grant, and partly by STEG administering the amortization of the loan on behalf of the banks, which reduces the costs of transaction for the banks and eliminates the need for collateral. Installers are in principle authorized: ANME gives short-

[23] The state budget provides USD 2.5m to finance the cost of the subsidy, the two donor-financed programs MEREP and MEDREC an additional USD2m. The state provided subsidy amount is, however, compensated by replaced LPG-consumption, which saves the state USD 2.5m per year when the 700,000 m^2 target has been reached!

term training courses (1–3 day courses) to installers, but in practice the criteria for authorization are applied softly in order not to slow down the development of the market. ANME also gives training courses to SWH consultants for dimensioning systems for commercial buildings[24] and for supervising the construction work; an authorization system is also used here. Consumers get a one-year guarantee for installation, a 5-year guarantee for the water tank and a 10-year guarantee for the solar collector.

Local Government as Facilitator of Supply Chain Networks

In many CT promotion programs, a central government agency acts as coordinator. But partly inspired by Agenda 21[25] initiatives, municipalities across the world have become increasingly engaged as local promoters and coordinators of EERE finance. Rooftop PV, solar water heaters, geo-exchange cooling, EE-projects, and water supply and waste disposal projects are implemented everywhere; hence the importance of including local government as actors in market transformation programs. Their role can be described as follows:

- A 'one-stop shop' for householders, accessed by calling a freephone number.
- KES provided householders with advice on energy efficiency measures, discount prices for installation and access to cashback and preferential loan schemes.
- Householders would be referred to an approved installer, from the network set up by KES, who would inspect the property and recommend appropriate energy efficiency work.
- Once the work was completed, the householder paid the installer, and would then be eligible for cashback payments from KES.
- The quality of the scheme was monitored through inspections of 10% of the works, questionnaires sent out with cashback payments, and telephone surveys.
- The installers – of measures such as cavity wall insulation, loft insulation, draught-proofing of doors and windows, heating controls, hot-water tank insulation, floor insulation and condensing boilers – were selected following a tender published in local newspapers.
- The successful installers received specific energy efficiency training to help householders identify the areas where work could be most beneficial. Installers paid a referral fee of 5% to KES, to fund the scheme's administration.
- Three local credit unions became partners in the scheme, offering preferential loan facilities for householders to install energy efficiency measures. Without this access to dedicated finance, it is likely that many householders would not have been able to improve their homes' energy efficiency.

Fig. 4. "Kirklees Energy Services" (KES)

---

[24] In the previous GEF project suppliers tended to over-dimension the system to charge higher prices.

[25] The programme action plan that came out of the 1992 United Nations Conference on Environment and Development, the Rio Summit. It was given the title Agenda 21 because of the 21 chapters dealing with a wide range of aspects relating to sustainable development.

- To execute their planning and regulatory functions for approvals of CT projects efficiently; this lowers project risk and pre-investment costs;
- Provision of information to consumers;
- Quality control of implemented CT-work; and
- Organisation of PPPs for program implementation. Several successful PPPs can be identified worldwide.

Figure 4 gives an example of a scheme for promoting EE in the building sector: the "one-stop clearing house" administered by the British municipality of Kirklees. It is composed of (i) impartial information to consumers about AE, (ii) the administration of subsidy payments to AE, (iii) technical assistance to the supply side, (iv) quality control with performance and (v) bank loans to consumers for investments in environmental finance.

5 Bank Engagement Programs: Overcoming Hurdles to Entry

5.1 Justification for Bank Engagement Programs

The financial community is seldom in want of demand for its products. It has alternative business opportunities other than environmental finance to expand into. During the pilot phases of initial market development, transactions are small and start-up costs are high. At this stage, most RE companies in developing countries are frustrated by the lack of bank interest in their businesses, either to finance their operations or to lend to their customers.[26] For this phase, *a bank sector- specific framework to overcome the entry hurdles* is usually required to ensure bank engagement.

A typical support program includes the components discussed below.

5.2 Refinancing

Refinance facilities are found in almost all countries, normally financed by soft loans and grants from donors and international development banks. They may be the most important instrument of all. They give the banks a direct economic incentive to engage in environmental finance: because of refinance, the bank's involvement in environmental finance adds to its overall financial volume and does not reduce its financial engagement in conventional lending activities. Their terms can match the longer tenor of loans for EE&RE.

[26] "They claim that banks don't understand their business, their technology or their customers and generally lack incentive to innovate the financial services they have on offer." Usher & Touhami (2006).

KfW's environmental finance line for investments by home and apartment owners in the EE of buildings is an interesting example of a well conceived and integrated refinancing program, which is led and organised by a national development bank. A few aspects are highlighted below.

- KfW provides a refinance line for loans by homeowners in EE.
- Households go to their local banks to apply for a loan. Loans have 10 years duration, low rate of interest (subsidized by KfW) and a grace period.
- The loans finance only specified packages of typical EE measures in "older houses".
- A certified energy engineer approves a priori the package and after finalisation of the works, the quality of implementation.
- If the implemented package results in an EE standard equal to the norms of new buildings, the home owner gets a 5% reduction in the repayment of principle, and a 12.5% reduction if the EE standard is 30% better than the building norm for new houses.

5.3 Information and Awareness Building, Capacity Building

Information and moral persuasion by government is required in all countries. The process involves multi-actor discussions between, on the one hand the financial sector, and on the other hand the ministries responsible for finance and energy as well as stakeholder representatives from the private sector. The government lays out its EE&RE policy goals and implementation, specifying the roles of each major actor. With the help of the donor community and foreign technical assistance, the government can inform the financial sector about quantified estimates of the future market demand for environment finance once the government policies are implemented.

With the help of the donor community and foreign consultants, governments can provide cost-shared capacity building (i) in the design and administration of new environmental finance and (ii) in basic technical appraisal of EE&RE projects.

5.4 Reducing Risks for Banks

Guarantee facilities for loans to customers who have little collateral to offer have been developed in several countries. In theory, partial risk guarantees to local banks for loan repayment as a collateral substitute are a good instrument; but in practice they result often in serious moral hazard.

Sustainable Energy Authority (SEA) in Sri Lanka provides a 75% guarantee on loans for RE and EE investments for up to USD 100,000. For this it charges the banks an annual premium of 0.5% of the amount guaranteed or loan amount outstanding. The premium is expected to mainly meet the cost of facility management. The scheme helps to solve the problem of lack of collateral of small-scale investors. The banks perform the financial due diligence review of the investor and the project; if it is positive, the bank forwards the project proposal to the Guarantee Fund to undertake the technical review and approve the guarantee. Normally, the loan repayment period will be the project payback period guaranteed by the ESCO plus one year; the maximum repayment period is 6 years. SEA's guarantee facility is endowed with USD 500,000. A fund reserve of 15% of loans guaranteed, based on the highest non-performing loan portfolio of leading banks in Sri Lanka, is set aside as a loan loss reserve. Based on this and the 75% guarantee limit, the fund can leverage close to USD 5 million in loans for EE&RE projects.

Guarantee schemes for loans to solar home PV systems, usually with involvement of vendors for the recycling of recovered systems by banks, have also been put in place in Sri Lanka as in other countries.

5.5 Facilitating Financing Channels for Bank Loans to CT-Investments

In the Tunisian PROSOL program, the government used its regulatory powers to persuade the state owned power utility STEG to channel bank loans to consumers for investments in solar water heaters. Consumers paid back their loans, including payment of interest, through a fee on the monthly electricity bill. This turns a multitude of tiny loan transactions for the financing institution into one single large loan which is given to the utility.

Another and by now well-tested avenue is for the government to act as originator of collaboration and *financial links between established commercial institutions* which provide the basic finance and *microfinance institutions,* which provide loans to small-scale business and households investing in EE&RE.

6 Concluding Remarks

The prospects for environmental finance look promising even in the short term. The need for coherent frameworks is increasingly understood by governments, the designers of integrated policy packages can draw for inspiration and evidence on a large number of proven tools and implementation approaches and the financing community sees a market which grows from year to year!

References

AID-EE (2007) Success and Failure in Energy Efficiency Policies. Ex-post Evaluation of 20 Instruments to Improve Energy Efficiency Across Europe.

CBI (2007) Climate Change; Everyone's Business.

Economist (2008) Not Everybody Is Paying Higher Prices for Oil. May 29.

Friedman (2008) Letter From Cairo. New York Times, June 15.

Hamilton, K., Sonntag-O'Brien, V. (2004) Financial Sector: Statement on Renewable Energy. Finance Sector Presentation at Bonn Conference 2004.

HM Treasury (2005) Energy Efficiency Innovation Review. Summary Report, December 2005.

IEA (2006) Renewable Energy Technology Deployment – RETD, Barriers, Challenges and Opportunities. May 2006.

IEA (2008) Deploying Renewables. Principles for Effective Policies.

Enkvist, P.-A., Nauclèr, T., Rosander, J. (2007) A Cost Curve for Greenhouse Cost Reductions. McKinsey Quarterly 2007(1).

Kruger, R. (2005) Sustainable Development – The Banking and Finance Sector.

Lindlein, P., Mostert, W. (2005) Financing Renewable Energy. Instruments, Strategies, Practice Approaches. KfW Discussion Paper 38.

Mostert, W. (2007) Unlocking Potential, Reducing Risk. Renewable Energy Policies for Nicaragua. ESMAP 2007.

OPTRES (2008) Final Report. Assessment and Optimisation of Renewables Energy Support Schemes in the European Electricity Market.

Sonntag-O'Brien, V., Usher, E. (2004) Mobilising Finance for Renewable Energies. Thematic Background Paper, Bonn Conference 2004.

Sri Lanka Sustainable Energy Authority Act, No. 35 of 2007.

Usher, E., Touhami, M. (2006) Engaging the Banks. Financing Small-Scale Renewables in the Developing World. In: Renewable Energy World, May–June 2006.

CHAPTER 3

Mainstreaming Environmental Finance Markets (I) – Small-Scale Energy Efficiency and Renewable Energy Finance

John MacLean[*]

Abstract

Energy efficiency and small-scale renewable energy (EERE) projects have huge and essential contributions to make to create a sustainable, low-carbon economy and achieve the Millennium Development Goals. But there remains a large gap between the strong economic and environmental potential of EERE projects versus their limited commercial realization. A major cause of this gap is the lack of effective project delivery and financing mechanisms, adapted to national and local market conditions.

The EERE market encompasses a diverse set of markets which fundamentally consist of large numbers of small, dispersed projects in a wide range of market segments. These markets are best approached programmatically, with market aggregation strategies. Successful programs combine a) access to finance with financial products structured and adapted to the target market, with b) marketing, project development and project delivery mechanisms that generate a steady flow of investment-ready projects, along with programs that build capacities of market participants to expand this business on a commercial basis. That is, they address both the supply side and the demand side of EERE financing.

A substantial body of experience exists with commercial financing of EERE projects and with EERE finance programs. These are conducted by commercial financial institutions (CFIs) in partnership with development finance institutions (DFIs) that organize and systematically deliver EERE projects, services and financing for the implementation of multiple projects in target markets. Such programs a) engage and mobilize financing from local CFIs, and b) are frequently supported by credit lines, risk sharing facilities and/or other investment instruments and technical assistance programs provided by DFIs. Further, CFIs can partner with EERE businesses, energy utilities, associations of energy users and

[*] Managing Director, Energy Efficiency Finance Corp.

D. Köhn (ed.), *Greening the Financial Sector: How to Mainstream Environmental Finance in Developing Countries*, DOI 10.1007/978-3-642-05087-9_3,

governments acting on behalf of energy users to market their financial products and generate substantial flows of well structured projects for financing.

The public good features of clean energy produce a strong rationale for public investment to develop EERE finance markets. The urgency of scaling up EERE investments makes it imperative to assess experience and lessons of commercial EERE financing and EERE finance programs. It is important to share effective methods and define and implement scale-up strategies to capture the economic and environmental potential of EERE.

After characterizing EERE markets, the challenges of EERE financing and the rationale for development finance initiatives in this field (Section 1), this chapter reports on a range of methods to structure and market commercial financing of EERE projects (Section 2); and successful EERE finance program models involving partnerships between CFIs and DFIs, including technical assistance programs (Section 3). The chapter contends that sufficient experience exists with successful EERE transaction structures and finance programs to justify roll out and scale-up, provided such programs are properly adapted to country and target market conditions. Initial ideas on scale-up strategies are provided in Section 4. This chapter is intended to inform commercial FIs of the possibilities for building profitable business lines in this field, to provide ideas and recommendations to DFIs for design of future EERE finance programs, and to be useful to other national and international development agencies concerned with promoting EERE finance market development.

1 Overview: Promise and Challenges of EERE Finance

1.1 Innovative EERE Finance and Delivery Mechanisms: Getting Ready for Scale-Up

Energy efficiency and small-scale renewable energy (EERE) projects have huge and essential contributions to create a sustainable, low-carbon economy and achieve the Millennium Development Goals. However, there remains a large gap between the strong economic and environmental potential of EERE projects versus their limited commercial realization. A major cause of this gap is the lack of effective project delivery and financing mechanisms, adapted to national and local market conditions. The good news is that a substantial body of experience exists with innovative and effective mechanisms for a) commercial financing of EERE projects, and b) EERE finance programs which organize and systematically deliver EERE projects, services and financing to implement multiple projects in target markets. Many EERE finance programs have been implemented by governments, development agencies and development finance institutions (DFIs) in partnership with commercial financial institutions (CFIs).

This paper reports on a) a range of methods to structure and market the commercial financing of EERE projects (Section 2), and b) successful EERE finance program models involving partnerships between CFIs and DFIs, including technical assistance programs (Section 3). Further, this chapter contends that sufficient experience exists with successful EERE transaction structures and programs to justify roll out and scale-up, provided such programs are properly adapted to country and target market conditions. Initial ideas on scale-up strategies are provided in Section 4.

1.2 EERE Market Definition

For the purposes of this chapter, energy efficiency and small-scale renewable energy (EERE) projects are defined as all forms of energy efficiency investment retrofitting a) existing equipment and facilities (as distinguished from construction of new facilities) b) in all end-user sectors (residential, commercial, industrial, agricultural, municipal/institutional) and c) including a full range of end-use equipment such as boilers, thermal plants, lighting, motors, controls, heating and air conditioning, industrial process systems, waste heat recovery, refrigeration, compressors, etc. plus d) small-scale cogeneration, distributed generation, and renewable energy systems in the size range of up to 5–15 MW.

Small-scale RE also includes household and community scale projects such as solar photovoltaic bio-gas systems targeting the 'energy access' market, to deliver energy services in off-grid and underserved communities and rural areas. These benefits have essential roles to play in meeting the Millennium Development Goals.[1] Single EERE project investment costs range from the micro (e.g., USD 250–500 for a solar home system) to USD 5–15 million, e.g., for an industrial biomass cogeneration system. The upper limit of the definition of "small-scale" is not a hard and fast number but is defined operationally by commercial FIs based on projects which are sufficiently large to be financed on a single, one-off project finance basis, such as larger 15–25+ MW grid-connected RE projects. This size will vary by country, market and institution.

1.3 EERE's Essential Contributions to a Low-Carbon Economy

Energy efficiency investments in lighting, heating and cooling, pumping, motors, cogeneration, thermal plants, control systems and other end-use technologies are economic and readily available. In its 2006 *World Energy Outlook* Alternative Policy Scenario, the International Energy Agency (IEA) estimated that efficiency measures could account for more than 65% of energy-related GHG emissions savings up to 2030. Furthermore, these investments will generate an estimated net savings of USD 386 billion between 2006 and 2030. In its *Energy Technology*

1 See, for example, Worldwatch Institute, REN 21 Renewable Energy Policy Network, "Energy for Development: The Potential Role of Renewable Energy in Meeting the Millennium Development Goals", 2005.

Perspectives 2008 the IEA estimates that end-use efficiency can account for 36% of the emissions reduction required to return emissions to current levels by 2050. This is the largest share of any option.

The IEA's recent report *Deploying Renewables* (2008) finds that many renewables are commercial or near commercial and justified for deployment on a "massive scale". These renewables consist of on-shore wind, small hydropower, solid bio-mass combustion for heat, power and cogeneration, geothermal, bio-gas electricity and solar photovoltaics in many applications. Renewables, given an aggressive effort, as outlined in the IEA's *Alternative Policy Scenario 2007* and *Energy Technology Perspectives* BLUE scenario, are projected to produce 29% of global power generation by 2030 and 50% by 2050. Further, in its *Energy Technology Perspectives 2008*, the IEA estimates that renewables can create 21% of the emissions reduction needed to return emissions to current levels by 2050. This is the second largest share, after efficiency, of any option. Carbon capture and sequestration (CCS) represents 14% of the reductions, and nuclear energy, 6%.

1.4 Market Barriers to EERE Project Finance

Many EERE technologies are proven, economic and actionable for scaled-up deployment. Properly financed, they can pay for themselves from energy cost savings. Yet, many thousands and millions of projects with compelling economic returns remain unimplemented. With some exemplary exceptions, EERE has not yet been targeted strategically at a level of effort and investment warranted by its technical and economic benefits. A major cause of this gap is the lack of EERE finance and delivery mechanisms that are adapted to national and local market conditions. The reasons for this gap in the capital market are well-documented. EERE is not a single market, but constitutes a diverse range of end-user sectors, end-use equipment and technologies and, similarly, consists of very large numbers of small, dispersed projects. High pre-investment development and transaction costs, lack of customer awareness, complicated technical information requirements, long marketing cycles associated with selling EERE and the early stage of development of the EERE industry all result in a relative paucity of investment-ready projects.

Further, commercial financial institutions often lack experience with EERE. High perceived and real end-user credit risks, lack of collateral offered by EERE equipment and difficulties creating creditworthy financing structures discourage CFI entry into this market. These and other characteristics of EERE financing create marketing barriers, increase development risk and costs, reduce financial institution interest in this sector and contribute to the gap between EERE's technical/economic potential versus its commercial achievement. In some cases, local financial market conditions, e.g., lack of long-term capital, legal environments that negatively affect loan security or high interest rates may discourage borrowing generally. These factors may or may not be amenable to intervention by a DFI.

1.5 The Importance of EERE Finance Programs

The EERE market consists of a diverse range of end-users, each with their own institutional and financial characteristics. Financing must be adapted to each target market segment. A *programmatic* approach to EERE project financing is needed that *aggregates* end-users and projects, and that assembles sufficiently large demand for capital to attract commercial financing. Successful EERE finance programs combine a) access to finance with financial products structured and adapted to the target market, with b) marketing, project development and project delivery mechanisms that generate a steady flow of investment-ready projects. These must be complemented with programs that build the capacities of market participants to develop and structure finance for projects. That is, they must address both the supply side and the demand side of EERE financing.

The availability of finance to energy users is important because it overcomes the high initial costs and makes it possible for end-users to pay for projects out of the savings they have generated. But financing alone is not sufficient. EERE finance programs must also reach further into the project development cycle and generate a pipeline of investment-ready and creditworthy projects. Insufficient project pipeline development was a major weakness of many early EERE finance programs. An EERE finance program organizes and systematically delivers EERE project development services and financing to implement projects in a specific target market sector or sectors. Programs can target housing, SMEs, industry, public/institutional sector, energy access or other market segments.

1.6 Mobilizing Commercial Financing and Roles for Development Finance Institutions

The vast majority of EERE project finance must come from private sector commercial financial institutions.[2] This requires the mobilization of commercial financial institutions (FIs) that can offer properly structured EERE financial products. The commercial banking systems in many developing countries have ample liquidity and financial resources but are not mobilized for EERE lending. Commercial FIs are in the business to book profitable assets. If properly organized, CFIs will respond to demonstrated, ready, substantial and creditworthy demand for financing with manageable transaction costs. DFIs can be instrumental in mobilizing the resources and capacities of commercial FIs for EERE financing.

Where sufficient liquidity exists, credit enhancement and risk sharing products can be used to mobilize funding from commercial FIs. Where it does not, DFIs can provide credit facilities. In some cases, both may be required. Further, DFIs

---

2 See, for example, United Nations Framework Convention on Climate Change, "Investment and Financial Flows to Address Climate Change", 2007, which prominently highlights this same conclusion.

can organize the market by designing and implementing EERE finance programs to generate demand for the financing facilities it arranges or supports with partner FIs. DFIs can arrange donor funding for technical assistance and capacity building and can also work with governments to formulate enabling policies.

2 EERE Financial Products and Marketing Strategies for Commercial FIs

This section presents several EERE financial products which local CFIs have offered – and can offer – in their markets. Further, marketing strategies that can generate a steady flow of demand are discussed. The financial products presented all use successful commercial financing methods. A general discussion of commercial FI perspectives on EERE finance, design of EERE financial products, structuring security, and marketing are provided.

2.1 Developing EERE Financial Products by Commercial FIs

Components of a Financial Product

Because the EERE market is so diverse, FIs should take a "financial product" approach to EE finance, designing specific financial products to selected markets. This facilitates standardized financing. Considerable financial engineering and product design are often required to serve these markets. Design of a financial product starts with assessment and selection. Choice of target market should be based on matching the CFI's interests and capacities with those of the prospective market. The EERE project economics should be strong and the CFI knowledgeable. The CFI should be able to assemble adequate security for the contemplated transactions, perhaps with support from a DFI.

The financial product design must define: tenor, pricing, down payment, required security and underwriting guidelines, required documentation and origination procedures. The objective is to design a financial product that is a) attractive, even compelling to the target borrowers, b) easy to use, and c) with reasonable security terms. Loan terms, tenors and payments should be matched with the target project benefit streams so that loans can be self-amortizing. To devise a well designed product, CFIs often do initial transactions to gain experience, then roll out the product through its branch network. Training for loan officers is helpful.

Typical EERE Finance Products

The most common EERE financial product is a loan directly to the energy end-user. When the end-user is the borrower, the project is implemented with two agreements, one for turnkey project installation and services between the end-user and contractor,[3] and one for project financing between end-user and the financial institution. End-user credit risks are separated from project performance and project technical risks. The FI assumes all of the end-user credit risk, in which it has expertise, while all technical and performance matters are addressed between the contractor or energy service company (ESCO)[4] and the end-user directly. The end-user is obligated to make fixed loan payments. The loan payment amount is set to amortize the loan regardless of project performance. Guarantees of project performance are made between the ESCO and the end-user. The loan is on the balance sheet of the end-user.

The end-user assumes responsibility for equipment maintenance, repair, insurance, taxes and risks of loss or damage associated with the equipment. Provision for equipment operations, maintenance services and warranties can be addressed in an end-user/contractor agreement. Loan financing can be combined with savings guarantees from the contractor, effectively making the total arrangement a performance contract.

A second common alternative is for the ESCO to be the borrower. The ESCO packages financing with its turnkey project implementation and services agreement. The loan is on the balance sheet of the ESCO, not the end-user. In lending to the ESCO, the CFI's due diligence agenda is greatly expanded, similar to project financing. It includes the end-user credit risk because the ESCO's ability to repay its debt is strongly dependent on the payment performance of the end-user. This is a function of a) project economics, b) project engineering and technical performance, c) ESCO financials and equity contribution, d) ESCO management and performance track record, and e) all project contracts including critically the Energy Services Agreement. A variety of energy services or sales agreement structures are possible. Lending to ESCOs is discussed briefly below.[5]

Most commercial FIs offer term lending for plant and equipment. Some have leasing units. Others use structured finance and project finance capacities and thus may be familiar with lending similar to that used in EERE projects. Engaging CFIs may be a matter of learning their existing interests and capacities and seeing how these can be adapted and applied to EERE markets. In many markets, finance leasing can be used for EE/RE equipment, even when the equipment lacks collateral value. Leasing companies, often bank subsidiaries, have experience with vendor finance programs and other forms of equipment finance that are analogous to EE. They are often much more aggressive in marketing their financial services, and some have structured finance capabilities.

---

3 This agreement may also include provisions for operations and maintenance, savings monitoring and guarantees of project performance.

4 The term "ESCO" is used broadly to refer to the EE project developer and contractor.

5 Typical due diligence and appraisal agenda and related guidance materials on lending to ESCOs for EERE projects are available on request.

Security and Special Features of Credit Analysis for EERE Project Loans

- *Low Collateral Value*

  EERE equipment often has relatively low collateral asset value. For most EERE projects, equipment represents 60–65% of total project cost; EERE projects have high portions of engineering, development and installation costs.[6] EERE equipment is installed in the end-user's facilities, for example, lighting and motors and industrial process equipment, and is often difficult and uneconomic to remove and use elsewhere. For these reasons, EERE project lending is most frequently not based on the equipment asset value, but on the credit-worthiness of the energy end-user.

- *Positive Credit Features of EERE Equipment: Essential Use and Energy Cost Savings*

  EERE equipment has two important positive credit features. First, EERE equipment is "essential use" equipment, e.g., commercial buildings cannot operate without their lighting, controls and air conditioning, and the industry cannot operate without its motors or bio-mass thermal plants for processing energy. Because of this characteristic, the end-user's willingness to pay on EERE loans is enhanced. Second, EERE projects save money and these savings improve the end-user's ability to repay. Energy cost savings should be incorporated into lenders' analysis of free cash flow and ability of borrowers and end-users to meet debt service payments.

  In addition to full recourse to the end-user/borrower, major techniques for securing EERE equipment and project loans to end-users include the following:

- *Preferred Drawing Rights and Special Escrow Accounts*

  A preferred drawing right agreement or provision is included in the loan documentation whereby the borrower agrees that the lender is paid automatically at a defined payment date each payment period (monthly, quarterly), and this amount is automatically withdrawn from the borrower's bank account. Lenders can establish special escrow accounts where borrowers deposit cash flows from defined revenue sources. The lender would have first call on funds in the escrow account for debt service.

- *Reserve Funds*

  A common project finance technique is to establish dedicated reserves for debt service, repair and replacement of equipment or other purposes. Similar reserves can apply in EERE project financing. For example, debt ser-

[6] Some EERE project equipment, such as package cogeneration systems, or PV panels as a component of solar home systems, does have some collateral value, but considerably below project cost.

vice reserves can be combined with the escrow account method by requiring minimum balances in the escrow account, equal to, say, two to three months of loan payments.

- *Security Interest in Equipment and Project*

  Although EERE equipment may have relatively low collateral value, lenders should still perfect a security interest in equipment to assure that the lender's interests are protected. If a borrower defaults, a security interest in equipment may allow a lender to deny access to or use of equipment even if it is not repossessed. In defaults, the facilities in which the EERE equipment is installed may be foreclosed, vacated or sold. If the building itself is viable, i.e., in a good location and well-constructed, it is likely that the building will be re-occupied by another owner or tenant. This new occupant will use and benefit from the improvements made by the prior defaulting owner/tenant. Lenders with a perfected security interest or mortgagor waiver can require the new owner or tenant to assume the remaining payment obligation as a condition of use of the building. That party can therefore recover the loss due to default, providing an alternative way out of a defaulted loan.

- *Recourse to Equipment Vendor*

  Because equipment finance can increase the vendor's sales and profits, the equipment vendor has an interest in supporting the financing. This can be in the form of direct, limited or partial recourse, or repurchase or resale of equipment in default or impairment.

- *Portfolio Approach to Credit Structure*

  When many small financings can be pooled, credit analysis using a portfolio or statistical approach becomes possible. The large number of small transactions can become a virtue: no single default can cause the lender to fail to recover principal. Reasonable worst case default rates can be estimated for the structure and pricing of the overall program, with added reserves coming from fees, vendor recourse or even concessional risk sharing programs. Portfolio approaches to credit enhancement have been used to finance energy access equipment such as household-scale solar PV and biogas home systems, single- and multi-family residential EE finance products and vendor finance programs targeting SMEs and other loan portfolios.

- *Collections via Utility Bills or Property Taxes*

  Utilities can be important partners or originators for EERE equipment loan financing. If the utility can collect payments via utility bills, the credit structure of the loans will be enhanced. The convenience, habit and regularity of utility bill payment by customers result in dependable collections. The customer's utility bill payment history can be checked quickly and easily.

A major incentive to repay and improve collections may be used if the utility is able and willing to terminate utility service in the event of customer default. Utility participation in such a program also lends credibility, which enhances marketing. Banks can partner with utilities for this purpose. Similarly, banks are beginning to cooperate with local governments to collect EERE loan payments via property tax collections.

- *Extra collateral from the borrower*

  As a condition of lending, many lenders require borrowers to pledge hard or liquid asset collateral equal to a multiple, e.g., 150%, of the loan amount. Of course, extra collateral can be requested and obtained where possible; however, this requirement is often difficult for a borrower to fulfil and generally discourages borrowing. EERE finance marketing will prosper where lenders can make credit decisions on the basis of free cash flow and ability to pay, and realizing a prudent portion, e.g., 70%, of the estimated energy cost savings. Many DFI EERE finance programs that offer guarantees emphasize this point: help the partner FIs to create secure transactions that require less extra collateral from borrowers. Instead, underwrite the loans based on the project's benefit stream and the borrowers' ability to pay.

- *Guarantees and credit enhancement programs*

  In some cases, DFIs or other government agencies may offer credit guarantees to support EERE financing. When the terms are attractive, these can be used by the CFIs to share risks, making them a very effective tool to support expanded EERE lending. Further discussion of DFI guarantee products is provided in Section 3.

Security techniques for lending to ESCOs are discussed below.

Marketing

An EERE financial product must be launched around a marketing strategy and plan. Marketing strategies should include partnering with EERE equipment vendors, ESCOs, utilities and end-user associations to generate deal flow. Such partnerships are critical to generate and aggregate demand for financing. Multiple marketing channels can be used.

This approach is well-illustrated by the IFC China Utility-based Energy Efficiency Finance program. IFC has helped its partner CFIs establish EERE financial product marketing relationships with a gas utility, ESCOs and EERE project developers, and EERE equipment vendors. FIs can market their financial products directly and systematically to their existing customers. They can survey their existing customers, starting with those with whom they are willing to take on additional term credit exposure, to evaluate their potential for EERE investments. Most industrial and commercial companies will have some potential for cost effective EE projects. To take a proactive approach, the FI can partner with EE/ESCO companies[7] and offer to conduct an EE audit, the first step to develop a project. This type of offer can be included in a donor-supported technical assistance program.

2.2 Creating Demand for EERE Finance: Marketing Strategies for Commercial Financial Institutions

EERE markets consist of large numbers of small projects. Therefore, commercial FIs are recommended to apply programmatic methods for marketing their financial services. This is achieved by aligning with market aggregators and others whose activities could create effective demand for the EERE financial products the commercial FI offers. Partnerships can be created between CFIs and several types of market actors pursuant to strategies to aggregate the market. Examples include:

- vendor finance programs, partnering with EERE equipment suppliers
- energy service company (ESCO) programs
- utility-based programs supporting EE, demand side management (DSM), and renewable/distributed energy investments
- pooled energy end-user procurement programs which organize effective market demand and develop investment ready projects, partnering with governments or associations to aggregate groups of end-users
- housing EERE project finance programs
- EERE finance programs targeting small and medium enterprises (SMEs)
- energy access finance programs which mobilize capacities of microfinance institutions to deliver energy equipment financing

Each of these strategies work on the "demand side" of EERE finance to prepare a series of projects for investment that will meet the lending criteria of the CFI.

Vendor Finance Programs

A vendor finance program is a relationship between a company selling EERE equipment and a financial institution, whereby the FI provides financing for customers to purchase the vendor's equipment. Vendor finance programs are applica-

[7] EERE and ESCO firms should be qualified by the FI for such partnerships. The FI should assess: services/products offered, business methods used including form contracts, the firms' target end-user market and customer profile including related end-user credit characteristics, the company's reference projects and current project pipeline, their current and estimated project financing and projections as well as general corporate and financial statement information. Resource materials for conducting such assessments are available on request.

ble for virtually every end-user. For the FI, the vendor finance program creates a flow of financing business, aggregating demand for many small projects. The vendor markets the FI's financial services and performs certain finance origination functions which lower FI transaction costs. In some cases, the vendor can provide credit support, thus helping the FI to offer financing to more customers. For the vendor, such a program supports increased sales. The customer pays for the equipment over time, matching payments with energy cost savings benefits. (See Annex, Example 1: Vendor Financing Examples in IFC EERE Finance Programs.)

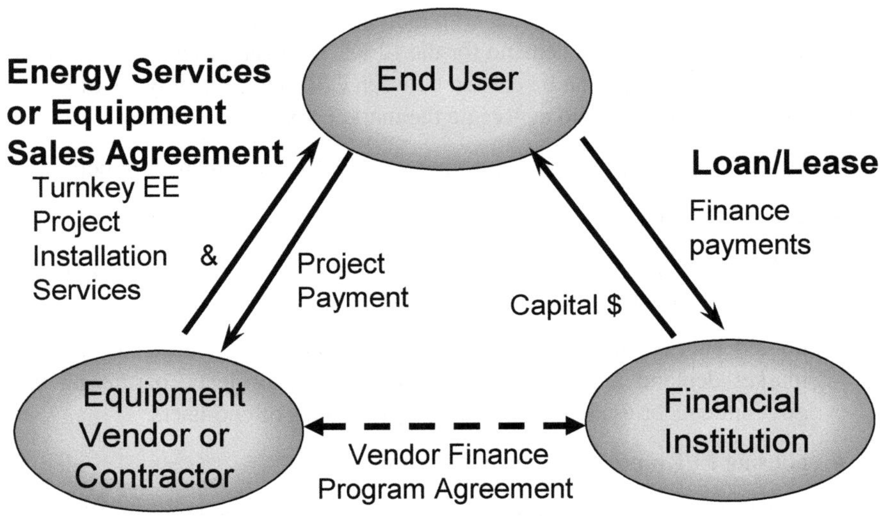

Fig. 1. End-user as Borrower: Vendor finance program

Alternative structures can be considered, for example: 1) Vendor borrows from FI and on-lends to Customer or otherwise has a long-term Energy Services Agreement with Customer; or, 2) Vendor enters into loan, rental or instalment purchase agreement with Customer, and then Vendor *sells* this payment stream to FI. This structure is called forfeiting. These alternative structures can be very effective for marketing by the vendor, as the vendor combines equipment sale with financing. They are depicted below.

ESCO Programs

An Energy Service Company (ESCO) is a business that develops, engineers, and installs clean energy projects in a variety of end-user sectors. For the energy user, the ESCO packages a complete turnkey offering. By combining financing with turnkey implementation, an ESCO has powerful marketing. ESCOs operate with a range of business models. The ESCO often provides or arranges financing for their projects. ESCO's are not a source of financing *per se*, as they in turn require both debt and equity. Thus, ESCOs and/or their customers need debt financing from commercial financial institutions. ESCOs can form an important bridge between the energy user and the FI, especially in developing countries where finance is less accessible. ESCOs can structure their projects using a range of business models. Those that create the most secure financing include some fixed payment obligation from the customer to amortize the project capital investment.

The typical structure is depicted in Fig. 2:

- The end-user enters into an Energy Services Agreement (ESA) with the ESCO; a variety of ESAs are possible.
- The end-user payment obligation may be determined based on project performance, savings, delivered energy or the value of capital and services.
- The loan is typically on the ESCO's balance sheet. The ESCO assumes end-user credit risk and may require lender assistance to evaluate.
- The ESCO will typically fund a portion of the project with equity, typically 10–30%.

In lending to the ESCO, the FI must assess end-user credit risk, the ESCO's technical, managerial and financial capacities and the project economics, contracts and risks, which are similar to a project financing. Common alternative structures are depicted in Fig. 2 and 3.

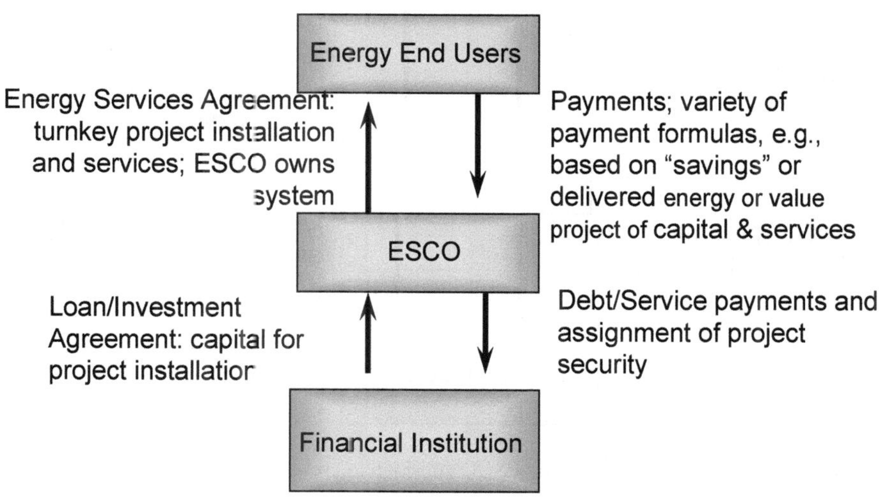

Fig. 2. ESCO as Borrower, Typical Performance Contract Structure

- End-user makes a fixed payment to ESCO, matched to amortize ESCO's investment.
- ESCO sells this payment stream to FI.

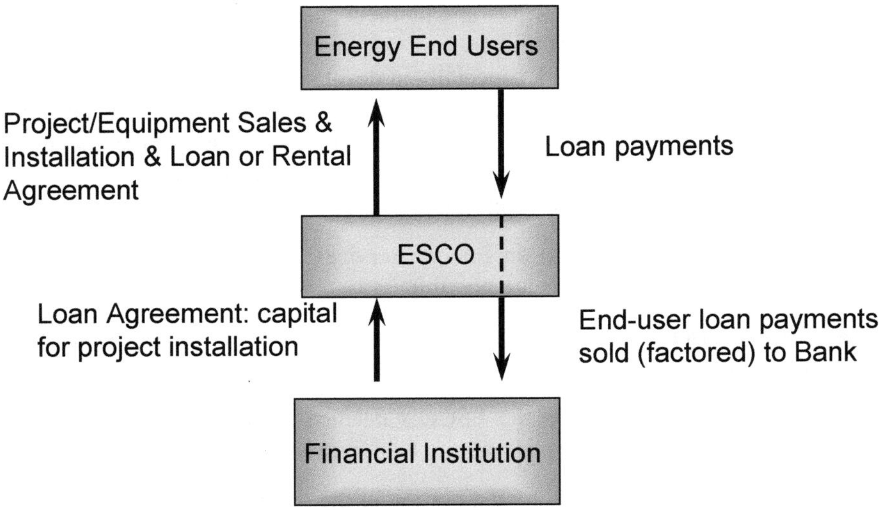

Fig. 3. ESCO loan to end-user; ESCO sells this payment stream to bank, factoring or forfeiting

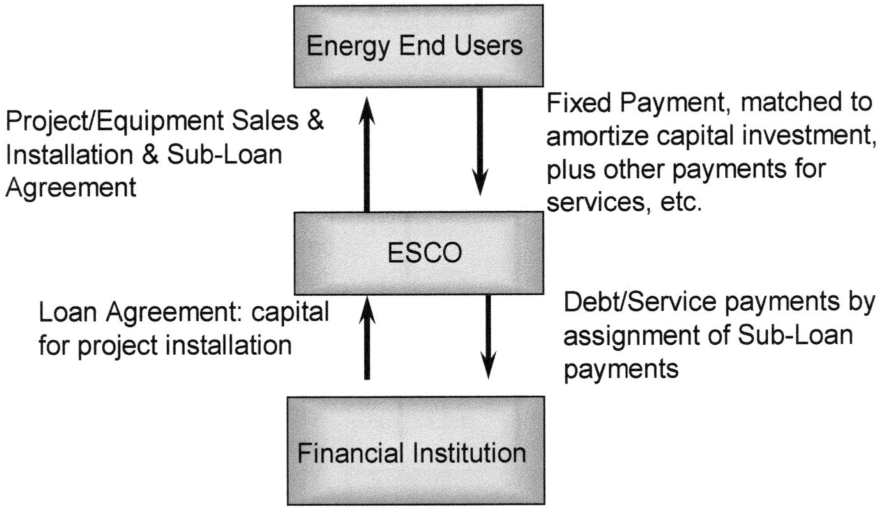

Fig. 4. Bank loan to ESCO, matching ESCO sub-loan to end-user

- End-user makes a fixed payment to ESCO, matched to amortize ESCO's investment.
- ESCO assigns these payments to lender.

- *Multi-project finance facilities for ESCOs*

  When financing an ESCO project, FIs should explore the possibility of financing a series of projects with a multi-project loan facility. To establish an ESCO project finance facility, a master loan agreement is executed between the ESCO and the financier. The master loan agreement commits the lender to provide a certain volume of funding according to defined terms and conditions. It would a) reflect the lender's acceptance of standard end-user agreements (ESAs), b) set parameters for project economics financed under the facility, c) define financing terms including rates, fees, financing amounts and security provisions, and d) lay out procedures and conditions precedent for closing transactions under the facility. Approval of financing for each specific project would typically be required based on a) due diligence demonstrating that the project meets the defined criteria, and b) credit approval of the end-user. Construction financing may also be provided, typically with a portion of funding withheld until completion, commissioning and acceptance. With a master loan facility commitment, the ESCO can develop projects that meet these criteria with confidence that funding will be available when the criteria are met.

  Many EERE programs have focused on developing ESCOs or have otherwise included ESCOs as a delivery mechanism. The World Bank China Energy Conservation program started three ESCOs in its first phase, and directly supported their capacity building, capitalization and project financing. In its second phase, it supported the development of many new ESCOs (building on existing EE firms with core capacities in project engineering, equipment supply and turnkey installation), established an ESCO association and also set up a guarantee program to support loans to ESCOs. This program has been instrumental in creating the ESCO business in China. In all markets, the viability of and potential for developing an ESCO industry should be researched. A broad definition of ESCO projects should be used, including mechanical and electrical contractors, along with a range of business models for structuring ESCOs.

Utility-Based EERE Finance Programs

Energy utilities – electric, gas, heat – can be effective agents and aggregators for marketing and delivering EE and customer-sited RE equipment, projects and financing. Utilities can partner with commercial FIs for funding. The utility billing and collections mechanism can be used to collect payments from end-users. This method can enhance credit structure and collections performance. It can also reduce collection costs which is useful especially in the case of smaller end-users. All customers can be targeted: large/small, commercial/industrial, governmental and residential. Utilities can act as financial intermediaries or establish them to finance EE projects for their customers, partnering with CFIs. Utilities can also directly purchase or dispatch the saved or produced energy (e.g., kW and kWh) as part of integrated resource plans where this benefits their system. (See Annex, Examples #2–5: Utility-Based EE Finance Example, Pacificorp, USA; Tunisia PROSOL Solar Water Heating Equipment Finance Program; Opportunity Example: Agriculture Demand Side Management with Power Utilities in India; Opportunity Example: India Pooled Mini-Hydro Development & Finance Program.)

- Utility acts as FI and provides or offers financing to its customers.
- Customer makes payment via utility bill surcharge. Collections are less expensive and collections performance is enhanced.
- EE equipment and service companies are qualified to co-market and deliver projects.
- EE project development services and energy audits can be provided to customers.
- Financial institution provides debt finance to utility, full or limited recourse.
- IFC program operating in China, with Industrial Bank and Bank of Beijing.
- Xinao Gas is utility partner; program just beginning.
- Utility markets program and EE projects to customers; EE project development services provided to customers.

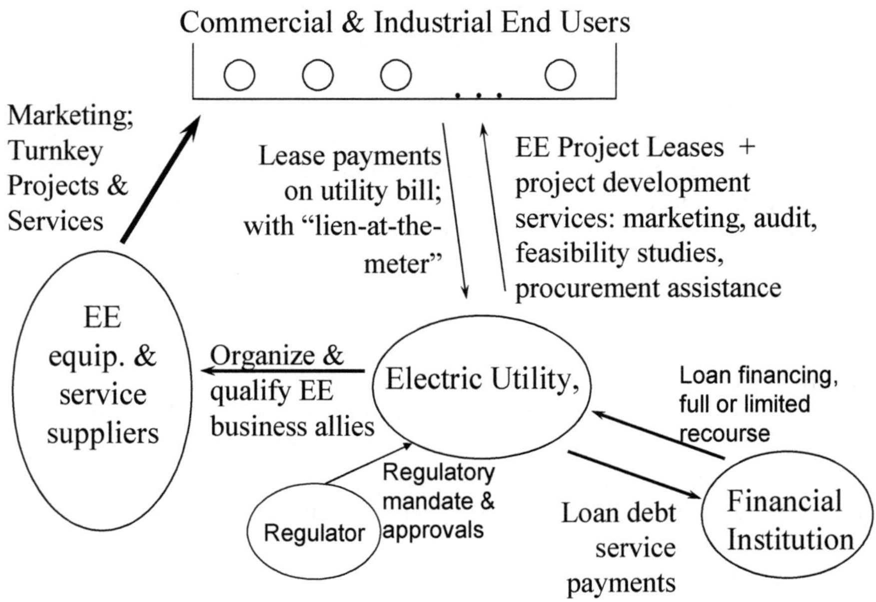

Fig. 5. Utility as Financial Intermediary

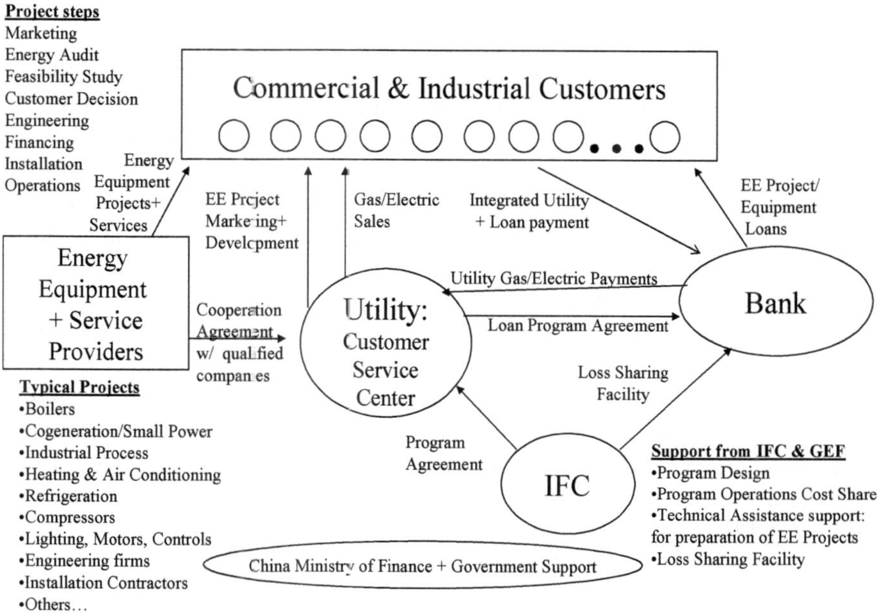

Fig. 6. IFC China EE Finance Program

- Bank partner provides financing to utility customers.
- Loan payments and collections are integrated with the utility bill. Default leads to suspension of gas service.

- *Use of Utility Collections Mechanism*

  The utility billing and collections mechanism can be used to collect payments from end-users. This method can enhance credit structure and collections performance and reduce collection costs which is useful, especially in the case of smaller end-users. In some cases, the utility can impose a "lien-at-the-meter": if the customer defaults, the utility service is suspended; it would be restored when the payments are brought current. If a customer defaults, a new occupant of the facility where the EERE equipment has been installed can be required to assume the remaining balance of payments as a condition of new service. This method is applied in many cases, in both developed and developing countries, as an effective means of delivering credit, and enhancing security and collections. In some cases, the FI can make the collections of an integrated utility bill and loan payment. This method is used in the IFC China Utility-based Energy Efficiency Finance program. The method chosen must be consistent with applicable utility regulation and loan agreement terms with customers.

Pooled Procurements

Market aggregation is crucial for scaling up EERE finance. Pooled procurement programs organize groups of end-users, get them ready to purchase EERE projects and services, and conduct procurement on their behalf. This approach can be and has been used in many sectors. End-user associations – in industry, housing, commercial real estate and state and local governments in particular – can be important coordinating partners. Cities are increasingly important actors in organizing local action and mobilizing investment in climate change. This applies to municipal facilities as well as residential, commercial, industrial and institutional end-users. Organizations such as the Clinton Climate Initiative and the International Council for Local Energy Initiatives (ICLEI) are promoting this approach.

Two exemplary and instructive new initiatives are in Berkeley, California and Cambridge, Massachusetts. In Germany, the Berlin Energy Agency is a successful model. (See Annex, Examples #6–10: Berlin Energy Agency; Cambridge Energy Alliance; Berkeley Sustainable Energy Financing District; Opportunity Example: Pooled Bond EE Finance Program for Local Governments in India; IFC Hungary, National Schools EE Finance Program.)

Small and Medium Enterprise (SME) EERE Programs

SMEs can be a target for clean energy finance programs as energy end-users and as EERE businesses. The tools described in this chapter – guarantees, vendor finance programs, ESCOs, utility-based programs, etc. – can be applied to the SME sector. Many nations have programs to improve access to finance for SMEs. These can be applied directly to EERE finance. In India, a creative example of an EE finance program business model targeting SMEs and cooperating with SME business associations is under development. The history of India has resulted in many SMEs in the same industry group clustered in the same geographic location. These "cluster associations", of which there are many, are a natural marketing partner and aggregator. They are a nodal point for communication and organization of EE projects with groups of end-users. Industries can use common technical solutions. An example for textiles would consist of a package of motor efficiency, power factor correction, smart metering, lighting, and solar thermal for dye-processing hot water. These elements can make an attractive and rather standard technical solution offering combined average payback periods of typically two years.

Several commercial banks in India are developing EERE finance business lines, in part because of priority sector lending policies of the Government of India (See Section 4.4 on supporting financial system regulation and policies). The Small Industries Development Bank of India (SIDBI) can apply its term loan guarantee program to share in the risk of bank loans. (See Annex, Example #11: Small and Medium Enterprise EERE Finance, India SME Industry Cluster Program.)

Housing EERE Finance Programs

Housing is a large energy user and a market with multiple ownership structures, relevant financing instruments and sub-sectors: single family, small multi-family, large multi-family, retrofit and new construction. Many examples of housing EERE finance programs include loans provided by commercial FIs to households or to homeowner associations (e.g. condominiums and co-operatives) for EE investments in individual dwellings or common areas of multi-family residential buildings. Loan products are typically first or second mortgages, or, in the case of multi-family housing, secured by a pledge and assignment of common charges. Cooperation with district heating utility companies has also been arranged to facilitate marketing and financing.

DFIs have worked with commercial FIs to support housing EERE finance via credit lines, risk sharing facilities, and equity or quasi-equity to the FIs. Some initiatives also focus on developing new EE mortgage finance products, and incorporating EE into underwriting criteria for secondary mortgage market funding sources.

- *Single Family*

  Loans to single family households are typically structured as second mortgages. Loans can be secured simply by a security interest in the equipment being financed, e.g., if the equipment is the building's primary heating system. Loans for EE retrofits can also be included within the first mortgage. One strategy is to work with primary mortgage lenders to fund this type of facility, and include expanded EE project loans as an option when new first mortgages are originated. (See Annex, Example #12: IFC Hungary Retail Gas Program.)

- *Multi-family*

  Multi-family housing can pose challenges in obtaining proper security. Often the common areas of buildings are owned proportionately by the individual homeowners and not by the homeowners' association, precluding mortgage on real estate. Ownership and institutional and legal structures pertinent to a nation's multi-family housing stock and to particular buildings must be researched to develop an appropriate financing product: a) who owns the property, b) how is it governed, c) who pays the energy bills and how are they paid, d) is there a homeowners' or condominium association, e) does it have borrowing powers, f) what are the rules governing borrowing, g) can it levy common charges to collect debt service payments, h) what are the enforcement mechanisms for collections, I) is there an association of homeowners associations which can act as a market aggregator, etc.

  EERE finance credit structuring for housing co-ops can involve: a) access to and analysis of utility bill payment history, b) tenant/owner payment history of common charges, c) analysis of the co-op income statement, d) assignment and use of building reserve funds, e) analysis of energy cost savings for estimating the ability to pay and security as real estate, f) security in assignment of rental incomes from service/retail stores in the coop, and g) cooperation with the district heating company serving the co-op in delivering credit or performing billing and collections functions. (See Annex, Example #13: Financing Energy Efficiency for Low Income Blockhouses in Central Europe.)

Energy Access Finance

"Energy access" refers to providing energy services to communities and households in rural, off-grid areas as a key component of programs to end poverty and promote economic development. Energy is an essential input for a productive enterprise. Examples include valued-added processing of agricultural products and cottage industries and for social services, including lighting for education, power for information and communication technologies, refrigeration for clinics and vaccines, and purification of drinking water. Finance for energy access equipment has multiple dimensions: end-user equipment finance, finance for EERE enterprises, and small-scale project finance for small grid-connected or off-grid/community power systems.

End-user or consumer finance is a vital instrument for the delivery of energy equipment to households and micro-enterprises. This equipment is typically less than 100 kW in size, such as solar PV and bio-gas systems, cook stoves and other equipment integrating energy supply and productive equipment. Access to finance enables end-users to acquire equipment by paying over time, with monthly or periodic payments that are affordable.[8] EERE businesses that have achieved high levels of market penetration selling household energy systems have a very high portion of their sales purchased by credit. A notable example is India.

However, consumer finance must be applied and promoted only in cases where market conditions are right and ready. There must be capable EERE vendors to deliver equipment and services. EERE enterprises drive the market by selling systems, and market development must generate sufficient and consistent demand to attract FIs to offer end-user financing. Second, institutional capacities in the market must be able to deliver EERE equipment finance. Such capacities could include rural banking networks, microfinance organizations, agricultural cooperatives, or even electric utilities

The design of effective, appropriate end-user finance and risk sharing mechanisms begins with the observation that the EERE consumer equipment market consists of very large numbers of very small projects. This creates challenges for consumer finance due to relatively high transaction costs per project. However,

---

8 Grants and subsidies are often used to buy down the capital costs of energy systems and are combined with consumer financing programs to make energy systems affordable, as per the ability to pay of target market groups.

when pooled in a portfolio, the large number of small transactions can become a virtue from a credit analysis point of view if a portfolio approach to is used to structure credit.

Based on these characteristics, the main elements of the most accepted and recommended methods to structure credit enhancements for EERE equipment consumer finance can be summarized as follows: a) structure the credit enhancement either as a first loss portfolio guarantee or a loss reserve scheme, both of which take advantage of a portfolio approach to credit structuring, with appropriate risk sharing amongst the several parties (FI, vendors, and donor); and, b) have the FI undertake vendor finance agreements with qualified vendors, and require vendors to provide after-sale service and credit enhancements including buyback guarantees to repurchase equipment repossessed in loan defaults. Complementary technical assistance program elements include banker training, bank transaction cost support, incentives/subsidies to end customers, and EERE business development programs.

A promising method for end-user finance is to mobilize microfinance institutions (MFIs) to deliver energy access. MFIs have developed tremendous capacities and networks to deliver small-scale finance and microfinance. These can potentially be tapped to deliver EERE systems and finance. Mobilizing MFIs for energy access finance has been called "a convergence waiting to happen". MFIs can be a delivery mechanism. Their main product is typically short-term working capital loans for micro enterprises, often in urban areas. Several issues arise in adapting MFI lending capacities to the energy market. Term lending for energy equipment may be a new financial product, involving new risks, lending practices and security, and also requiring additional wholesale funding resources. Thus, MFIs will require assistance to develop and offer new EERE equipment loan products. Because energy access has such positive developmental benefits, an EERE financial product is aligned with MFI objectives.

Some MFIs are becoming deposit-taking institutions, pursuant to evolving MFI financial regulation. However, most MFIs rely on DFIs or commercial FIs for wholesale funds. To offer a new EERE loan product, MFIs will need matching wholesale loan resources. UNEP has developed an approach to work with wholesale lenders, offering a two-tiered credit enhancement mechanism. Through this a) end-borrower credit risk is assumed by the MFI when making equipment loans, and b) MFI credit and other risks are assumed by a wholesale lender that provides funds to MFIs for on-lending as EERE equipment loans. Wholesale MFI finance as a field has made major strides in the last two to three years; working with wholesale lenders to support a network of MFIs that offer EERE finance can therefore be a good scale-up strategy. (See Annex, Example #14 Palawan, Philippines Solar Home Systems Finance Program.) Another promising strategy for energy access finance is to work with mobile phone service companies, which have built and are building networks of cell towers that require power solutions. This capacity can be used to deliver energy services in adjacent communities.

3 EERE Finance Which Development Finance Institutions Can Provide to Commercial Financial Institutions

The second aspect of this discussion concerns investment instruments and technical assistance programs that development finance institutions can offer to local CFIs for EERE finance. DFIs can be multilateral (World Bank, IFC, ADB, IADB, EBRD, AfDB), bilateral (e.g., KfW, FMO), national development banks (e.g., Nafinsa in Mexico, IREDA in India) or even sub-national development banks, (e.g., Maharashtra State Energy Conservation Fund in India). DFI's have a mandate to invest with development impact. Hence, to build EERE finance markets, DFI funding should be used within commercial structures and market processes. DFIs are capable of assuming risks and mobilizing substantial donor funds to blend with their investments and to fund technical assistance and capacity building programs. EERE projects are usually far too small for DFIs to finance directly, but DFIs can be instrumental in supporting local FIs to provide EERE financing. DFIs offer a range of investment instruments to commercial FIs including credit lines, credit enhancement products, and equity investments.[9]

3.1 DFI EERE Finance Programs and the Financing Chain

Proper design of EERE finance mechanisms requires understanding the full chain of financial intermediation, from the DFI instrument offered to the CFI, to the CFI financial product offered to its target EERE markets, to the structure and security details of the underlying transactions. DFIs use public grant monies to blend with their investment instruments, to provide softer terms and/or to accept greater risks, and for technical assistance, capacity building and program operations costs. The typical chain of financing is depicted simply as follows:

Grant/public monies → DFI → CFI → projects

Public funds are typically provided as grants to the DFI. The DFI provides the public finance mechanism to the CFI, blending grant funds with its own resources, equity and debt raised on capital markets. The CFI provides structured, adapted financing to the EERE project sponsors. The sequence in the chain will vary for different mechanisms, applications and circumstances. For example, DFIs could invest directly in projects, which is common for larger grid-connected RE. But,

[9] DFIs can also offer financial products directly to EERE businesses, most frequently in the form of equity investments. In many cases, the DFI will invest in a clean energy equity fund, with professional fund management, which will make a series of clean energy corporate and project equity investments. DFIs may also provide loan facilities to EERE businesses, e.g., for projects or manufacturing facilities, but these are less common. Equity investments may also be made through special enterprise development funds targeting seed capital and early stage EERE enterprises. The DFI manages concessional funds, blended with its own investment, and has grant support to cover the high transaction costs.

the general point remains: design of successful public finance mechanisms should plan the entire chain of financial intermediation, including the last step where the project investments are made. An example is illustrated in Fig. 7.

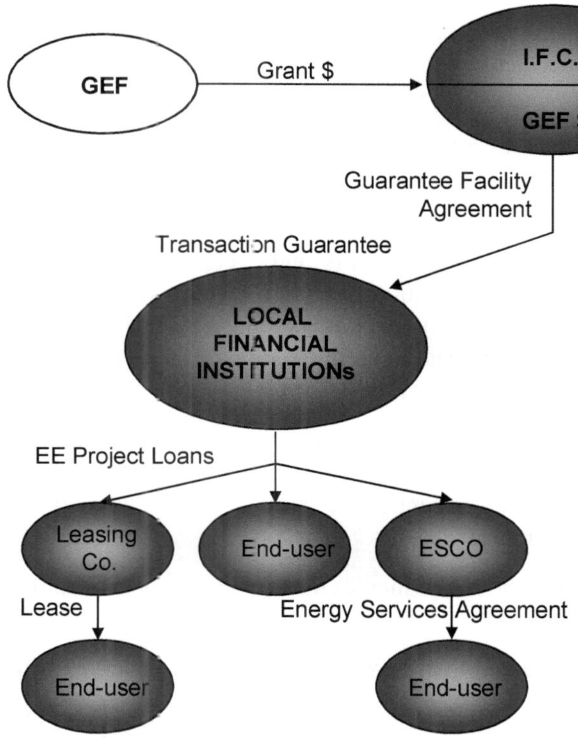

Fig. 7. Chain of Financing Example

1. The International Finance Corporation (IFC) operates energy efficiency (EE) finance programs using partial credit guarantees (PCGs) in seven countries. These programs employ the following chain of financial intermediation:

2. The Global Environment Facility (GEF) provided grant funding to IFC. These funds are used (a) as reserves backing a portion of IFC guarantee liabilities, and (b) technical assistance and program operations costs.

3. IFC provides guarantees to local FIs. (Although one local FI is shown, multiple FIs are participating.)

4. Local FIs use the risk sharing support from IFC to provide financing to various EE market segments, including residential, commercial, industrial, municipal, energy supply and distribution. Multiple financial products have been used.

Over time, the guarantees from IFC can be phased out as familiarity with these sectors improves and risk perceptions decrease. When effectively structured, one dollar in GEF funds can directly leverage 12–15 dollars of commercial investment into EE projects and indirectly catalyze long-term growth of financial commitments to the sector.

This example illustrates several principles in the design and operation of effective public finance mechanisms:

- the catalytic role of public funding (from the GEF in this case) to assume extra risks within the investment structure, and to fund the costs of program operations, technical assistance and capacity building
- the role of the DFI to a) provide a tailored public finance mechanism (guarantees in this case) to local FIs, and b) combine this with technical assistance to structure transactions, c) turn individual transactions into replicable financial products, d) create marketing relationships between the FIs and the EE companies, and e) build EE finance into a commercially viable business line for the partner FIs
- the "branching" effects within the program design, that is, the DFI works with multiple FIs, and each FI can offer a series of financial products to various EE market segments. The success of this work takes time and grows with experience
- the leveraging of the public monies through the financing chain

3.2 Objectives and Design Criteria for DFI EERE Finance Programs

Effective EERE finance programs seek a) to support directly the financing of EERE projects, and (b) to build EERE finance markets and the capacities of CFIs and other market actors – EERE businesses, utilities, energy users, government policymakers – to develop and implement an on-going series of projects on a market basis after the public program has concluded. To make best use of public funding, it is essential that both these direct and indirect outcomes are sought when designing and implementing clean energy public finance mechanisms.

EERE finance programs must be designed using in-depth analysis of country market conditions and based on the specific institutional and credit characteristics of the target end-user sector(s) within the country. Target sectors – industry, SME, commercial, single and multi-family residential, public/institutional/municipal, agriculture – vary widely, and each has its own special circumstances that have to be addressed in designing an appropriate finance/credit structure and program marketing plan.

Market research for an EERE finance program design must include assessment of: a) the economics of individual EERE investments from the point of view of all parties, especially the end-user; b) the commercial contract, finance and credit structure of the investments, especially to satisfy CFI lending criteria; c) definition of a marketing strategy and plan; d) consultation and negotiation with market actors and specific arrangements with market aggregation partners; e) conduct of a complete roles and risk analysis of the entire project development and implementation cycle and definition of a clear allocation of project roles and responsibilities amongst the various parties to the transactions, consistent with their respective objectives and capacities; f) identification of structures that have scale-up potential; and g) definition of the DFI and donor development role and how the public grant and DFI investment instrument(s) will leverage commercial financing. The EERE program design must address all of these levels.

CFIs want and will respond to a sufficiently large, steady, creditworthy demand for capital with manageable transaction costs. These three points – deal and market size, credit, and transaction costs – are key to meeting lender criteria. Strategies to aggregate projects and the demand for capital through market aggregators, development and provision of credit enhancement to create creditworthy finance structures, and preparation of projects to reduce transaction costs, should all be considered as part of an EERE finance program design. EERE finance programs should work with and support commercial parties, incorporate commercial financing, and strengthen rather than distort the marketplace. The program should define a pathway and vision for how EERE financing systems can proceed on a full- or near-commercial basis following completion of the program and how the capacities of all parties to do so will be enhanced.

3.3 Credit Lines

Provision of credit lines to FIs for on-lending to EERE projects is a common DFI investment instrument. The following questions are useful in determining whether credit lines are an appropriate instrument.

- Does the FI lack liquidity, especially finance for medium-to-long tenors (three to seven, or even 10+ years) that are required by EERE projects? If so, then a credit line can be an effective and necessary DFI instrument, with the tenor matched to the target market. DFI resources can be used to fund sub-loans, in full or blended with FI resources. Eligible projects and use of proceeds must be defined, and the target EERE market selected, based on market research.

- Is the credit line full recourse to the FI? Or, does the DFI share in the credit risk of the sub-loans funded with the credit line? Full-recourse lending is far more common and much simpler to originate and administer. If the DFI loans are full recourse to the FI, the only barrier the program would address is the lack of available capital in the market, not the credit risk of the project loans. If the DFI shares in the credit risk, then the DFI will typically prescribe underwriting guidelines, and it must have procedures to comply with them. Even with full recourse credit lines, DFIs will prescribe underwriting guidelines to assure that development objectives are met.

- What is the pricing of the credit line? Will it allow the CFI to on-lend at rates that are attractive to end-borrowers and make a profitable margin? Some DFIs provide EERE credit lines at below-market interest rates. The pricing of the EERE loans which the CFI makes is then prescribed to assure that a) the end borrower enjoys the interest rate subsidy, and b) the CFI is allowed to make higher than normal margins on the portion of their loans funded with the DFI credit line. Thus, the interest rate subsidy can benefit both the borrower and the FI, giving them an added incentive to make the EERE project loan. This is the case in the Thailand Energy Conservation Fund, operated by the Government of Thailand.

Interest rate subsidies are unacceptable for some DFIs due to concern about distorting financial markets, driving out or delaying entry of other non-participating FIs, or causing borrowers to delay or gear project decisions according to the availability of the subsidy. Also, interest rate subsidies by themselves do not address other barriers to EERE finance, e.g., end-user credit risks. In countries having financial markets that are less mature, or that have very high prevailing market interest rates, an interest rate subsidy can be instrumental in stimulating borrowing and EERE investments. (See Annex, Example #15: Thailand Energy Efficiency Revolving Fund.)

Debt co-financing addresses barriers associated with lack of medium and long-term funds available in the market, and in some cases with high interest rates. While debt co-financing can be effective, it is relatively resource intensive and therefore tends to have lower leverage ratios (ratio of public grant and DFI funds to total CFI financing mobilized).

3.4 Mezzanine Debt Facilities

DFIs can offer subordinated or mezzanine debt facilities to support small-scale (e.g., <15 MW) renewable energy project lending through local CFIs. "Subordination" refers to the order of or priority for repayment. Subordinated debt is structured so that it is repaid from project revenues after all project operating costs and senior debt service has been paid. The senior lender gets paid first, and then the subordinated lender. Thus, the subordinated lender assumes greater risk, but still has a claim on project revenues that ranks before that of the project equity owners. Subordinated debt provides capital to a project finance structure and is typically in the range of 10–25% of a project's sources of funds. Use of subordinated debt in a project's source of funds can substitute for and reduce the amount of senior debt. This will improve the loan-to-value ratio and the debt service coverage ratio for the senior lender, thereby reducing risk and strengthening the project's financial structure from the senior lender's viewpoint.

Subordinated debt can be undertaken in partnership with senior lenders and thus is incorporated in the loan origination capacities of the senior lender. The CFI acts as manager of the subordinated loan funds and an aggregator of capital demand. Subordinated debt facilities could readily incorporate concessional and donor fund components. Concessional funds could be blended with DFI monies and provided on a "first loss" basis, thereby improving the DFI's risk position on the subordinated loan facility.

The subordinated loan can be made alongside senior loans. This structure gives the senior lender an effective tool to increase debt financing of EERE projects prudently while making the senior debt component of the loan more secure. Subordination can also be effected by having all sub-debt principal repayment deferred until after the senior loan principal is fully repaid. This allows the senior lender to have a shorter loan tenor, also reducing the senior lender's risk time horizon. The subordinate loan typically commands a premium over the senior loan rate, e.g., 400+ basis points. Subordinated lenders can also often get some form of equity-like returns, e.g., a share of project profits in addition to their loan coupon.

Use of subordinated debt can also substitute for and reduce project sponsor equity requirements. For many project sponsors and developers of EERE projects, a key limiting factor to project financing is a lack of available equity for investment. Subordinated debt can fill this gap and lower a sponsor's equity requirement. It also allows the project developer to preserve controlling ownership interests in its project or company. (See Annex, Example #19: E+Co Central America RE Investment Fund Using Mezzanine Financing Instruments.)

3.5 Guarantee and Risk Sharing Facility Programs

Guarantees can be well adapted and are a good match to support financing for EERE projects. Financial institutions in many developing countries have adequate, even ample medium and long-term liquidity. The DFI's development role is to mobilize these domestic funds for EERE finance. Guarantees support CFI lending by sharing in the credit risk of project loans which the FIs make with their own resources. Guarantees address the credit risk barrier, which are common in many EERE market segments. In financial markets that are developing, gaps often exist between perceived credit risks, as reflected in credit underwriting practices, and actual credit risks. Guarantees can help bridge these gaps. Further, guarantees support local currency lending, thus avoiding foreign exchange risks associated with hard currency lending, risks which many borrowers are ill-equipped to assume.

Financial market conditions where guarantees are best applied include: a) adequate liquidity, especially for medium to long-term funds; b) reasonably attractive market interest rates, that is, rates not so high that they represent *prima facie* a deterrent to borrowing; c) competition and reasonably mature FIs interested in EERE financing; d) conservative credit practices, which typically use a fixed asset collateral approach to loan security, and e) existence of credit risk barriers. A guarantee is a risk management tool that supports the FI to provide financing on more attractive terms to borrowers.

Development agencies and multi-lateral development banks often use concessional funds in guarantee structures. Typical structures include: a) pari passu partial guarantees, b) subordinated recovery guarantees, c) portfolio first loss and second loss guarantees, d) loss reserves acting as first loss guarantees, and e) liquidity support guarantees. In all of these cases, the concessional funds are used as reserves against guarantee liabilities. (See Annex, Examples #16–18: IFC/GEF Hungary Energy Efficiency Co-Financing Program (HEECP); West Nile (Uganda) Hydro Project Financing; International Finance Corp. (IFC) Senior Loan Guarantee for EERE Projects in the Czech Republic.)

A summary table of DFI co-financing instruments for CFIs to support financing of EERE projects is provided below. These finance program options are not mutually exclusive, i.e. more than one can be used. This list is not exhaustive. Alternative versions or hybrids can be developed.

Table 1. Summary of Select DFI EERE Co-financing

Instruments for CFIs				
Option	**Description**	**Barriers Addressed**	**Leverage Potential**	**Examples**
1. Senior Debt Co-financing to FIs	Provide senior debt facilities to CFIs for on-lending to end-users & ESCOs for EERE projects	(i) Lack of available long-term funds; also, possibly (ii) high interest rates	Low to medium	DFI credit lines to CFIs in Russia & E. Europe
2. Subordinated Debt Co-finance	Loans to FIs for on-lending to projects in combination with FI senior debt; subordination leverages and improves security for senior lender	(i) Credit risk barriers, via subordination; (ii) lack of available financing including for long term; (iii) lack of project sponsor equity	Medium	E+Co Central America RE Investment Fund
3. Interest Rate Subsidies	Below market rate credit lines or direct buy-down of interest rates on funds provided by CFIs	high interest rates; induce interest of FIs in lending and end-users & ESCOs in borrowing	Low	Thailand EE Revolving Fund, credit lines
4. Partial Guaranttees on Parity	DFI provides pari passu risk sharing, e.g., 50–80%, on loans CFI makes with its own resources; concessional funds used as reserves for guarantees	(i) credit risk barrier; (ii) can also structure guarantee to lengthen FI loan term; (iii) stimulate FI interest in market	Low to medium	IFC Hungary EE Co-financing Program

Table 1 (continued)

Instruments for CFIs				
Option	**Description**	**Barriers Addressed**	**Leverage Potential**	**Examples**
5. Subordinated Recovery Guarantees	Same as #4, except that FI has first claim on all recovered monies in default events; (concessional funder subordinates in recovery)	(i) credit risk barrier; (ii) can also structure guarantee to lengthen FI loan term	Medium	IFC Hungary EE Co-financing Program
6. First Loss & Second Loss Portfolio Guarantees	Like #4 except risk sharing formula defined on a portfolio basis and includes first loss & second loss components; grant funds can be first loss cover for the DFI	credit risk barrier	High	IFC China EE Finance Program
7. Loss Reserves	Concessional monies used to establish dedicated loss reserves to cover portion of first losses in a loan portfolio	credit risk barrier	High	UNDP Philippines Palawan Solar Home Systems Finance Program
8. Liquidity Support Guarantees	Guarantor keeps loan current in late pay events and institutes work out remedies; appropriate where borrower is a public utility	credit risk barrier	Medium	World Bank Philippines System Loss Reduction Rural Electric Cooperative Loan guarantee program

3.6 Supporting Technical Assistance Programs

Finance is necessary, but not sufficient to stimulate EERE investments. Other barriers – e.g., project development risks and costs, failure to aggregate projects, marketing and education of end-users to get them "decision-ready" to buy EERE projects, transaction structuring, credit structuring and enhancement – must be addressed. EERE finance programs, in addition to organizing access to finance, must also reach back into the project development cycle and promote systematic project development by capable parties who can generate a pipeline of investment ready and creditworthy projects.

A typical agenda of possible supporting technical assistance (TA) activities for FIs is described below. Strategies for recruiting, engaging and working with FIs are also summarized. Key components of TA to support FIs in EERE finance include: a) market research, b) marketing support, c) transaction structuring support, d) development of new financial products, e) staff training and business planning, f) establishing technical standards and engineering due diligence, and g) development of market aggregation programs to build deal flow and carbon finance.

- *Market Research and Marketing Support*

  Thorough market studies can be valuable and useful to FIs. Market studies can a) assess demand for various EERE equipment and financial and non-financial products, b) analyze equipment and project economics, c) identify active and qualified EERE system vendors and project developers, d) identify and assess target markets and their credit characteristics, and e) evaluate perspectives and programs of other key government, NGO, donor and policy actors which affect the market. Such studies can demonstrate to the FI its market and the potential demand for EERE financing. TA programs with FIs can focus particularly on marketing, especially by assisting FIs to establish relationships with EERE businesses, equipment vendors, contractors and project developers; and these companies need FI financing to support their sales.

  A primary means for FIs to market EERE finance services is through relationships with EERE businesses. Assistance can be provided to FIs to establish relationships and structure vendor finance programs and multi-project finance facilities with EERE and ESCO businesses. Other marketing and market aggregation partners include utilities, end-user associations and local governments. TA programs can help develop these programs and link partner CFIs to them. These programs include the provision of financing facilities. Implementing such strategies can help aggregate demand for financing, build quality deal flow for EERE finance programs and be beneficial to participating FIs.

- *Transaction Support and Development of New Financial Products*

  EERE finance may be new to prospective partner FIs. In these cases, TA is highly valued to structure initial transactions. An FI can proceed opportunistically to finance initial transactions which meet their credit criteria, while seeking to define target markets and design financial products with strong replication potential. TA can help FIs learn from international experience and best practices, and create new products adapted to their internal credit procedures.

- *Training and Business Planning*

  EERE finance training for FIs can cover a) EERE technologies and applications, b) EERE project economics, c) structuring EERE equipment and project loans, d) lending to ESCOs, special risk and credit features, e) case studies, f) marketing FI financial services, and g) other topics. Training can be offered initially for an FI's headquarters staff. Then, as financial products are defined and adopted, ready to roll out, branch staff can be trained in promoting those specific products. Some FIs can use tailored assistance to prepare business and marketing plans for the implementation of their EERE finance programs. Many DFIs (EBRD, IFC, World Bank) and other development agencies have developed and implemented EERE finance training programs for FIs. Compilation of best practices in this field is recommended.

- *Engineering Due Diligence*

  FIs will require set technical standards and due diligence procedures for the EERE projects they will finance. FIs have a material interest to ensure the equipment and systems are technically sound, durable, well-designed and installed, backed by strong warranties and with accessible after-sale service. Borrower willingness to repay is strongest if the equipment works properly and can weaken significantly if it breaks or fails to perform as expected. Participating EERE vendors can be selected on the basis of their ability to meet minimum standards and be required to follow the standards in practice. This will mitigate potential loan portfolio risks. A TA program can help establish the standards and support FIs with technical knowledge, vendor criteria and selection, training of loan officers and lead staff and support for product development and necessary changes in internal processes. For EERE project financings, a TA program can provide engineering due diligence on equipment and systems, and independent engineering reviews to confirm technical viability and economics of given projects. This type of service is highly valued by FIs. Post-project implementation performance reviews are valuable to FIs as a means of monitoring their loan portfolios.

- *Technical Assistance for Financial Institutions on Carbon Finance*

  Most EERE projects and equipment will reduce greenhouse gas (GHG) emissions. Capturing these carbon values as Certified Emissions Reductions (CERs) through the Clean Development Mechanism (CDM) can help make many EERE projects and investment programs more economic and easier to finance. Selling CERs can provide important revenue support and upside profit potential for project sponsors, or be passed through to customers to make projects more affordable. There is strong potential for FIs to act as carbon aggregators and market makers for carbon credits for

EERE projects.[10] FIs financing projects are natural aggregators for small-scale projects; as a capable nodal agency, an FI, will have a formal contractual relationship with a series of project sponsors. A TA program could help FIs develop this type of program, work on specific EERE markets, help gain approval for the CDM methodology, and assist the FIs to create CER purchase agreements and relationships with qualified buyers. (See Annex, Example #20: India Compact Fluorescent Lamp Program of Activities.)

3.7 Engaging Commercial FIs to Participate

Many EERE systems are capital intensive. Most projects and end-users require initial financing for start-up for initial operation. At the same time, EERE projects can be self-financing from the costs savings or energy production benefit stream. Most EERE companies market on this basis. If given the financing tools, EERE and ESCO firms will market financing at the point of sale of their projects and services to end-users.

FIs' motivation is to book profitable assets. Attracting commercial FIs to EERE finance requires a substantial, steady, and creditworthy flow of demand for their financial products that can be originated profitably, with manageable transactions costs. These, in turn, require marketing, project investment preparation, market aggregation and use of secure transaction structures and in some cases credit enhancement. So, regarding FI perspectives: a) borrower credit-worthiness, transaction structure and security are primary considerations; b) technical assistance to educate banks on engineering and technical aspects and due diligence of EERE projects is very useful and may be instrumental; c) banks must be convinced there is a real business which can best be accomplished by bringing banks real transactions for funding through established relationships with equipment vendors and ESCOs that seek financing for their projects and sales; d) FIs are often interested in cross-selling other services – opportunities to do so should be explored in an EERE finance program brings them new customers and deposits. Generally, FIs do not initiate projects and cannot drive the market or be the market protagonist. But they can be brought to the table to finance EERE projects provided their underwriting criteria, appraisal methods, technical information requirements and market strategies can be addressed.

- *Developing Programs by Building Business Relationships*

  In developing EERE finance programs, DFIs and development agencies must conduct research and interviews with prospective partner CFIs. Many commercial parties have been wearied and become wary of development

[10] Canara Bank (India) is financing solar domestic hot water heating systems that typically displace LPG or electricity use, estimated at USD 10 million per year (source, personal conversation with senior bank officer, May 2006) and has expressed interest in being a CER aggregator.

agencies, and rightly concerned about the time spent responding to development agency research requests. Thus, it is important to treat the research process in the same way as if one were establishing a business relationship. The value proposition for the CFI must be clear from the beginning. One way to achieve this is to conduct EERE market research in advance, provide valuable market information to the CFI in initial contacts, and even put potential transactions on the table, basing the relationship with real financing opportunities.

- *Introducing and Effecting Innovation Within an FI*

  FIs should be understood as large corporate organizations acting in a policy and regulatory environment. Getting FIs to readily adopt and promote EERE financial products involves an organizational process that introduces innovation. This requires leadership at the Board level, plus active understanding and advocacy by senior management. Further, to get middle management to implement the program, senior management must provide a clear mandate, especially when the innovation involves new credit risk management practices. New financial products are usually tested and originated initially at the headquarters level. Then, when the new products, including underwriting guidelines are defined, they can be rolled out through training at the branch level. Middle management needs to be recognized and rewarded for promoting the new product line. This support must come from the top of the organization and followed through with reporting and recognitions. Supporting government and central bank policies and regulations can be instrumental in mobilizing and directing the resources of commercial FIs to this market. These are discussed in Section 4.

4 Challenges and Strategies for Scale-Up

EERE project investment needs and opportunities are pervasive, diverse and dispersed. They involve changes and retrofit in the economy's capital stock in all sectors and thus touch the lives of virtually every citizen and organization. Many effective transaction structures and programmatic models that aggregate the market have been demonstrated which enable EERE investments. The challenge is that implementation of each model in each respective target market requires sustained attention and capacity building. Scale-up does not imply blind replication, but rather adaptation and application of good transaction structuring and program design principles. In many ways, the challenge of scale-up is an institutional development and human resource challenge. As the World Bank has concluded in its recent and important study on financing energy efficiency:

Development and operation of energy efficiency investment delivery mechanisms is an *institutional development issue* [emphasis added] ... Lack of domestic sources of capital is rarely the true barrier; inadequate organizational and institutional systems for developing projects and accessing funds are actually the main problem. Therefore, mechanisms to capture the opportunities for energy efficiency investment need to be created and strengthened. This entails sustained effort over years ...[11]

Likewise, financial product standardization, the high set-up cost of introducing EERE finance and the low level of potential client awareness constitute further challenges for scale-up.

4.1 Knowledge Management and Capacity Building

A compilation of EERE transaction structures and finance program best practices is needed as a ready reference for commercial and development practitioners. This can be done on an "open source" basis that assesses experience and lessons and compiles effective methods in a ready-to-share format. This compilation would thoroughly document a) a range of EERE finance transactions, that is, the structures of individual deals between commercial parties, and, b) EERE finance programs of the type that governments, DFIs and development agencies undertake, which organize and systematically deliver EE project development services and financing. Such a compilation would include case studies of EERE transactions and programs. The case studies should go well beyond introductory descriptions and would be linked to substantive resource materials. Implementation of each finance transaction and program involve certain documents which could be called collectively "resource materials" or "business tools".

These include: a) energy service agreements, b) bank appraisal and due diligence guidelines, loan appraisal and underwriting guidelines, c) specialized loan agreements and term sheets, d) guarantee and risk sharing agreements, e) project financial analyses, f) procurement documents, g) program design documents, h) vendor finance program agreements, i) utility DSM contracts, j) program design documents for specific end-user markets such as multi-family housing and municipal end-users, etc. The resource materials would include: a) market research and diagnostic methods of the kind used to assess EERE market and sector-specific conditions, and productively engage various stakeholders in the process of program design, and b) technical assistance (TA) materials and methods useful during program operations. To make a tool kit useful, it should include an extensive library of these resource materials to enable development agencies and commercial practitioners to see exactly how transactions and programs have been implemented. It must also be able to apply and adapt these methods to their own applications.

Assembled materials could be refined through a process of peer compilation and review, with a view to making the resulting product practical and useful. The activity would first assemble, and then build on, materials already compiled. Additional in-kind contributions from participating institutions, including the DFIs,

---

[11] Robert P. Taylor et al., *Financing Energy Efficiency: Lessons Learned from Brazil, China, India and Beyond*, The World Bank, 2008, p.7.

would be requested including: a) participation in peer review processes, and b) assistance in compiling materials and case studies from experience which would be sanitized of confidential information and cleared prior to use.

This compilation would be designed to have immediate value to clean energy finance practitioners generally. Resulting resource materials could be made available through an appropriately sponsored on-line service. Preparing the initial compilation would produce solid value in and of itself. However it is not a terminal activity: it could become the core of an on-going activity. Further case studies and resource materials can continue to be compiled, by accretion, to deepen the body of materials. Thus, the tool kit would be a living document.

Applications and Replication Services

To place this information in the hands of practitioners, an on-going service should be established to link practitioners to relevant resource materials and provide follow-up remote and on-site consultation. This compilation could become the "go to" source for information, tools and resource materials on EE finance transaction structuring and program design. The on-line information service could include "application assessment forms", where users may prepare summary descriptions of their specific applications and situations in an organized format. These would be transmitted to the on-line EE/RE finance information service to initiate customized guidance on their transactions and programs.

This guidance can be provided remotely through written and phone consultations. The service could link the user/applicant to relevant resource materials and distribute them to practitioners. As needed, and subject to funding, deeper customized and even on-site guidance could be provided. Over time, a network of country-based financial advisors could be established to provide direct, local hands-on guidance. Country teams could be sponsored by an appropriate government agency or development bank, and include local consultants. Networks such as PFAN (Project Finance Assistance Network, providing financial advisory services on RE project finance) can expand to assist country agencies and practitioners at the project level. Similar initiatives would be used to develop and launch EE finance programs.

4.2 Recommendations for Development Finance Institutions

DFIs play a critical role in the EERE field. Because of the nature of the EERE market, DFIs must work through financial intermediaries. DFIs could:

- collaborate in the development of a thorough EERE finance tool kit and establishment of an advisory service
- expand staffing and strengthen the institutional placement of clean energy finance program offices within DFIs to assist development and commercial practitioners in adapting and applying EERE finance program models to their markets

- devote a portion of profits, alongside donor funds, for use similar to equity in higher risk position in combination with DFIs' investment funds; these could be utilized to implement and expand clean energy finance programs, working with local commercial FIs and other market actors
- incorporate EERE finance program lessons into the design and operations of new climate investment funds being proposed and developed in the UNFCCC, G-8 and in other contexts

These ideas are not new and many are being implemented.

4.3 Design of New Climate Mitigation Funds and Country-Based Programs

Commitment of substantial new public funding for climate mitigation and/or adaptation investment in developing countries is being considered in the context of the UNFCCC negotiations, and within the G-8, multilateral, bilateral and other forums. As new public funding is being considered, key questions arise: a) How can it be organized and deployed? b) What investment mechanisms, instruments and vehicles are available that are scalable and replicable for the climate mitigation objectives at hand? c) How can public monies be used to mobilize commercial finance, and deliver this financing to implement climate mitigation projects? Answers to these questions begin by identifying EERE transaction structures and finance program models.

If the design and scale-up of EERE finance programs is considered a priority, and the international community devotes considerable new resources to support such programs, then an institutional structure is needed, both within the MDBs and the countries being assisted. Much of this institutional infrastructure already exists, but it requires designation and capacity building to take the next steps. Expanded EERE finance programs will combine funding from new public grant resources, investment instruments from DFIs (multilateral, bilateral and national) and the resources of local CFIs.

As with the CDM and GEF mechanisms, a designated lead national agency is needed for each participating country. A logical country-based coordinator for EERE finance programs could be each country's national development bank or similar institution. The local lead agency, with support from international agencies, would become the lead agency to a) conduct market research, b) define investment priorities, c) develop program designs, d) become the knowledge leader and institutional home for applying the EERE finance tool kit, e) liaise with commercial FIs and other market actors, and f) provide program operations oversight along with the international donors and investors.

4.4 Supporting Financial System Regulations and Policies

National banking and financial system regulation often prescribes commercial bank loan portfolio limits and sets loan portfolio targets. For example, a prescribed maximum percentage of a bank's assets could consist of term loans greater than 1 year. In China this percentage is 30%. Loan underwriting guidelines are also often set, and rules are defined setting risk weightings for certain types of assets. To promote lending in socially important areas, such as housing, agriculture, rural economic development and even clean energy and other "green" investments, bank regulators a) often set targets for these priority types of lending as a percentage of banks' portfolios, and b) may differentiate reserve requirements for lending in different sectors as a function of risk.

India has an extensive system of "priority sector lending" to direct loans to specific economic sectors. For domestic banks, priority sector lending policies prescribe targets for a full 40% of bank lending. In the US, the Community Reinvestment Act promotes bank lending for housing by requiring lenders to invest a minimum portion of their portfolio in the communities in which they accept deposits. In China, "green credit" policies carve out certain types of lending, for new green buildings, for example, from certain lending limits. Clean energy financing by commercial FIs could similarly be promoted, based on its national macroeconomic, energy security, economic development and environmental public goods benefits. Such policies can be very effective in assuring that senior management of commercial FIs direct attention to this type of lending, and they provide additional motivation for expanded lending in this socially important area.

4.5 Conclusion: Financing for a Sustainable Low-Carbon Economy

Patterns of energy and resource use and waste outputs are imbedded in an economy's capital stock, which includes everything from buildings, factories and manufacturing equipment, appliances and vehicles, to transportation, water, energy and power infrastructure. Creating a green, low-carbon economy will require comprehensive investment over many years to transform our capital stock so that it provides economic services with far greater energy efficiency and wiser resource use, and far less generation of wastes, GHG emissions, environmental impact and depletion of natural capital.

This is a tremendous, long-term, systemic challenge. Capital stock is inherently capital intensive. Further, virtually every item of capital stock has investment and financial system analogs; that is, financial products and finance delivery mechanisms, whether they be commercial loan products, leases, bond financing, mortgages, consumer credit, or microcredit, that enabled the capital purchase. To make the green economy transition, we need to develop and implement investment programs that target and deliver financing with financial products adapted for green economy projects, including prominently EERE projects, wherever these projects are located.

5 Epilogue: Link Creation of New International Reserve Currency to Financing Global Public Goods

A proposal which dates to the mid-1970s, has recently been resurrected by George Soros, Joseph Stiglitz[12] and others. It proposes linking the creation of a new international reserve currency with purchases and investments in global public goods, such as EERE finance programs. The author strongly recommends this proposal for further development and consideration in light of the current financial system crises, the need to address imbalances in the international monetary system and the needs for public investment in a sustainable low-carbon economy.

ANNEX: EERE Financing and Program Examples

This Annex provides abbreviated examples of EERE project finance and program examples. Further information is available upon request. A list of all examples is provided following the table of contents.

A.1 Vendor Finance Programs

Vendor Financing in IFC EERE Finance Programs

IFC has used vendor finance programs frequently in its EERE finance programs that work with commercial FIs in providing credit lines and guarantees.

Russia – Centre Invest Bank, UNK Agroproduct: IFC has had a credit line with Centre Invest, a commercial FI in southern Russia, dedicated to EERE financing. An important target market for Centre Invest is loans to agro-industrial SMEs. A vendor finance program was developed with UNK Agroproduct, a supplier of small bio-mass fueled boiler systems, and multiple transactions were supported for agro-processors.

Hungary – OTP Bank, Tivi Street Lighting: IFC has a Guarantee Facility Agreement (GFA) with OTP supporting loans to small and medium size municipalities to acquire turnkey street lighting system retrofits. A vendor finance program was successfully implemented with Tivi, Kvt., a small firm specializing in municipal street lighting. Tivi's target market is small and medium size cities. The OTP finance facility financed a series of Tivi projects, using a fixed payment energy services agreement vendor finance structure.

Czech Republic – Cseka Sporitelna Bank (CSB), Siemens Building Technologies (SBT): IFC has a GFA with CSB supporting factoring of SBT long-term receivables on EERE projects being implemented with industrial Sees.

[12] See, for example, Joseph E. Stiglitz, "Reforming the Global Reserve System", Chapter 9 in *Making Globalization Work*, W.W. Norton & Company, New York, 2006.

A.2 Utility-Based EERE Finance Programs

Utility-Based EE Finance Example, Pacificorp, USA

A US investor-owned electric utility, PacifiCorp, serves customers in seven states of the Pacific Northwest and Utah. Pacificorp is interested in promoting energy efficient motors, lighting and other technologies to commercial and industrial sector end-users in its Oregon service territory as a means of meeting its demand management goals. In designing this program, PacifiCorp was motivated to reduce ratepayer financed rebates and shift more of its EE program costs to the participating end-user while maintaining competitive rates. The utility organized a group of equipment vendors, engineers and contractors who offer EE products and services. The utility then provides these trade allies with two tools: a) funding for energy audits to assess the EE potential for qualified technologies with customers in the utility service area, and b) a lease financing program. The utility also provides technical assistance to end-users on project engineering, development and contracting.

Under the lease financing program, the utility provides financing to customers to implement the EE projects. The customer makes payments as an "energy service charge" on their utility bill based on a four or five-year term lease. The financing services are marketed by the trade allies to the end-user clients. When a customer signs up for the program, the trade ally completes the documentation, which is verified by the utility. The financing is then closed and the lease payment begins on the customer bill the following month. The utility takes the risk of customer non-payment but, because it has a "lien-at-the-meter" whereby power service can be cut in the event of non-payment, the default rate is very low. This program started operations in late 1992. In its first three years of operation, the program provided financing for over USD 32 million of projects. The utility eventually packaged and sold a portfolio of these lease assets to a major commercial bank.

Tunisia PROSOL Solar Water Heating Equipment Finance Program[13]

UNEP is implementing PROSOL, an effective and innovative program for financing domestic solar water heater (SWH) equipment in Tunisia as part of its Mediterranean Renewable Energies Programme (MEDREP). The high initial cost of SWHs was a substantial market barrier when compared to cheaper water heating alternatives. To address this market barrier, PROSOL introduced a credit mechanism that has resulted in greatly increased sales.

PROSOL was launched by UNEP and the Tunisia National Agency for Energy Management (ANME) with the support of the Italian Ministry for the Environment and Territory. PROSOL employs a range of institutional and financial support to develop and sustain the solar water heating market. These include a credit mechanism for SWH buyers, with loans provided of up to a 5-year term with col-

---

[13] This summary is based on information provided by Myriem Touhami, UNEP/Paris, "PROSOL Heats Up Tunisian Solar Water Heating Market", December, 2006.

lection of principal and interest through the customer's electricity bill. PROSOL also provides a subsidy of 20% of the system cost, funded by the Tunisian government. Finally, discounted interest rates are offered on SWH loans for the year 2005–2006 with funds from MEDREP.[14]

The PROSOL credit programme works as follows. First, a customer decides to purchase a solar water heater from a supplier who installs the solar water heater at the customer's home. The customer pays the loan processing costs and any residual system costs. After installation, the supplier receives the subsidy payment from ANME. The supplier then receives the remaining cost of the system directly from the bank. This sum is a credit granted indirectly to the buyers of the solar water heater, via the SWH suppliers, which will be refunded through the customer's Société Tunisienne de l'Electricité et de Gaz (STEG) electricity bill. The SWH suppliers carry the loans on their balance sheets. The PROSOL account at the Société Tunisienne de Banque (STB) receives the sums collected from STEG out of the loan principal and interest. These funds are then disbursed to the bank accounts of the solar water heater suppliers concerned, who use these funds to repay the loans.

Overall, about 70% of the costs of the SWHs are paid via the loan, with the balance from the subsidy and upfront deposits from customers. Once the SHW's are installed, customers benefit through reduced costs of water heating. An extensive communications and advertising campaign to market the program is included, paid in part by MEDREP. PROSOL creates three decisive advantages. First, SWH subsidies and loans have led to a substantial increase in solar water heater sales, with domestic sales reaching a record 23,000 m² over the period April-December 2005. Second, credit recovery through STEG electricity bills lowers collection costs and makes credit available to a broad class of domestic customers, including those without salaried employment or bank accounts. It reduces the risk of credit default. Taken together, these advantages reduce interest rates. Third, the local banking sector is effectively engaged in financing SWHs and has the resources and abilities for making loans and scaling up the program.

This structure has the potential to create a long-term, commercially sustainable program that can deliver credit even when the subsidies end. The program has ambitious growth targets and can also expand to financing SHWs for multi-family housing, commercial building and hotel applications. There is one limiting factor which could potentially hamper the ambitious growth targets of the program: suppliers, in effect, take on debt on behalf of their customers and they have limited ability to do so. UNEP is assessing various options to potential application of a loss reserve fund credit enhancement mechanism and other commercial finance methods such as forfeiting which would resolve this constraint.

---

[14] Once the US$1 million MEDREP fund is exhausted, the repayments via STEG on all sales will have to be increased, because interest rates will no longer be discounted. On 1 April 2006, the interest rate support was reduced from 7% to 4% in order to gradually diminish the subsidy and bring PROSOL financing up to market rates. The overall impact of this reduction was minimal as loan repayments increased only by about 2 Tunisian dinars per month.

Opportunity Example: Agriculture Demand Side Management with Power Utilities in India

The economics and investment opportunities of agricultural water pumping efficiency (Ag DSM) in India are compelling. India's agriculture sector typically consumes 30+% of State Electric Board (SEB) total electricity units sold and as much as 40% of connected load, but as little as 5% of revenue realization. Power tariffs for agriculture water pumping are far below the costs of service, which includes distribution costs and losses Utilities incur large losses for every unit sold, which are made up by State government subsidies, which, nationwide, total an estimated Rs. 40,000 crores or approximately $10 billion per year.[15] Irrigation pumping systems are highly inefficient. Demonstration projects indicate that the energy required to deliver a given amount of water can be reduced by up to 55 percent by replacing the pump set with a smaller, efficient and correctly-sized pump set and installing a low-friction foot valve and piping, amongst other measures. Pumping systems also have very low power factors, often less than 0.65, increasing distribution losses.

Yet, farmers have little incentive to conserve, given the low costs of power, and poor voltage conditions preclude it. There are an estimated 20 million electricly powered agriculture water pumps nationwide with a total connected load in the range of 70 GW. Average investment costs for replacing pump sets are in the range of Rs 40,000 per pump set. An investment program to replace half of the pump sets would cost about $10 billion and have a simple payback period of about 4 years (prior to incorporating carbon values), assuming that savings of 45% in power consumption could be achieved and sustained.[16] Properly financed, these projects can yield net savings to State governments and SEBs as well as improve power and water pumping service to farmers. The projects can also open the way to metered tariffs that, over time, would approach the full costs of service. Innovative EERE business models for structuring win-win transactions and overcoming barriers to exploiting this potential are needed.[17]

Opportunity Example: India Pooled Mini-hydro Development and Finance Program

A final example is drawn from the field of small-scale renewable energy (RE), which is an important part of the clean energy field. RE and EE have similar economic and environmental benefits while facing similar market and financing

---

15 Economic Survey, 2006–07, as quoted in *National Workshop on Developing Road Map for DSM in India*, Section III on 'Agriculture DSM", Bureau of Energy Efficiency, presented at the National Workshop on DSM, Pune, October 1–2, 2007.

16 This is a simplified calculation, and requires further analysis and commercial validation in specific State applications. Fully loaded project costs, including all necessary social components of a successful investment program, may lengthen the payback period.

17 See MacLean, John and Hogan, Jim, *Financing Agriculture Demand Side Management Projects in India*, USAID, PA Consulting, February, 2008.

barriers. Several State Electric Boards (SEBs) in India (Karnataka, Himal Pradesh, Uttaranchal) have identified hundreds of small and mini-hydro sites (typically 1–5 MW) which currently operate as hydro plants and/or grain mills with the potential to be upgraded for greater power production.

Individual project sizes are small (typically 1–10 MW), but in aggregate they could provide significant power contribution to the local grid, contribute to peak power supply, all while avoiding high transmission and distribution costs. ADB has estimated the new power potential of such small sites in Himal Pradesh alone to exceed 1 gig watt. Thus, the state utilities (SEBs) are keen to license these projects, offer power purchase agreements and promote their development. A program could be developed that would consist of a finance facility combined with technical assistance (TA) to develop this market. An integrated program would work with the SEBs, FIs, system/equipment vendors, project developers and the local project sponsors. The project development process must begin with the party that has site control, typically the local government or local industry. If each individual site owner is required to learn, fund and suffer through the project development process, the potential of this resource will likely never be exploited to its potential. Thus, a programmatic approach is needed.

An integrated service package could include: a) resource assessment, b) feasibility studies, c) choice of turnkey project contractors, d) a standard offer power purchase contract with the relevant utility, and e) a financing facility. Financing could come from local FIs, perhaps supported by a partial credit guarantee. The program team could conduct an RFQ to select and qualify turnkey project contractors and system vendors. If project equity finance is needed, that could also be assembled. Or, project contractors which can build, own and operate can be identified and qualified to undertake such contracts with the site owner. The electric utility could be a main program sponsor and market aggregator, if the utility wants to promote this type of new power generation. The development agency could conduct program design and then help fund project marketing and development TA costs. Credit enhancement for the project loan facilities may also require concessional support.

A.3 Local and State Government Initiatives Using Pooled Procurements

Berlin Energy Agency

The Berlin Energy Agency (BEA) acts as an independent project manager to develop EERE projects in public and private buildings in the City of Berlin. Funded by the State and District Municipal Governments, the BEA pools a number of buildings and conducts pooled procurements for ESCOs to make EERE investments. The winning ESCO pays for the upfront cost of the retrofit project, costing the building owners nothing. Average savings have been 26% of energy use. The ESCO is repaid over an average of 8–12 years from these savings. The ESCO is able to shoulder the upfront costs through a loan provided by a financial institution.

The BEA has been operating since 1997 and has implemented over 43 million Euros in investment in 1400 buildings. These projects are saving over 10 million Euro per year in energy cost savings. BEA conducts the initial energy audits at no cost to the end-user and this information is used for the ESCO procurement. BEA used government grant funds to pay for these services. An average of 20 buildings are pooled for each procurement. The BEA program has been highly successful and is being replicated in Bulgaria, Romania, Slovenia and Chile. It demonstrates the power of local government to act as a market aggregator and procurement agent for EERE projects.

Cambridge Energy Alliance

In March 2007, Cambridge, Massachusetts launched the Cambridge Energy Alliance (CEA). CEA is a city-sponsored non-profit organization that offers comprehensive services to develop, finance and implement EERE and water conservation projects for end-users in multiple sectors: residential, commercial, industrial, institutional, and governmental. Pooled procurement methods are used. CEA has conducted a procurement process and selected ESCOs for small residential, large residential, small commercial/industrial (C/I) and large C/I end-users. For the ESCOs, CEA delivers organized demand; in the process, CEA gains better pricing and service terms for end-users by aggregating their purchasing power.

The ESCOs provide: energy audits, feasibility studies, and then turnkey installation of end-users' chosen investment program. To end-users, CEA provides a) independent expertise, b) project management, c) guidance through the full project cycle, d) procurement assistance, e) access to funding, f) inspection of completed installations, and g) project monitoring. Over five years, CEA targets $100 million in investments and a 10% city-wide reduction in both energy use (approximately 50 MW) and emissions (approximately 150,000 tons per year CO2). Moreover, CEA targets 50% market participation. The city actively markets the program. A financing facility has been arranged with a consortium of local commercial banks. Loan tenors up to 10 years are available, which are made directly to end-users.

Berkeley Sustainable Energy Financing District

The City of Berkeley, California is establishing a Sustainable Energy Financing District. The city will issue bonds and use the proceeds to provide loans to residential and commercial property owners to install solar PV systems and EE improvements in their buildings. The program is being developed in response to the "Measure G" ballot initiative passed in 2007 which sets GHG emissions reduction targets for the city. Loans to property owners will have 20 year terms with an estimated interest rate of 6%. This addresses the high up-front cost barrier which end-users face when considering making such investments. It also allows end-users to match their loan payments with the projects' benefit stream, i.e. the energy savings resulting from the new EERE project.

The city bears the credit risk of the loans, but, in an important innovation, it will collect loan payments with the property tax bill. The city will assess and obtain a lien on property for the loan amount. All property tax enforcement mechanisms apply: liens, transferability of liens, right to repayment at resale, foreclosure rights to enforce payment, plus the historic payment collection performance on property tax collections. The city is negotiating a private placement of the bonds with a green investment fund. In addition, a loss reserve fund is being raised to help cover the city's credit risk exposure.

The city is also responsible for qualifying participating PV system installers, operating the program and also helping property owners tap State of California incentive payments for solar PV. The City earns a service fee from property owners to offset the costs of the program. The program design can be used to fund EE measures as well. This mechanism is being followed closely by many interested governments in the USA and, given its integration with property tax collections, has great replication potential.

Opportunity Example: Pooled Bond EE Finance Program for Local Governments in India

State governments can be instrumental in pooling projects amongst their local governments. Several state governments in India (for example, Karnataka, Andra Pradesh, Tamil Nadu, Maharashtra) are interested in programs to develop and finance municipal energy efficiency (EE) projects for cities within their respective states. State governments have a responsibility and certain programs and budget authority for development of municipal infrastructure. State governments have a duty to promote municipal EE as part of good governance, prudent fiscal policies and infrastructure development. There may be direct fiscal benefits for states which have some financial responsibility for infrastructure, operations or energy expenditures of the municipalities.

Project types include: efficient street lighting (including use of dimming technologies), efficient pumping of water and wastewater facilities, and EE in public buildings and facilities. Many states have already sponsored studies for municipal EE projects, providing an initial project pipeline. The state government acts as the market aggregator and marketing partner. The program could be led by appropriate state government nodal agencies (Urban Development, Energy, Water Supply and Sanitation, Urban Development Investment and Finance Corporation, as applicable) and would offer a) access to EE project finance, and b) project development TA services to a pool of municipalities.

The State may also play a role in the financing structure. One efficient method of raising capital budget money for state and municipal projects is through bond financing. The state could issue bonds and on-lend the proceeds to participating municipalities, using pre-defined credit and underwriting guidelines. To create a sound credit structure, the borrowing municipality must typically pledge a defined revenue stream and dedicate it to debt service. In some cases, it may consider allowing the municipalities to pledge revenues they receive from the state government. For example, the state government of Karnataka directly pays municipal electricity bills. These funds could be placed in escrow as part of the loan security. Such an instrument could apply to all municipalities receiving this subsidy, thereby enhancing their creditworthiness. DFI guarantees may also be required to enhance the sale of local currency bonds in the capital markets. Providing such guarantees would mobilize local savings and contribute to financial market deepening. This practice has been adopted by IFC, ADB and others. The state may also offer grants and incentives for municipal EE capital investments.

For example, Maharashtra State offers 75% funding support to municipalities that conduct energy audits and 23.33% capital grants to implement EE projects for their water supply and sanitation systems. Procurement of EE projects could also be pooled amongst the several municipalities. This aggregates demand for EE project and services, as well. This type of program could significantly support ESCO development, a key barrier to which are the high project sales and development costs and risks. The program would prepare projects for investment and get the end-users "decision-ready". The project could then be the subject of a competitive procurement, as required in the public sector, via a "request for proposal" (RFP) process. The RFP would present the project to the EE and ESCO business community, reducing costs. A well-designed project will find a ready response.

Many EE and contracting firms have core capacities in EE systems, engineering and turnkey construction, but do not self-identify yet as "ESCOs". But they can be recruited to respond. Typical municipal projects will be in the range of $250,000 on the very small end to $10–15 million, with a typical average of $1–3 million. In aggregate this market can be sufficiently large to attract the larger, most capable contracting firms and also to justify the transaction costs of a bond issue. The sponsoring State agencies will need assistance to implement and institutionalize the program, building their capacities to sustain it in the medium to long term.

Development agencies can provide such assistance. States will need help in program design and structuring the financing mechanism. In operations, municipalities will typically need assistance such as: a) preparing system inventories, energy cost and consumption data and load profiles for participating municipalities; b) assessing EE investment opportunities at a preliminary feasibility level; c) supporting decision-making to determine appropriate project implementation plans ("detailed project reports" or DPRs), including desired levels of outsourcing, and project financing plans; d) assistance arranging project financing through the municipal fund mechanism; e) preparation of the RFP documents, including appropriate RFP provisions and evaluation methodologies for ESCO contracting, and advice in conducting the procurement process and evaluating proposals; f) preparation and negotiation of project implementing contracts, e.g., turnkey construction contracts, service agreements, performance guarantees, and/or ESCO Energy Services Agreements; and g) providing independent engineering reviews of project systems and savings estimates.

Investments of this type may also include assessment, development and sale of carbon credits, (CERs or "certified emissions reductions") and development of cooperative agreements with electric utilities which want to acquire demand side management and load management resources. Concessional funding could support the financing structure, help cover costs of structuring the financing program, and provide some credit support for the bond issue, such as first loss reserve funding within a DFI guarantee. Such a program is highly replicable amongst the many Indian states and in other countries. The public sector can be a leader in the development of the ESCO industry, as in the case in the USA, Canada, Europe and other markets where ESCOs have matured.

IFC Hungary, National Schools EE Finance Program

The Hungarian National Ministry of Education conducted a pooled procurement for ESCO projects and services in 2005 on behalf of medium and small school districts in the country. OTP Bank provided a $200 million project debt facility, to provide loans to school districts, supported by an IFC partial credit guarantee.

A.4 EERE Finance Programs for Small and Medium Enterprises

Small and Medium Enterprise EERE Finance, India SME Industry Cluster Program

A new initiative of the World Bank to develop and finance EE investments for small and medium enterprises (SMEs) is an example of an EE finance program business model. The industrial history of India has resulted in many SMEs clustered in the same geographic location and makingt the same product. These "cluster associations" are a natural marketing partner and aggregator. They are a nodal point for communication and organization of EE projects with groups of end-users. Main components of this business model are summarized below.

World Bank SME Cluster Association EE Program Model

Business Model Component	**Methods**
Target Market & Typical Deal Size	SMEs in industrial clusters, e.g., textile, metallurgy; range of EE measures (motors & VSDs, lighting, cogeneration, efficient boilers, etc.); typical investment size per end-user is $50–500,000, with $125,000 estimated as an average. Each industry cluster typically has several hundred SMEs, so the market size for each target cluster will be in the tens of millions total investment.
Market Aggregation Partner & Marketing Plan	Cluster Associations serve as market aggregators and marketing partners. A series of seminars will be conducted to market the program to SMEs.

Business Model Component	Methods
Project Development Cycle & TA Program	Interested and eligible SMEs will be offered engineering TA step-wise to assist them through the project development cycle.
Financing Mechanism & Credit Structure	Loans to end-users are offered by commercial banks. Banks will be drawn from those participating in prior WB/GEF EE finance programs[18]. A partial credit guarantee with SIDBI (Small Industries Development Bank of India) is being developed to enhance the credit structure and may include guarantee reserves from GEF funds. ESCOs can also be organized to offer financing packaged with turnkey projects, e.g., for cogeneration systems.
EE Project Design	EE project measures will be selected by individual participating SMEs. Many SMEs have common energy use patterns/systems, e.g., need for power factor correction and motor efficiency plus solar thermal water heating for textile plants. Standard packages of equipment & systems will be prepared which are cost-effective and technically suitable for each industry group. This will accelerate marketing and decision making and reduce development costs.
EE Project Implementation	A set of qualified EE equipment and service firms will be selected by the cluster associations via a "request for qualifications" (RFQ), assisting SME end-users to make purchase decisions. Cost advantages from pooled procurements will be explored. All purchasing decisions will be made on a market basis by the individual SME end-users.

This example illustrates the several components of an effective business model. Concessional and development agencies can apply their resources to design such programs, assemble the participants, fund operations of the TA program and provide grant or concessional finance components of the financing mechanism.

A.5 Housing EERE Finance Programs, Single- and Multi-family

IFC Hungary "Retail Gas" Program

As of its Hungary Energy Efficiency Co-Financing Program, IFC developed a product with Raiffeisen Leasing, a subsidiary of Raiffeisen Bank, to finance gas-fired heating systems for single family homes,packaged with other EE improvements, such as lighting, weather-stripping and hot water heater insulation. The program was marketed with a local gas utility in Szeged, Hungary. A set of equipment vendors were qualified and they marketed the leasing product at the

[18] For example, State Bank of India, Canara Bank, Bank of Baroda, Union Bank, etc.

point of sale to the household. A loss reserve portfolio guarantee was used. The program was successfully marketed in 1998–2000, consisting of several thousand projects, averaging approximately $1500 each.

Financing Energy Efficiency for Low Income Blockhouses in Central Europe

GreenMax Capital Advisors, based in Warsaw, has developed a Housing Energy Efficiency Financing Facility (HEEFF) which works with local commercial FIs to lend to condominium associations for investments in energy efficiency. The HEEFF is a financing facility operated under agreement between the Dutch International Guarantees for Housing (DIGH), a local housing agency, and the participating financial institutions. DIGH provides a cash deposit fund (CDF) to the participating bank as a financial security. The CDF which is initially funded by DIGH at 2 million Euros is used solely to back energy efficiency renovation loans to condominium associations. For each individual loan, a Project Cash Deposit (PCD) is allocated from the cash deposit fund. The PCD is used to replace the 20% owners' equity normally required from the borrowers and to cover the first 20% of losses of principal on each loan. An international financial institution (IFC) provides additional credit support to the participating bank which covers 80% of the loans not backed by DIGH. Through the backing provided by the CDF of DIGH and the IFI, the participating bank achieves a level of comfort to finance 100% of the investment required by the condominium associations.

A.6 Mobilizing Microfinance Institutions for Energy Access Finance

Palawan, Philippines Solar Home Systems Finance Program

With a small grant from the GEF, UNDP is operating a solar home systems financing program in Palawan, Philippines since 2004. This is part of an effort to promote the use of renewable energy and to increase support of livelihoods in rural areas. Because of Palawan's island geography, more than 60% of all villages lack grid power. Many households rely solely on stand-alone household energy systems because of their remote locations, which provide an excellent application of Solar PV home systems.

Shell Solar Philippines Corp. (SSPC), the sole vendor in the region, has been active marketing and selling SHSs, but sales momentum was hard to achieve due to lack of consumer financing. UNDP has established a vendor finance program involving SSPC and the Cooperative Bank of Palawan (CBP or Bank). This small local rural bank has total assets of approximately USD$3 million equivalent. CBP. It is experienced in capital loans to farmers and fishers, but had not yet provided term loans to households for consumer equipment.

The program design uses a loss reserve fund (LRF), co-funded by UNDP with GEF monies, to provide credit enhancement for backing loans to households that acquire SHSs. The vendor, SSPC, committed to buy back any SHS's repossessed from defaulting borrowers. The price was matched to the value of the PV panel alone and was equal to at least 50% of the remaining principal balance of the loan.

The LRF was sized to cover all the net losses, net of the proceeds from SSPC's buyback of the PV panel, with an estimated default rate of 20%. This default rate was greater than the level expected. The LRF was funded primarily by UNDP with the balance contributed by both the vendor and the bank. The typical loan term is four years. Customer down payments are small, but a minimum of 10% is required, plus a security deposit of two month's payments. On these terms the household's monthly payments are generally considered to be affordable.

SSPC provides system warranties and training for local technicians to provide after-sale services. The program was implemented on a pilot scale with an initial deposit $35,000 by UNDP,, which could support financing of over $400,000 in SHS systems, approximately 1200 SHSs. The LRF was deposited with the Development Bank of the Philippines (DBP) which served as escrow agent. DBP is also considering providing wholesale loan funds to CBP to expand its lending resources for this program. The design of this program is depicted in Fig. 8. Loan defaults have been less than 4% of total loans to date. Successor programs can therefore use a smaller planned default rate to size the LRF and therefore achieve greater leverage of donor funds.

Similar program designs are underway by UNEP for several countries in Africa.[19]

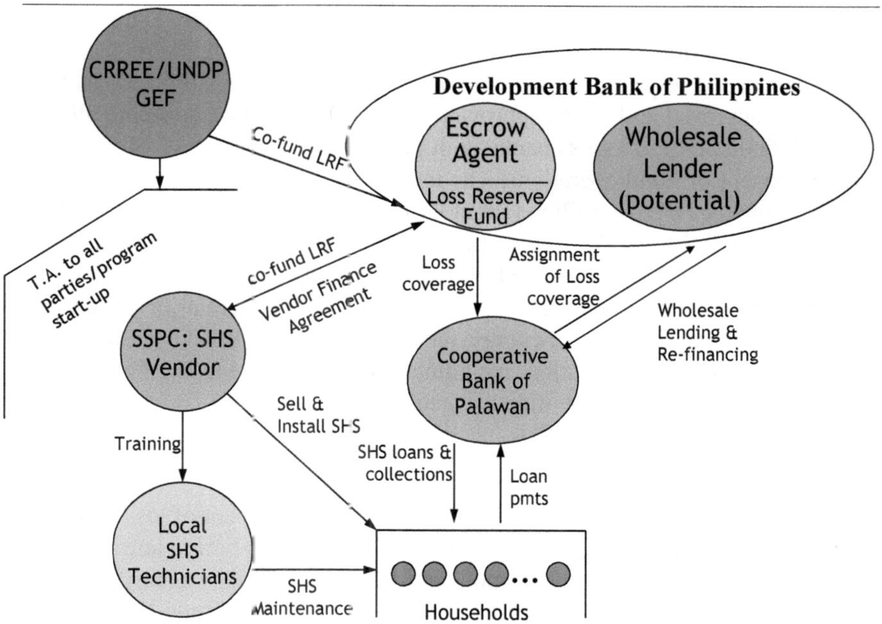

Fig. 8. UNDP/GEF SHS Direct Sales Finance Scheme, Palawan

[19] See MacLean, John and Siegel, Judith, *Financing Mechanisms and Public/Private Risk Sharing Instruments for Financing Small Scale Renewable Energy Equipment & Projects*, UNEP, Paris, 2007.

A.7 DFI Credit Lines to CFIs

Thailand Energy Efficiency Revolving Fund

The Thailand Energy Efficiency Revolving Fund has been established by the Government of Thailand, and managed by the Ministry of Energy, Department of Alternative Energy Development and Efficiency (DEDE). The Fund receives revenues from a petroleum tax (USD 0.0001 per liter) on all petroleum products sold in Thailand, which was first levied in 1993. This tax yields approximately USD $50 million per year. The Fund also pays for EE and RE technical assistance programs, such as funding for energy audits and project feasibility studies. It presently has an accumulated balance of approximately $350 million.

The Fund initially (2003–2007) provided up to 50% of a project's total loan requirements, and fund monies are blended with the bank's own resources. In its second phase of operations, the Fund reduced its share to 30%. The Fund lends to banks on a full recourse basis. The Fund provides loan capital on up to seven year terms and at a below market interest rate (between 0–4%) to participating banks. Banks must pass through most, but not all of this lower interest cost to the project borrowers. Thus, the banks are able to make a higher margin on their loans funded in part by the Fund. Six major Thai commercial banks namely Bank Thai, Bangkok Bank PCL, Sri Ayutthaya Bank, TMB Bank, Siam City Bank, Siam Commercial Bank participate in the program.

The banks are responsible for most aspects of the lending process, including marketing, appraisal and credit approval, loan collections and enforcing all remedies in defaults. DEDE assists banks with project appraisals, which are an important component of Fund operations. The maximum size of any single project loan from the Fund is THB 50 million (about USD 1.25 million). Setting the maximum loan size at THB 50 million ensures that money from the Fund will be distributed to a large number of medium-sized projects rather than being taken up by a few large projects. Eligible borrowers include owners of commercial or industrial facility and third parties such as energy service companies (ESCOs). Eligible projects include energy conservation, including renewable energy. The Fund has supported many bio-mass cogeneration projects.

DFI Guarantees with CFIs

Important features of a guarantee include: a) definition of event of loss which triggers the guarantee payment, b) the risk-sharing formula, c) timing and calculation of guarantee claim payment, d) responsibilities for collections against defaulting borrowers, e) disposition of recovered monies, e) maximum single loan guarantee exposures, f) guarantee approval and issuance procedures, and g) guarantee fees. Typically guarantees are partial, covering less than 100% of the outstanding loan principal, with 50–80% being typical. This assures that the FI remains at risk for a portion of its lending as a means to assure sound credit practices. The FI typically retains responsibility for exercising remedies and taking collection actions in events of default, as the FI is typically better equipped to do so.

Guarantee pricing is typically expressed as a percentage per annum of the guarantee liability and paid semi-annually or annually. Some guarantee pricing formulas call for a single guarantee payment at origination. The role of the guarantor in approving each guarantee transaction is an important topic. For larger guarantees, the guarantor may have loan-by-loan approval rights. In some cases, e.g., portfolio guarantees, the guarantor and lender agree on loan underwriting criteria in advance, and the lender can automatically include new loans meeting these criteria in the loan portfolio covered by the guarantee.

- *Pari Passu Partial Credit Guarantees*

  In the case of a pari passu partial guarantee, recovered monies net of an appropriate allowance for collection costs are distributed in the same proportion that the loss was distributed. Because the CFI must share recovered monies proportionally with the guarantor, the pari passu structure is weaker as a credit risk management tool. For the CFI to be made whole, and have a "second way out" of a defaulted loan, it still must require full security for the loan, in addition to the guarantee.

- *Subordinated Recovery Guarantee*

  A subordinated recovery guarantee serves like a pari passu partial guarantee except in the disposition of recovered monies. With a subordinated recovery guarantee the FI can apply all monies collected from a defaulting borrower, (recovered from legal action, from liquidation of collateral, etc.) first to recover the FI's own losses of principal, (typically including reasonable collection costs), before any recovered monies are repaid back to the guarantor. This approach makes the subordinated recovery guarantee more powerful for the CFI as a tool to create creditworthy financing packages, even at lower percentages of guarantee coverage.

- *Portfolio Guarantees*

  Portfolio guarantees are applied to portfolios of loans and typically distinguish between first losses and second losses on the whole loan portfolio. Portfolio guarantees are useful when the loan portfolio being covered consists of a very large number of smaller and relatively homogenous loans, as is the case in the EERE equipment consumer market. Thus, a statistical approach to credit risk for the portfolio as a whole can be taken. An estimated default rate can be planned in the credit structure of the portfolio as a whole. By covering a large share of first losses, and sizing the definition of first losses to be a comfortably high proportion of the loan portfolio – higher than the estimated default/loss rate – a first loss portfolio guarantee can provide very meaningful risk coverage to the FI, with low levels of total guarantee liability relative to the total size of the portfolio.

- *Loss Reserves*

  Concessional funds can also be used to create or supplement loss reserves to provide risk coverage. The loss reserves also would be applied to cover an FI's losses on a portfolio of concessional loans which an FI would make with its own resources. Loss reserves provide risk coverage very similar to a first loss portfolio guarantee. They are best used when the loan portfolio consists of large numbers of smaller loan transactions where a statistical approach can be taken to the credit structure of the loan portfolio as a whole. For example, if a loan portfolio consists of 2000 equal size transactions, a single default results in a maximum 0.05% loss. A reserve of 5%, for example, where the FI estimates default rates at <5%, would be very meaningful as a credit enhancement instrument.

- *Liquidity Support Guarantees*

  In some cases, a guarantee or some portion of it can be structured as a liquidity support guarantee. Guarantee payments could be drawn down to keep the loan current, extending time periods for effecting recoveries, if it is possible in avoiding final default and loss. This approach is being used in a World Bank GEF guarantee program in the Philippines that supports loans to rural electric cooperatives (RECs) for power distribution system upgrades and loss reduction investments. A liquidity support feature to the guarantee structure is used because an REC provides an essential service and will not go out of business. Hence rather than immediately declaring default and accelerating a loan for which payments are past due, it is better to seek work out remedies. Loan acceleration always remains an option.

  Design of an appropriate guarantee structure supported by concessional financing should meet several criteria.

- *Appropriate Risk Sharing*

  The instrument must provide levels of risk sharing sufficient to attract and motivate FIs and expand their risk profiles and horizons while also maintaining and aligning incentives of the parties concerned for good loan origination and administration.

- *Leverage*

  Concessional funding sources seek good leverage for their monies, usually measured in terms of a) the total energy project and equipment financing accomplished through a program, in ratio to b) the amount of concessional funding provided. In guarantee structures, leverage can be achieved at several levels of financial intermediation.

- *Flexibility, Suitability, Replicability*

  The instrument should be suitable and matched to the types of financial products that meet address the target market, market barriers and conditions. It should also be flexible to support the range of financial products that can be developed to meet market needs.

- *Alignment of Incentives*

  Guarantees should be structured to maintain incentives for the CFI for prudent, effective underwriting and loan administration practices and to avoid moral hazard.

- *Administration*

  The instrument should be designed to be easy to administer and responsive to commercial needs and timing, and to provide for proper reporting and accountability.

- *National Banking Regulations*

  Guarantees should be structured in consultation with banking regulators to maximize regulatory benefits to the beneficiary CFI, e.g., to allow the guarantee to substitute for CFI loss provisioning.

IFC/GEF Hungary Energy Efficiency Co-financing Program (HEECP)

This program was initiated by the IFC Environmental Finance Group (EFG) and was funded with a total of US$5.0 million by GEF. In 2003, similar guarantee programs were rolled out in five additional Central European countries. HEECP is designed to overcome barriers to EERE project finance and development, primarily credit risk and the lack of well-prepared projects. To address these barriers, HEECP has two tools: a) a guarantee program, supporting and sharing in the credit risk of EERE financing undertaken by domestic FIs with their own funds; and b) a technical assistance program to help prepare projects for investment and aid general EE market development. HEECP aims to support projects which a) are economic and achieve energy savings and greenhouse gas (GHG) emissions reductions; b) promote the entry of domestic FIs in the EERE financing market, and increase the ability of domestic FIs to provide such financing; c) support FIs to develop and use innovative financing structures and provide more favorable credit terms to borrowers; d) promote development of the EE market and commercial ESCO industry; and, e) develop and demonstrate new non-grant finance tools for the GEF, including methods of leveraging commercial finance.

Under the guarantee program, participating FIs execute Guarantee Facility Agreements (GFAs) with IFC. FIs propose EERE project transactions to IFC, which in turn reviews the transaction for approval. Each Guarantee Facility Agreement defines the maximum amount of guarantee claims that IFC would ever pay out under a GFA (a "Facility Liability Limit" or FLL). IFC makes the guarantee payment within 90 days. Thereafter, the FI has responsibility to continue legal remedies, take collections actions and sell collateral to recover the loss from the defaulting borrower. HEECP has developed a second guarantee product structured on a portfolio basis where large numbers of small projects are being financed systematically. This guarantee program gives participating FIs a risk management tool to create creditworthy financing and allow projects to be funded that otherwise might not be funded because of credit risk concerns.

In conjunction with its FI partners, HEECP has developed financing products and supporting guarantee structures for EERE financing for a) multi-family housing, b) single family housing, c) municipal street-lighting, d) district heating, e) industrial cogeneration implemented pursuant to energy sales agreements, and f) hospitals, with financing offered both direct to end-users and to ESCOs. Financing structures have been adapted to the institutional and credit requirements of each type of end-user and include direct recourse to end-users, direct recourse to ESCOs and limited recourse project financing. The complementary technical assistance (TA) program is essential to the program's success through its support of the marketing of EE finance services by participating FIs and its help in identifying EE projects through energy audits. The TA program also supports EE project development and investment preparation, corporate finance advisory services to ESCOs and general EE market promotion and program evaluation activities.

West Nile (Uganda) Hydro Project Financing

Providing longer loan tenors can often address the need for long term debt capital that can reduce annual debt service to a level that better matches a project's stream of benefits. This need is often manifest for RE power generation systems. This approach can be critical to create affordable energy services. For example, in Uganda the West Nile Rural Energy Agency implemented a 5 MW small hydro project with support from a World Bank program that used concessional funds to allow Barclays, a commercial lender, to extend the loan tenor from seven to 14 years. This made the price per kWh affordable.

Given their lack of experience with this type of project and other financial market conditions, Barclays was willing to undertake a maximum seven year loan term for the project. The World Bank provided a form of partial guarantee on the loan. The guarantee amount was sized and structured to fully repay the remaining principal balance on the loan after seven years. By assuming all the loan exposure risk after seven years, the guarantee allowed a 14 year loan term to be used. To make the guarantee, the World Bank provided a cash instrument equal to the full guarantee liability amount. A zero-coupon bond was used that would have a future redemption value in seven years, equal to the agreed amount. At Barclay's option, this instrument can be redeemed at the end of the first seven year loan term to prepay the loan. If the project performs well and meets its debt service obligations, the parties expect that at the end of the first seven years, Barclays can simply extend its loan for the remaining second seven year term, and the WB guarantee can be retired.[20]

[20] This type of guarantee is very useful. In this case, however, because a cash-type instrument was used, it also required a large sum from the World Bank to implement. After seven years, the remaining principal on a 14 year loan will equal about 67% of the original loan principal. Depending on the effective yield on the zero-coupon bond, the purchase price of the bond will approximate 65% of the planned seventh year redemption

International Finance Corp. (IFC) Senior Loan Guarantee for EERE Projects in the Czech Republic

IFC, through its Commercializing Energy Efficiency Finance (CEEF) guarantee program has financed several grid-connected EERE projects by Cseka Sporitelna Bank (CSB) in the Czech Republic. These include wind, small hydro and bio-mass projects, all less than 5 MW in size. IFC has a Guarantee Facility Agreement (GFA) to provide a 50% pari passu (on equal terms) partial credit guarantee to CSB, facilitating the bank's financing many EERE projects. One 2 MW wind project was financed on a limited recourse project finance basis. IFC has $15 million in GEF funds in a first loss position supporting its guarantee liabilities, where any claims to the fund would come first from IFC and secondarily from CSB. IFC has approved undertaking guarantee liabilities of up to five times the amount of its GEF reserve funds. IFC has also developed first loss, subordinated recovery and portfolio guarantee structures for use in the CEEF program and the related Hungary Energy Efficiency Co-Financing Program, although the pari passu guarantee structure has primarily been employed for EERE project financing. IFC also provides technical assistance in loan structuring and appraisal, development of new financial products, and marketing and project pipeline development. These TA services have been critical and instrumental in engaging CSB effectively and making the CSB program successful.

A.8 DFI Mezzanine Finance Facilities

E+Co Central America RE Investment Fund Using Mezzanine Financing Instruments

E+Co has recently established an investment vehicle to provide innovative mezzanine and debt financing to clean energy enterprises in Central America and the Caribbean. The Central American Renewable Energy and Cleaner Production Facility (CAREC) signed their partners' agreement in August, 2006 to fund US$17 million of a total targeted capitalization of US$20 million. The target market is mainly RE projects, <5 MW typically, and mostly grid connected, but also including a range of

value based on a 6% yield. Therefore, the sum required to purchase the bond will be about 45% of the total loan amount. Thus, it would be costly in terms of concessional and development funds to replicate on a large scale. If this type of instrument were replicated, a guarantee program would be established whereby a local guarantor offers similar partial loan guarantee instruments for a series of transactions; concessional funds could be used as equity or as a first loss reserve by the guarantor to support undertaking such liabilities. The parties would need to agree in advance that the redemption option is available only if the project loan does not perform. Then, it can be estimated that only a portion of the guarantee liabilities will in fact be called. Then, total guarantee liabilities could be a multiple of the concessional reserve funds and the concessional funder would achieve better leverage of its resources.

clean energy enterprises. The CAREC facility will use mainly mezzanine-financing mechanisms such as subordinated debt, convertible debt, preferred shares and other quasi-equity structures. These instruments will strengthen the projects' financial structures and successfully leverage the always-needed senior debt component. The instruments are typically designed to earn a fixed rate of return, matched to the given project's revenue stream, and paid from revenues net of operating costs and senior debt service, plus additional returns in the form of profit sharing, ownership shares, and, potentially, acquisition and sale of carbon emission reduction credits. A maximum 25% of a project's capital cost can be financed.

CAREC provides flexible capital, like a strategic investor, that can help mobilize commercial and development bank debt from both local and international sources, thus helping to fill an important financing gap. E+Co Capital Latin America has secured a loan guarantee facility from the USAID Development Credit Authority (DCA) for support of private sector debt to the CAREC fund.[21] CAREC, managed by E+Co Capital Ltd., a subsidiary of E+Co, Inc., was initiated with core financial and institutional support from the Multilateral Investment Fund (MIF) of the Inter-American Development Bank (IDB). Also, with grant funding from MIF and the Netherlands Development Finance Company (FMO) the fund will have a Technical Assistance facility to help cover investment preparation and project and business financial advisory services.

A.9 Carbon Finance

India Compact Fluorescent Lamp Program of Activities

The Indian Bureau of Energy Efficiency (BEE) is piloting a program in Pune, India to support replacement of incandescent lighting with compact florescent lamps (CFLs) in the household and commercial sectors. Revenues from the sale of Certified Emissions Reductions (CERs) finance the program. The project distributes 500,000 CFLs manufactured by Siemens Osram to household customers of the Maharashtra State Electricity Board. Up to 450,000 households are eligible to receive up to two CFLs each of 15 or 20 watts to replace high usage incandescent bulbs, at a price roughly equal to that of an incandescent on the Indian market, or $0.32 USD. Program marketing will use door to door canvassing as well as being accompanied by an awareness campaign. This project achieves demonstrable GHG emission savings. Conservative estimates provided by the program designers calculate a total of 299,881 tonnes of CO2 will be avoided, producing an equal amount of CER's[22]. CFL's sold to households through this program must involve an exchange of the incandescent that is being replaced, which will then be destroyed to prevent future use.

---

[21] For more information, please see http://eandco.org/.

[22] 1 CER = 1 tonne CO2e.

The CFLs will be produced in India with German/Italian parts and technology which will create jobs and lower the mercury content compared to current Indian CFL production methods. Financially, the program is not profitable without the revenues available from the sale of CER's. The estimated full cost per distributed CFL for this project is approximately $4.20, and overall the project is estimated to cost approximately $2.2 million. Present value of CER revenues are estimated $4.2 million based at $24.00/CER, sufficient to buy down the costs of the CFLs to the price of the incandescent bulbs and pay for program operating costs. This approach appears to be a highly replicable production and distribution model.[23]

A.10 Specialized National Development Bank EERE Project Funds

The Bulgaria Energy Efficiency Fund (BEEF)

The BEEF was established in 2005 as a self-sustaining, public-private partnership to finance EE projects in the municipal, residential, commercial and industrial sectors. Seed funding of $10 million was provided by the Global Environment Facility (GEF) with additional funds from the governments of Austria and Bulgaria. BEEF provides technical assistance to its energy user clients to help prepare projects, and then provides loans for project implementation. BEEF built a project portfolio of over $32 million in just over two years of operation (as of June, 2008), many in the municipal and district heating sector. BEEF is considering ways to increase its capitalization, and could become a vehicle for commercial FIs to channel funds into EE projects. Its success, though small, demonstrates demand for adapted financing, and the importance of combining technical engineering capacity with funding capacity.

India Renewable Energy Development Agency (IREDA)

IREDA provides debt financing for RE and EE projects. It was incorporated as a government-owned company in 1987. It has received credit lines from the World Bank, ADB and KfW, amongst others, as well as grant support from the GEF. IREDA has built up its capability to originate clean energy project investments. It has developed significant experience and project finance capacities. Eligible borrowers include energy end-users, ESCOs, equipment manufacturers and vendors, and electric utilities. Small and medium projects are eligible. Projects as small as $200,000 and as large as $25 million have been funded.

IREDA also makes technical assistance funding available to help prospective project sponsors develop projects. This serves IREDA's development functions and builds the pipeline of prospective investments. IREDA invests mainly as a

[23] See Pune (India) OSRAM CFL distribution CDM Project, CDM Project Design Document, Version 03 – in effect as of: 22 December 2007; and, A. Mathur, "Cooperation for CM Project", 2nd Meeting of the Indo-German Energy Forum, 2007.

senior lender, loaning up to 80% of a project's total investment cost on terms up to 10 years with up to two year grace periods. IREDA has applied project finance principles to its investment structuring and underwriting, lending to special purpose project companies and ESCOs for example. Funded projects total over USD $1 billion and have included wind, hydro, bio-mass cogeneration, industrial waste heat recovery power plants, and industrial process efficiency. Industries include: steel, cement, sugar, chemicals, paper, textile and power generation. Special programs working with local commercial banks to fund energy efficiency projects with SMEs are also being developed to further extend IREDA's financial products to the SME sector. In India, the Energy Conservation Act of 2002 authorizes state governments to establish state energy conservation funds. IREDA, as a national entity, has the potential to replicate its capability by supporting the development of these funds.

Chapter 4

The Roles of Weather Insurance and the Carbon Market

Jerry R. Skees[*] *and Benjamin Collier*[**]

Abstract

This chapter discusses two financial markets — the carbon and weather markets — and their potential role in helping stakeholders address climate change more effectively. While this chapter focuses on how these markets can benefit the poor in developing countries, it also examines the major constraints that must be addressed before the poor can gain access to carbon and weather markets. It also suggests how governments and donors might effectively facilitate sustainable carbon and weather market activity in developing countries.

Poor households in developing countries are particularly vulnerable to weather shocks. To the extent that climate change may make such shocks more frequent, weather shocks and climate change are particularly troublesome given that proportionally more of the poor live in marginal areas and under marginal conditions. Furthermore, many of the world's poor rely on rain-fed agriculture with limited ability to adapt to climate change (Corbera et al., 2006; Nicholls et al., 2007; Stern, 2006). What is not understood are the specific impacts climate change will have at sub-regional or local levels; therefore, planning for these future events remains a challenge for households, firms, and policy makers (IPCC [International Panel for Climate Change], 2007a; Lobell et al., 2008; Morton, 2007).

Climate change projections depend on a variety of assumptions made by researchers regarding uncertain future weather patterns and feedback effects of reduced emissions (Hare and Meinhausen, 2006; Hulme et al., 2001; Stern, 2006; Yohe, 2006). This uncertainty challenges stakeholders trying to prioritize their efforts based on two overarching strategies for addressing climate change (IPCC, 2007a): *mitigation* to reduce anthropogenic contributions to climate change; and *adaptation* to adjust to the physical impacts of climate change. The authors argue that investments in adaptation are probably more critical for developing countries than investments in mitigation. This argument is based on the faster payoff of these investments relative to investments in mitigation.

[*] President, GlobalAgRisk, Inc.

[**] Project Associate, GlobalAgRisk, Inc.

D. Köhn (ed.), *Greening the Financial Sector: How to Mainstream Environmental Finance in Developing Countries*, DOI 10.1007/978-3-642-05087-9_4,

Carbon markets are a mitigation tool that uses price signals to reduce the overall rate of GHG (greenhouse gas) emissions. The right to emit GHGs is traded as a commodity on these markets. In theory, the use of price signals allows for the reduction of emissions at the lowest possible cost. Firms purchase carbon offsets when the cost of doing so is lower than the cost of changing production practices to meet emissions reduction regulations. Pricing pollution in this fashion also provides incentives for new technologies that will lower carbon emissions. The United Nations Convention on Climate Change (UNFCCC) has led mitigation efforts; the Kyoto Protocol establishes binding commitments for emissions reductions. Carbon markets have emerged from the mechanisms outlined in Kyoto and the specific regulations of the developed countries that have ratified Kyoto. Carbon markets primarily serve large firms in developing countries as these firms are the largest contributors to GHG emissions and must adhere to emissions reduction regulations (UNFCCC, 2007).

Carbon offsets are the instrument used in carbon markets that is most directly relevant to developing countries. The Kyoto Protocol does not require developing countries to reduce emissions; however, they can participate in mitigation efforts by reducing their GHG emissions. Credits for emissions reductions are sold on carbon markets to firms in developed countries that must meet emissions standards, or in the case of the United States, firms that seek to acquire carbon offsets at lower prices as a hedge against future restrictions. Thus, carbon emitting firms in developed countries finance global mitigation efforts. Large firms in China, India, and Brazil generate over 80 percent of the carbon offsets created through carbon offset projects in developing countries (Capoor and Ambrosi, 2008). The UNFCCC, the World Bank, and others are working to build capacity in the least developed countries so that they can also participate in carbon offset projects (UNFCCC, 2007).

Regarding adaptation, investments that reduce the vulnerability of the poor, especially infrastructure and new technology investments, are needed to manage the risk of specific climate change impacts. Many of these investments are badly needed irrespective of climate change. To be clear, weather shocks are common now and existing systems are vulnerable to those weather shocks. Climate change impacts will only serve to increase the vulnerability of the poor by increasing the frequency and/or severity of extreme weather events.

Weather markets, such as for weather insurance and weather derivatives, enhance risk management strategies. They can serve as an adaptation tool to aid decision makers at many levels by sending price signals regarding weather risk and by providing cash payments that can be used to adapt to changing climate impacts. Adaptation must occur in the form of a specific risk in a specific local context, which can require among other things changes in household production strategies (Fankhauser et al., 2008). Weather insurance reduces revenue volatility in weather sensitive industries. It may also serve as a tool to finance restoration of critical infrastructure that is designed to lessen the affects of extreme weather (e.g., levies, irrigation systems, etc.).

Weather index insurance is a relatively new form of weather insurance. It is gaining popularity in developing countries, creating new opportunities to protect the poor from the natural disasters that devastate their livelihoods and impede economic development (Barnett, Barrett, Skees, 2008). The most prevalent use of weather index insurance is for agriculture. Payouts are based on an important weather variable tied to agricultural production such as rainfall. Basing insurance payouts on an objective index reduces the loss adjustment and asymmetric information costs of traditional agricultural insurance. Weather index insurance protects against catastrophic risk (e.g., drought), and relies on international reinsurance markets to transfer the risk of extreme losses.

Challenges remain in providing weather index insurance at rates affordable to poor households: 1) the start-up costs of developing attractive weather index insurance for the working poor create a significant barrier to entry for local insurance companies; 2) insurance companies in developing countries are simply not ready to take on this special form of highly correlated risk, as they may have limited access to global reinsurers to transfer the risk out of the country; 3) insurance laws and regulations in developing countries are not in place to facilitate this special form of insurance; and 4) in many regions, the underlying weather risks overwhelm an insurance solution for risk management.

Index-based weather risk transfer products can be written either as insurance or derivatives. Over-the-counter weather index derivatives are becoming more common. Over-the-counter products are typically developed for a single user and have many of the characteristics of insurance (e.g., a well-defined event that triggers a payment in exchange for a fixed premium payment). Still, due to the difficulties associated with regulating over-the-counter weather derivatives, these instruments should not be sold directly to small households. Insurance regulators in developing countries are in a much stronger position to protect consumer interest when these products are structured as insurance rather than derivatives — much progress has been made in creating the proper regulatory environment for weather index insurance in developing countries (Carpenter and Skees, 2005).

Actively traded weather derivatives are also playing an important role in weather risk transfer, such as heating and cooling days for major US cities. In contrast to over-the-counter weather index insurance products, which are tailored to each client, actively traded weather derivatives are standardized weather derivatives contracts that are traded on financial exchange markets (e.g., the Chicago Mercantile Exchange). Actively traded weather derivatives are typically designed for large energy firms in developed countries. Lessons from these markets may improve the development of markets for the poor because experience with weather derivatives on financial exchange markets illustrates that actively trading weather risk improves price discovery and creates more efficient pricing.

Reinsurers that are actively involved in weather index insurance and weather derivatives markets are improving linkages between these markets to reduce the costs of weather index insurance. This may have important implications for developing countries, especially in regions where extreme weather events occur as a consequence of specific, global weather anomalies such as El Niño Southern Oscillation (ENSO). Climate change presents additional challenges to weather markets, especially in designing sustainable weather index insurance products that are affordable for poor households. The authors make four primary conclusions regarding climate change and weather markets:

1. when weather risk is increasing, weather markets can help stakeholders manage their associated revenue volatility;
2. to be viable, someone will ultimately have to pay for the increasing risk through premiums for weather insurance,
3. some public policy responses to higher premium costs such as premium subsidies can undermine the primary advantage of weather markets — pricing the risk in a way that leads to more rapid adaptation strategies; and
4. as risks increase due to climate change impacts, weather markets will continue to adjust the price of the underlying weather risk. Thus, in the long term, insureds pay for the cost associated with climate, and weather markets manage revenue volatility, not climate change. Insurers are uncertain about how climate change will affect the weather risk they are insuring; this uncertainty and the associated ambiguity creates upward pressure on the price of weather insurance.

A climate market — a financial exchange of products that can hedge against future climate risk — could potentially facilitate adaptation in several ways. These include alleviating some of the challenges climate change presents to weather insurance markets, which in turn could increase access to weather index insurance for the poor. By using financial exchange markets, the interaction of buyers and sellers would integrate myriad sources of information including climate change projections to develop a price for the risk under consideration. Such a market could reduce the pricing difficulties of insurers and allow firms, governments, and donors to hedge against extreme climate change effects.

To illustrate, we provide the case of a potential ENSO index — a product to hedge ENSO risk. ENSO has a strong influence on global weather patterns (McPhaden, 2003). Climate change effects on ENSO cycles would have economic impacts in many regions. Creating a short-term ENSO index that makes payments when El Niño events occur could help hedge the risk associated with ENSO, including the risk that climate change affects the ENSO cycle. Active trading in short-term climate markets could lead to trading longer-term climate risks, though it is fully acknowledged that creating longer-term exchange markets has been an illusive goal for many commodities.

As carbon and weather market activity increases in developing countries, a key question remains: to what extent will the poor be included in these markets? Currently, governments and donors are working to connect the poor to carbon and weather markets. The authors conclude that to increase the participation of the poor in these markets and to improve their ability to address climate change, decision makers can a) improve incentives for the poor to mitigate emissions, b) use mitigation and adaptation funds to seed environmental finance markets (especially credit and insurance) for the poor, c) increase the role of the private sector in developing countries as intermediaries between the poor and these markets, and d) create climate markets that facilitate adaptation.

1 Introduction

Financial markets provide important tools. These range from basic financial services such as credit, savings, and insurance, to more complex mechanisms such as derivatives, options, and securities, that can potentially help stakeholders address climate change more effectively. This chapter discusses the role of two financial markets — carbon and weather markets — and how these markets can benefit the poor in developing countries.[1] The authors also examine major constraints that must be addressed before the poor can gain access to carbon and weather markets, and how governments and donors might facilitate these markets in developing countries.[2] Recent applications in developing countries are used throughout as examples.

The overarching strategy to address climate change occurs on two fronts: *mitigaton* and *adaptation.* Mitigation refers to efforts to reduce anthropogenic (man-made) contributions to climate change. Adaptation refers to efforts to adjust to the physical impacts of climate change. (IPCC [International Panel for Climate Change], 2007a; Stern, 2006; UNFCCC [United Nations Framework Convention on Climate Change], 2007a). For financial markets, the distinction between mitigation and adaptation is important.

Mitigation requires investments and behavioral changes that reduce greenhouse gas (GHG) emissions (den Elzen et al., 2008). For example, improving energy efficiency among firms is a key mitigation effort that requires firms to change production strategies and invest in new technology. As other chapters in this book explain, firms need capital for these efforts. Credit is one important financial mechanism that facilitates mitigation.

Likewise, adaptation requires investments and behavioral changes to adjust to risks created by climate change (Lobell et al., 2008); however, these risks can also increase revenue volatility as weather shocks disrupt production and destroy assets (Lecocq and Shalizi, 2007). Thus for adaptation, both credit to fi-

1 Our focus is the working poor in developing countries. The majority of the working poor live in rural areas and operate small enterprises, in particular smallholder agriculture (World Bank, 2007).

2 By framing the question in this fashion, this paper does not investigate the relative benefits of a carbon market versus other choices for abatement. It is taken as a given that carbon markets will exist in some form in the future.

nance investments and behavioral changes, and insurance to manage weather risks and provide lump sum payments that may be used for adaptation investments, are important financial tools. For example, farmers may want to adjust their planting decisions or invest in irrigation due to erratic rainfall. They may need to purchase insurance for years of extreme drought when water shortages damage crops for non-irrigated agriculture and reduce access to water for irrigated agriculture (Leiva and Skees, 2008).

In this chapter, carbon markets that finance mitigation and weather markets are discussed. These markets can facilitate adaptation by managing the financial consequences of weather risk. The authors provide an overview that is relevant to the focus on how these markets might be better structured to serve the poor in developing countries. This chapter is divided into five sections: 1) setting the stage for how carbon markets aid mitigation and how weather markets aid adaptation to climate change; 2) a discussion of how carbon markets can be used by the poor; 3) a review of weather markets and how they may be used to facilitate adaptation by the poor; 4) an introduction some basic ideas about creating climate markets; and 5) final comments about the intersection of carbon and weather markets.

The authors view, developed later in this chapter, is that adaptation strategies will be more critical to the poor in developing countries than mitigation strategies. Also, weather markets are only one tool that may facilitate adaptation — and probably not the most important one.[3] Given that weather insurance markets are being widely touted as an adaptation mechanism for climate change, weather markets are examined more thoroughly than carbon markets.[4] *Weather insurance is not climate insurance.* Weather insurance is typically designed for a short time frame, often rainfall over the next year. However, longer-term climate change will have important implications for weather markets. The view emerging from climate change experts is that extreme weather events will occur more frequently in the future than in the past. If insurance underwriters also take this view, the price of weather insurance will rise. Consequently, these challenges may open the way for climate markets that would trade longer-term weather patterns.

The final section of this chapter highlights the intersection of carbon and weather markets. Carbon markets provide an explicit linkage to adaptation through a rule that designates that a percentage of carbon market funds must be contributed to an adaptation fund that finances adaptation in developing countries (Müller, 2008; UNFCCC, 2007). Among other things, these funds could be applied to assist in developing weather markets. In addition to links between carbon markets and adaptation, which may be imposed institutionally, there may be important overlaps in the delivery systems for carbon and weather markets for the poor.

---

3 See Müller (2008) for a comprehensive review of how to fund these strategies.

4 Weather markets can be structured as futures and/or options contracts traded on exchanges or as index-based insurance contracts.

2 Setting the Stage: Climate Change, Mitigation, Adaptation, and the Poor

Developing countries are more vulnerable to extreme weather events than developed countries (Carter et al., 2007; Morton, 2007; Fankhauser et al., 2008; Stern, 2006). The poor in developing countries are even more at risk, given where they live and that so many of them depend on rain-fed agriculture (Corbera et al., 2006; Nicholls et al., 2007; Stern, 2006). The poor tend to live where more affluent households choose not to settle — flood zones, vulnerable coastal areas, and regions where frequent droughts occur — which are the areas most affected by extreme weather events (Carter et al., 2007; Kundzewicz et al., 2007; Stern, 2006).

Increased frequency of extreme weather events may be the most significant concern associated with climate change (Corbera et al., 2006; Morton, 2007). Few models of the economic cost of climate change are adequate to examine the impact of extreme weather events (IPCC, 2007a). Most of this research is grounded in a framework that uses the expected values of important weather variables as the metric for examining the benefits and cost of mitigation and adaptation (Fankhauser et al., 2008; Yohe, 2006). Despite this focus on average future conditions, concerns about the potentially negative impacts of climate change are growing (Bindoff et al., 2007; Carter et al., 2007; IPCC, 2007a; Lobell et al., 2008). If increased frequency of extreme events could be modeled more effectively, the cost/benefit evaluation of mitigation and adaptation would probably change significantly.

Addressing climate change requires both mitigation and adaptation (IPCC, 2007a, Lecocq and Shalizi, 2007; UNFCCC, 2007). Mitigation involves multiple policy responses targeted at the abatement of GHGs, primarily carbon dioxide.[5] Adaptation involves a wide range of proactive and reactive strategies, both public and private, designed to buffer the adverse affects of climate change (Lacocq and Shalizi, 2007).[6]

2.1 Climate Change and Uncertainty

Uncertainty remains a significant challenge in preparing for climate change. Global circulation models inform climate change projections; however, these models are largely deterministic (primarily using trends in temperature from different climate

---

[5] To avoid confusion, "mitigation" is used by those working on climate change to mean efforts focused on reducing emissions of greenhouse gases. For those working on insurance, mitigation means efforts to reduce the exposure to a hazard; which is referred to as "adaptation" by those working on climate change. We use the terminology adopted by the climate change community.

[6] Many definitions of adaptation (e.g., IPCC, 2007b) are more generic and account for behavioral changes associated with positive or negative climate change outcomes. For example, farmers in some northern temperate climates may experience a longer growing season and adjust farm practices accordingly. We focus exclusively on adaptation for negative climate change outcomes.

models) while many of their assumptions remain uncertain (Hulme et al., 2001; Yohe, 2006). For example, the costs and effectiveness of various mitigation policies are dependent on assumptions of economic growth, implementation of technological advancements, and consumption patterns (Hare and Meinhausen, 2006; Stern, 2006). Additionally, the feedback effects of reduced emissions on the global climate are uncertain; this uncertainty greatly challenges long-term predictions of the effects of climate change and estimates of the level of mitigation required (IPCC, 2007a; Stern, 2006).

Preparation and prioritization of adaptation efforts should occur at sub-regional and local levels. However, climate change effects at a sub-regional level — and even a regional level for some variables such as rainfall — are nearly impossible to model (IPCC, 2007a; Lobell et al., 2008; Morton, 2007). For example, in 2007 the International Panel for Climate Change (IPCC) reported that by 2020, between 75 and 250 million people would experience increased water stress due to climate change in Africa. These kinds of general forecasts lack the specificity needed to plan adequate adaptation and safety net strategies (Lecocq and Shalizi, 2007). Additionally, projecting extreme events that have the largest impact on vulnerable populations, such as drought, extreme temperatures and rainfall, cyclones, etc., is more difficult than projecting average climate conditions (IPCC, 2007a). Nonetheless, the consensus view that extreme events will occur more frequently in some regions does require a public policy response to help the poor cope with extreme events (Corbera et al., 2006; IPCC, 2007a; Morton, 2007).

Leading organizations (e.g., IPCC, UNFCCC, etc.) agree that mitigation and adaptation must play a significant role in adapting to climate change; however, given the many uncertainties, it is difficult to determine how to prioritize climate change policies (Lecocq and Shalizi, 2007). Decisions regarding mitigation policies and adaptation investments impose real costs to households, firms, and governments (Perkins, 2008). Governments and multilateral organizations increasingly recognize the importance of a risk management approach to climate change policy that diversifies investments relative to the likelihood and severity of outcomes (IPCC, 2007a; Yohe, 2006).

2.2 Carbon and Weather Markets and Developing Countries

Carbon and weather markets fit squarely into a portfolio of responses to climate change. Carbon markets are a *mitigation* tool that use price signals to reduce the overall rate of GHG emissions. In theory, price signals allow for the reduction of emissions at the lowest possible cost. Carbon markets use tradable pollution permits to find least cost mechanisms to reduce emissions of GHGs. On the adaptation side, weather insurance markets are expanding in developing countries, and Article 4.8 of the UNFCCC explicitly mentions insurance to encourage adaptation to climate change. Weather markets are an *adaptation* tool that can aid decision makers. For weather risk, this is accomplished through price signals and by providing cash payments that may be used by those affected to adapt to a changing climate. Recent climate change discussions have addressed the potential for developed countries to assist developing countries in the creation of weather markets as a compensatory measure, given developed countries' inordinate contributions to carbon emissions. Table 1 compares and contrasts some important issues of mitigation and adaptation that are relevant for carbon and weather markets.

Table 1. Comparing and Contrasting Mitigation and Adaptation

	Mitigation	**Adaptation**
Definition	Reducing anthropogenic contributions to climate change	Reducing vulnerability to the physical impacts of climate change
Stakeholder focus	Big emitters (e.g., energy-inefficient firms, firms that reduce vegetation such as logging companies, etc.)	The most vulnerable (e.g., stakeholders living in marginal areas, those with agricultural livelihoods, low-skilled laborers, etc.)
Geographic focus	Global	Sub-regional/local
Timeframe	Long-term	Short and/or long-term
Can require that stakeholders	Change production strategies Adopt new technology	Change production strategies Adopt new technology Manage revenue volatility Improve infrastructure Relocate
Financial market role	Capital to finance investments Increase efficiency in emissions reductions	Capital to finance investments Smooth revenue volatility
Financial market mechanisms	Credit Carbon market	Credit Weather market (e.g., Weather insurance)

Source: Authors

Carbon and weather markets are different in many ways, but in developing countries these markets face similar challenges. Both markets are constrained by inadequately defined property rights or inappropriate regulatory policies. Delivering any market services to smallholders in remote locations is extremely costly. When transaction size is quite small, fixed transaction costs render it unprofitable to provide services to remote regions. In these situations, it may be more cost efficient to use an intermediary (e.g., a rural bank, donor organization, farmer cooperative, etc.) to aggregate carbon credits and weather insurance contracts. In some cases, a single entity may serve both markets. So far, donors and governments have been heavily involved in creating links between the poor and carbon and weather markets. In general, the private sector has limited incentives to foster these markets without government or donor help (Chapple, 2008).

Still, carbon and weather markets differ in a number of ways, including their origins, constructs, and reliance on government intervention. For example, carbon markets emerge when governments decide to impose restrictions on GHG emissions, or if it is expected that these restrictions will be imposed. However, weather markets have emerged to manage risks associated with extreme weather events. Carbon and weather markets also differ because the primary benefits for developing countries are likely to be on the selling side of carbon markets and on the buying side of weather markets.

3 Mitigation Using Carbon Markets

Mitigation is a long-term strategy aimed at curtailing future climate change effects. GHG levels are measured on a global scale in terms of atmospheric concentrations (parts per million) of their CO_2 equivalent (den Elzen et al., 2008; IPCC, 2007a). IPCC (2007a) reports with "high agreement and much evidence" that given current climate change policies on mitigation, GHG emissions will continue to grow. The global community is establishing standards for measurement and verification that have opened the way for carbon markets.

Since 1994, the UNFCCC has played a crucial role in efforts to mitigate GHGs. The Kyoto Protocol, enacted in 2005, created binding commitments for emissions reductions among participating developed countries. The thirty-seven countries that ratified the Kyoto Protocol commit to reducing greenhouse gases by roughly 5 percent on average of 1990 levels over the 2008–2012 period (Capoor and Ambrosi, 2008; UNFCCC, 2007).[7]

The rules and structure of the Kyoto Protocol provide the foundation for domestic, regional, and global carbon markets. A government places emissions caps on its producers so that it can meet its Kyoto emissions target, while markets have developed to facilitate emissions reductions in the private and public sectors.[8] Carbon markets reduce the cost of emissions reductions in four ways: 1) enabling firms that cannot cheaply lower emissions to abate emissions in other ways; 2) enabling cleaner and more efficient companies to profit from their contributions toward reduced emissions; 3) connecting buyers and sellers to reduce transaction costs; and 4) providing incentives for innovation in improved technologies that will lower emissions (UNFCCC, 2007).

---

7 Some economies in transition, such as those of the former Soviet Union, do not use 1990 as a target year.

8 The European Union-15 acts somewhat as a unit and has more flexibility than the country description provided here.

Kyoto establishes standards and mechanisms by which countries can mitigate their emissions.[9] For example, one influence on a country's emissions target is its level of vegetation that can act as a carbon sink — categorized as land use, land-use change, and forestry (UNFCCC, 2007). The basic idea is that developed countries can meet the targeted level of emissions in a number of ways (den Elzen et al., 2008). By creating a market to trade emission rights, emitters can adopt new technology that will lower their emissions, or they can purchase carbon offsets as a way to pay for the excess GHGs they emit.

Successful efforts to create this form of pollution trading with sulfur dioxide in the United States led the way for the development of carbon offset markets. Although the Kyoto Protocol promotes carbon markets, developments in the United States have demonstrated that a voluntary market can emerge, for example the Chicago Climate Exchange (CCX), even when the host country (the US) has not ratified the Protocol.

CCX members commit to a voluntary but binding emissions reduction of 6 percent of 1998–2001 levels by 2010. Because the voluntary carbon market is not governed by UNFCCC, some of its standards and guidelines differ, e.g., for carbon offset projects. Comparing the CCX to the European Union Emissions Trading Scheme (EU ETS) illustrates how the price to emit is clearly driven by the standards, rules, and units of trade on these exchanges. In 2007, for example, the EU ETS price ranged from USD 13 to USD 35 per carbon dioxide ton equivalent (tCO_2e), while the CCX price was roughly USD 3 per tCO_2e.

Carbon markets have grown significantly from USD 11 billion in 2005 to USD 65 billion in 2007. Of the USD 65 billion in carbon market volume in 2007, the vast majority of trades occurred in the EU ETS (USD 50 billion). The CCX accounted for only USD 72 million and the Australian New South Wales Exchange accounted for USD 224 million (Capoor and Ambrosi, 2008). A large institutional infrastructure has emerged to support carbon markets, brokers, firms that monitor and evaluate projects, advisors and consultants guiding carbon reduction projects, official exchange-markets, etc. Increasing financial sophistication is enabling firms to manage risks in the carbon market and more effectively plan for their carbon costs.

Kyoto Protocol commitments expire in 2012, creating uncertainty regarding the standards and mechanisms in place after 2012. This uncertainty is affecting carbon markets, especially projects and financial instruments that plan for carbon mitigation in the longer term (Capoor and Ambrosi, 2008). Without more certainty, the price of carbon will decline significantly. The largest source of volatility in carbon market prices is the uncertainly surrounding the rules that are imposed on allowable emissions (caps) and allowable offsets that create the opportunity to trade.

---

9 Greenhouse gas emissions and credits are measured in units of one ton of carbon dioxide equivalent: e.g., methane reductions are measured in terms of their carbon equivalent. The term "carbon markets" comes from this measurement. Carbon markets also include other greenhouse gases recognized by the Kyoto Protocol.

3.1 Clean Development Mechanisms (CDMs): The Potential for Developing Countries

Entities in developed countries can sell carbon emissions allowances to each other, or they may purchase carbon offsets created through GHG abatement projects in developing and transitioning countries. Most relevant for our discussion are carbon offsets from GHG abatement projects — Clean Development Mechanisms (CDMs) under the Kyoto Protocol. CDMs specifically target projects in developing countries where carbon caps and targets do not exist (UNFCCC, 2007). CDMs were developed, in part, because developing countries reported that they were being largely excluded from Kyoto's efforts (Bozmoski, Lemos, and Boyd, 2008).

CDMs must lead to real and measurable climate benefits. An underlying metric for CDMs is the principle of *additionality* — investments must fund emissions reductions or carbon sinks that would not have occurred otherwise. New types of mitigation projects (new "methodologies") are carefully managed by the CDM Executive Board — these projects must be funneled through the board of 10 members for final approval. CDMs require approval by all countries involved, and baseline estimates must follow approved methodologies, rigorous monitoring and evaluation, and quality control checks by authorities (UNFCCC, 2007). Critics of CDMs say the rules are too complex and change too often, resulting in increased regulatory risk. They also argue that the transaction costs of CDMs are too high (Capoor and Ambrosi, 2008).[10]

CDM transactions in 2007 were sold and traded for a value of roughly USD 13 billion; of that total, USD 7.4 billion were primary issuances of CDMs. China captured 73 percent of CDM transactions. India and Brazil were second and third in terms of CDM transactions, with 6 percent of the CDM market each. Africa as a whole accounts for 5 percent of CDM transactions. Energy efficiency projects such as those reducing emissions of a power plant dominated CDM transactions (40 percent of volume, Capoor and Ambrosi, 2008).

Mitigation efforts focus on the biggest GHG emitters and rapidly industrializing countries, such as China, that capture most of the benefits of CDMs. CDMs are intended to have the dual role of reducing emissions and creating sustainable development. CDM projects are much more concerned about regulating their emissions reductions than about their contributions to sustainable development. As a result, academics, NGOs, practitioners, and policymakers have accused CDM projects of emphasizing mitigation to the detriment of sustainable development (Bozmoski, Lemos, and Boyd, 2008; Chapple, 2008). The data support this contention to some extent, given that by 2012, 75 percent of CDM projects are expected to operate in China, India, or Brazil, while only 1 percent are expected to occur in sub-Saharan Africa (Bozmoski, Lemos, and Boyd, 2008).

---

[10] Capoor and Ambrosi (2008) report that firms that finance their own mitigation investments are more likely to pursue CDM projects. In contrast, firms that are unable to make mitigation investments without CDM financing are less able to bear the long delays and high transaction costs associated with the CDM review process.

After its initial implementation of CDMs, the UNFCCC (2007) quickly noted that developing countries could not participate equally in capturing CDM projects. Since then, UNFCCC has worked with the United Nations Development Programme, the United Nations Environment Programme, the World Bank Group, and the African Development Bank to engage in capacity building so that more developing countries participate in CDM projects. The World Bank Carbon Finance Unit (CFU) and the Global Environment Fund (GEF) hope to include more developing countries in carbon funds that are relevant to their situations (UNFCCC, 2007).

The World Bank Carbon Finance Unit (CFU)

The CFU leverages capital from carbon funds to engage in mitigation projects consistent with the larger sustainable development agenda of the World Bank. Carbon funds are publicly or privately supported and are intended to facilitate mitigation projects. The CFU includes a variety of carbon funds, such as the BioCarbon Fund, the Community Development Carbon Fund, and the Italian Carbon Fund. Fund participants purchase reductions of GHG emissions from these projects. The CFU acts as an honest broker between carbon offset buyers in developed countries and sellers in developing countries. The CFU also engages in capacity building in developing countries. It has created the first emissions reductions projects in several developing countries (CFU, 2006) that are not big GHG emitters.

Because the CFU works within the Kyoto framework, emissions mitigation must be a component of every project. Where possible the CFU also links into larger-scale World Bank projects designed to have sustainable outcomes. Some of the projects under the CFU engage in complementary mitigation, adaptation, and development efforts. For example, a CFU project supports the reforesting of 10,000 hectares of degraded land with gum-producing acacia trees in Mali (CFU, 2006). Part of this land will be managed by farmers who will receive training in sustaining the plantation while harvesting gum. Additionally, technical assistance will be provided on how to intercrop cowpeas, groundnuts, and other crops among the new trees. This project should 1) create a carbon sink through reforestation which is expected to sequester 1.5 million tCO_2e by 2035; 2) improve soils by increasing nitrogen levels and reducing water and wind erosion; and 3) create sustainable livelihoods for Malian farmers.

The Global Environment Fund (GEF)

The GEF was established in 1991. It funds projects in developing countries that have environmental benefits in coordination with the UNFCCC. This fund has leveraged USD 8.2 billion toward environmentally beneficial projects in developing countries. The UNFCCC Marrakesh Accords in 2001 created an emphasis on adaptation, especially for work that complements mitigation, and expanded opportunities for funding adaptation under the GEF. For example, the GEF now manages adaptation projects through a special Least Developed Countries Fund. This fund has support exceeding USD 100 million. Also, the Adaptation Fund for developing countries was created, supported by CDM projects. Two percent of payments for offsets from CDM projects are paid into the Fund. (UNFCCC, 2007).

As part of the GEF Small Grants Programme, farmer groups in Tanzania living near Lake Victoria received grants to develop wind-powered irrigation systems. Citing increased agricultural pollution in Lake Victoria, local stakeholders created drawing points for local communities to irrigate farms and water livestock. These points were selected to reduce pollution. Grants from the GEF created access to wind-powered irrigation systems, tools and skilled labor, and funded capacity building to train community members to operate and install them. Farmer groups provided in-kind labor to install the irrigation systems. As a result, communities received water at lower cost and with lower GHG emissions than those using electric- or gasoline-powered irrigation systems. Agricultural pollution in Lake Victoria has decreased and some farmers report more than doubled crop production as a result of access to local water (GEF, 2008).

Carbon Offsets on the CCX

Understanding carbon prices and regulatory differences between the EU ETS and voluntary markets such as the CCX is important for stakeholders planning carbon offset projects in developing countries. The CCX relies on independent sources for verification and monitoring of practices used to offset carbon emissions, which tend to require less rigorous regulation than UNFCCC standards. As a result, some projects are financed through the CCX until they can obtain UNFCCC approval. This can take as long as nine months after a project is certified by the UNFCCC, and perhaps longer for new methodologies. It can then move to the EU ETS, where it will receive a higher price for carbon offsets. Thus, the CCX provides a "bridge" to facilitate development for some carbon offset projects. In other cases, the standards for voluntary markets accommodate projects on the CCX that are ineligible for CDM status because they are difficult to monitor, but they may create important emissions reductions such as projects preventing deforestation, (Chapple, 2008).

A project selling carbon offsets on the CCX that contributes to sustainable development illustrates the potential of carbon offset projects outside the Kyoto framework. Andhyodaya, an NGO in southern India, connects smallholder farmers to the CCX. This project encourages farmers to use biogas digesters — small energy generators powered by animal manure and/or agricultural residues such as organic kitchen waste. These biogas digesters are primarily used to heat water and for cooking with gas. These produce less carbon emissions than generators powered by fossil fuels or that use wood for fuel that is not replanted. Biogas digesters are also 55 percent more efficient than wood burning stoves (CCX, 2007).

Because of the mitigation benefits, this project is funded through carbon credits sold on the CCX, and farmers are paid when these credits are bought. Over 15,000 farmers participated in the initial project phase, receiving roughly USD 1.2 million in gross revenues from 2003 to 2006, or roughly USD 27 per year per farmer. During the second phase, in progress in 2008, roughly 113,000 farmers were expected to displace 500,000 tCO_2e, in aggregate receiving USD 2 million per year or roughly USD 18 per year per farmer. Participants in the program are given carbon vouchers that can be cashed at any branch of the Federal Bank of Kerala, which partnered with the project.

Beyond the mitigation benefits associated with this project, the cleaner, more efficient biogas digesters reduce respiratory and eye problems associated with using traditional firewood; they also have the potential to increase household productivity as household members no longer have to travel to collect firewood. Additionally, manufacturing biogas digesters requires relatively low up-front investments, such that manufacturing plants could potentially be installed in remote rural areas (CCX, 2007).

The noteworthy feature of this type of project is that it may start spontaneously without donor support. Manufacturers of these forms of technology could potentially team with carbon aggregators to facilitate the joint sale of biogas digesters and carbon credits.

Creating Efficient and Scalable Mitigation Projects

As the projects described above illustrate, some mitigation technologies have immediate positive externalities for households, such as better air quality in the home. Stakeholders, especially donor organizations, are puzzling through the challenges of creating efficient and scalable projects using these technologies. Two considerations are noteworthy in this regard: the use of microfinance to increase household access to mitigation technologies and the size of carbon offset revenues for mitigating the emissions of poor households. (Box 1 profiles a successful example of a project that links mitigation technology for rural households, microfinance, and carbon markets.)

Box 1: Grameen Shakti: Microfinance and Energy Efficiency

Grameen Shakti (a subsidiary of Grameen Bank) provides energy-efficient technology to rural households in Bangladesh through microfinance (Chhabara, 2008; Grameen Shakti, 2007). Grameen Shakti sells solar and biogas energy systems and energy-efficient cooking stoves (Grameen Shakti, 2007). The solar-powered energy system has been the most popular item sold; consumers can choose among units that power from 10 to 75 watts. Households typically purchase the 50-watt system, which sells for USD 400 and can power a TV, radio, cell phone charger, or light a room. Households pay from 10 to 25 percent at the time of purchase and finance the remaining balance through a loan from Grameen Bank.

In 2007, the CFU of the World Bank agreed to purchase carbon offsets generated from solar home systems for EUR 9 per tCO_2e (Chhabara, 2008). The CFU (2008) predicts that 200,000 households will gain access to solar home systems by 2015 through this agreement, and that the project will generate over 16,300 tCO_2e per year. Each 50-watt solar home system will earn roughly EUR 4.50 per year at this carbon price. Grameen Shakti is using these revenues to reduce unit costs and improve loan terms for households (Chhabara, 2008).

Despite the positive externalities of some mitigation technologies, these products can be major expenditures for poor households. A biogas digester costs between USD 250 and 400 for households in Nepal, which is 25 to 40 percent of annual GDP per capita (CDM Executive Board, 2005; CIA, 2007). As a result, donors are experimenting with mitigation technologies that combine donor subsidies, household cash at point-of-sale, and microfinance (IIED, 2008). To the extent that microfinance is used instead of donor subsidies, the scalability and sustainability of these technologies may increase. In many cases a blend of cash, credit, and donor subsidies may enable households to purchase these products.

If households can earn revenue from carbon markets for their emissions reductions, they would have increased incentives to mitigate, including by purchasing energy-efficiency technology. However, as examples in this chapter illustrate, mitigating the carbon emissions of poor households through energy efficiency technology results in very low revenues per household from carbon markets. Poor households tend to consume very little energy in the home before gaining access to energy-efficiency technology. Instead of attempting to deliver payments such as the EUR 4.50 generated from solar home systems in Bangladesh (see Box 1), organizations like Grameen Shakti are using carbon offset revenues to increase access to microfinance for mitigation technologies at better rates (Chhabara, 2008).

Revenues for the poor may be feasible for land use projects,[11] which are relevant to the GHG emissions of poor households. Smallholder agriculture can result in deforestation to create more farmland, overuse of natural resources and important local ecosystems, GHG-emitting tilling practices, etc. Afforestation or reforestation projects on smallholder land are likely to go beyond the typical loan amounts of microcredit; therefore, these projects would probably have to attract the support of donors and/or the private sector.[12]

---

[11] Many factors complicate mitigation projects involving land use in developing countries. These include established property rights, which are beyond the scope of this chapter.

[12] As an example, see the CFU project, "India: Improving Rural Livelihoods," in which a paper company partners with local farmers to plant trees on marginal lands: http://wbcarbonfinance.org/Router.cfm?Page=Projport& ProjID=9636.

3.2 Summary Comments on Carbon Markets and Developing Countries

This cursory review of the current state of carbon markets offers a few key lessons: 1) these markets are still in their early stages of development; 2) rules and regulations will play a major role in how these market evolve and the level and stability of carbon prices; and 3) although there are positive examples and progress toward using carbon markets to benefit the poor in developing countries, results to date are quite limited.[13] But these markets should not be dismissed as being unimportant. They can complement any number of development projects and increase the income of poor households.

Additionally, financing from carbon offset projects has the potential to enhance financial sector development. As illustrated, some mitigation projects could be sustainable and provide income for households and firms; however, converting to these emissions-reducing technologies may be too costly for poor households (Chapple, 2008). Currently, donors often subsidize these costs, though increasing access to credit for carbon mitigation investments may be a more scalable solution than funding individual projects. The potential for environmental finance to become sustainable for poor households will depend on whether firms can profitably offer credit for mitigation projects. In turn, households would be likely to borrow for a mitigation project only if it increased household income or quality of life. Thus, the feasibility of sustainable environmental finance for poor households largely depends on the price of carbon offsets and the ability of firms in developing countries to enter carbon markets on behalf of households.

If funds from carbon markets increase access to credit for carbon mitigation projects, these investments can also enhance financial sector development more broadly, increasing access to credit, savings, and insurance for rural households and firms. Rural banks and microfinance organizations active among the working poor are logical intermediaries, and their local involvement could be leveraged for environmental finance. Enhanced financial services for rural households may also facilitate mechanisms for adaptation, which are explored in the following section.

Staying abreast of these developments and working to place these markets into a larger arena can be valuable for public and private decision makers considering projects that contribute to market development, a cleaner local environment, and/or the reduction of poverty.

4 Adaptation Using Weather Markets

Adaptation includes proactive efforts to prepare for expected long-term climate effects, such as improving coastal city infrastructure to prepare for rising sea levels (Müller, 2008). It also includes reactive adjustments to changing conditions such as in farming systems due to declining rainfall (Fankhauser et al., 2008; Lecocq

[13] See Chapple (2008) for further discussion about including the poor in carbon markets.

and Shalizi, 2007). Adapting to change is a hallmark of the human experience and a normal behavioral response to emerging conditions (IPCC, 2007b; Morton, 2007; Stern, 2006). Knowledge about changing conditions in weather and climate risk should improve public and private decision making and facilitate adaptation (Corbera et al., 2006; Morton, 2007).

The effects of climate change will vary greatly by region (Lobell et al., 2008; Stern, 2006). Unlike mitigation efforts, which contribute to global reductions in GHGs regardless of where they occur, adaptation efforts are sub-regional and local (Morton, 2007; Stern, 2006). Rising sea levels, higher temperatures, and more extreme weather events are among the commonly cited conditions that portend negative consequences for many sectors (IPCC, 2007a; Lobell et al., 2008; Stern, 2006). Because adaptation depends on geographical and climate risks in a particular region, the cost and effectiveness of adaptation are less understood than those for mitigation (IPCC, 2007a; Morton, 2007).

The adaptive ability of households, communities, countries, etc., is related to three major factors: 1) the extent to which climate change affects risk; 2) the presence of viable alternatives to current practices in the local context (e.g., can a farmer adopt new production practices given local conditions?); and 3) the ability to change behavior — determined in large part by the level of economic development, information and technology available to those most affected by climate change.

Adaptation is critical in developing countries, yet an obvious challenge is that the poor are the least equipped to adapt. Around 75 percent of the rural poor are engaged in some form of farming, making their livelihoods vulnerable to climate change (Anderson, 2002). The poor tend to live and farm on marginal lands and have less access to infrastructure that can protect against increasing weather risks. This makes them even more vulnerable to the negative consequences of climate change, reducing their options for viable livelihood alternatives (Nicholls et al., 2007; Stern, 2006). In addition, the poor are less able to make important behavioral changes such as technology adoption due to high opportunity costs (IPCC, 2007a; Skees and Collier, 2008). At the macro level, the least developed countries and regions are often less able to adapt to climate change than developed countries. At the micro level, poor households in developed and transitioning economies are often less able to adapt.

Many basic adaptation investments must be funded by governments, which may be aided by donors and multinational organizations. These public investments include infrastructure development (levees, water systems, health facilities, etc.), and safety net programs for catastrophic weather events. These investments should increase the availability of viable alternatives for vulnerable households and firms through agricultural research and development (R&D) investments, education and technical training or retraining (Fankhauser et al., 2008).

4.1 Adaptation and Insurance

Insurance facilitates adaptation efforts (Article 4.8 of the UNFCCC). Using insurance to reduce risk facilitate adaptation is consistent with the efforts of insurers who require improved building standards or other risk reducing activities as a precondition for certain types of coverage. For example, in areas prone to earthquakes, insurers may require that properties meet building codes and pass inspections before they are approved for cover. Likewise, insurance companies may give discounts to homeowners who purchase fire extinguishers or who live near a fire station. These links between insurance and risk reduction are far easier to enforce in developed countries than in developing countries.[14]

Weather insurance can help households in developing countries engage in adaptation efforts. First, the price of insurance can provide policy makers, households, and donors an estimate of the cost of risk, which can in turn prompt adaptation investments. Insurance prices are based on the expected losses of the insured. If the effects of climate change increase risk, the price of insurance will rise. Obtaining an explicit price for weather risks can provide stakeholders with new information about risks.

The insurance response to weather risks across time and space has significant potential value in prompting adaptation strategies. Underlying this model is the recognition that the cost of weather risk must be paid somewhere in the system — either directly by those most, such as households or firms, or by governments, donors or NGOs that intervene after a major weather event. The price may be very high in terms of human suffering, destruction of productive assets and the increased incidence of chronic poverty, government bailouts, disruptions in economic growth, etc.

For example, consider a situation where maps of flood risk along a river demonstrate that a particular area will be subjected to catastrophic flooding that could completely destroy property in that area in one out of every three years. Considering only the expected losses, an insurance product would cost at least 33 percent of the value of the property insured each year.[15] If decision makers understand that this risk is effectively uninsurable, the commitment to invest in alternative adaptation efforts may become more palatable. Making the cost explicit drives the point home: many of the most damaging aspects of climate change are simply not insur-

---

[14] The high cost of monitoring risk-reducing behavioral changes or investments diminishes the ability of insurers to provide these incentives in most developing countries. Infrastructure investments — both at the micro level (e.g., in irrigation systems) or at the macro level (e.g., in levies for coastal communities) — are one exception that is relatively easy for insurers to corroborate.

[15] In addition, insurers must include many other costs (e.g., costs of delivery and administrative costs) that will raise the price of insurance even higher.

able. These problems require other solutions such as building dams or relocating households and firms.

Second, if the event is insurable, cash payments from insurance payouts can help households to adopt new livelihood strategies. The ability of the poor to adapt is often limited. As a result, poor households may be better able to make marginal adjustments in response to climate change if they have indemnity payments. The fact that households receive these payments after experiencing an extreme loss may be a potent incentive, encouraging them to adapt to the exposure they face.

For example, our experiences include extensive work in livestock insurance in Mongolia. During the difficult years following the exit of the Soviets in Mongolia, many people resorted to herding animals as a source of livelihood. When extreme winter storms resulted in large livestock losses at the turn of the century, many herders were forced out of herding and had to find new livelihoods. In this scenario, insurance payments could be used to protect herders who continue to herd and to facilitate transitions to new livelihoods.

Third, insurance can be bundled with alternative production technologies, if there are any. For example, insurance has been bundled with loans for technologically advanced seed in Malawi (Hess and Syroka, 2005). The insurance product covers the value of the loan. If drought occurs and farmers experience low yields, the loan can still be repaid (Alderman and Haque, 2007). As a result, farmers gain access to higher yield seed. This model could be enhanced and used in adaptation: 1) to the extent that R&D advancements can provide seeds resilient to emerging climate change effects (e.g., reduced rainfall), these seeds could be sold to farmers through insurance-backed loans; 2) beyond repaying the bank, the insurance could be expanded to provide insurance payouts to cover household losses.

4.2 Weather Markets

Weather markets are important for considering how insurance can enhance adaptation in developing countries. First, we focus on weather index insurance, a weather market mechanism that is gaining popularity in developing countries. This insurance is flexible, offering a number of ways to protect household income and assets from catastrophic weather risk. Weather index insurance has primarily been used as a form of agricultural insurance, but it is relevant for almost any business that is affected by extreme weather risk. The fact that weather index insurance has primarily been used for agriculture makes it particularly promising for the poor in developing countries, because agriculture is the predominant livelihood of their households. Weather index insurance may be particularly relevant for climate change; many climate change effects result in differing weather conditions, including those that have profound consequences for farming.

Next, we suggest that innovations in actively traded weather markets may address challenges facing weather index insurance. In particular, actively traded weather derivatives have blended risk transfer markets and capital markets to obtain more efficient product pricing. Significant limitations currently prevent a blending of risk and capital markets for weather index insurance. However, investments that facilitate weather index insurance markets may also facilitate a convergence with capital markets. Learning from such innovations should improve the ability of weather index insurance programs to more efficiently manage challenges in pricing these products, given the uncertainty associated with climate change. This explanation of weather markets in developing and developed markets will be important for the discussion in the final section of the chapter regarding the potential for climate insurance.

Weather Index Insurance

Weather index insurance is a new tool that shows promise in developing countries. Traditional forms of agricultural insurance have been tried in developing countries for many years with little success (Hazell, 1992). Beyond the typical adverse selection and moral hazard problems[16] associated with traditional insurance, transaction costs (e.g., underwriting and loss adjusting) have proved to be too high for smallholder agriculture in developing countries. Feasibility studies of this problem began in the late 1990s. Weather index insurance uses a measure of a weather event as a proxy for losses. For example, weather index insurance that protects farmers from drought was introduced in India in 2003 (see Box 2). Payouts were based on the level of rainfall at the closest weather station (Manuamorn, 2007).

Weather index insurance should have lower transaction costs than traditional agricultural insurance because it avoids farm-level information problems: moral hazard, adverse selection, and individualized loss adjustment make traditional insurance so difficult to implement affordably. As a tradeoff to reduce costs, weather index insurance increases basis risk — the possibility that the insured's losses will not match the level of payout determined by the weather index. Weather index insurance has higher basis risk than traditional insurance because no individualized loss adjustment occurs. Rather, it relies on the weather index to determine payouts; increasing the likelihood of a mismatch between insurance payouts and losses of the insured. As a result, weather index insurance is appropriate only for insuring correlated weather risks — weather events that tend to affect a large geographic area in roughly the same way.

---

16 Adverse selection — the fact that the insured know more about their risk than the insurer — and moral hazard — the tendency of the insured to engage in riskier behavior after purchasing insurance — are problems for Multiple Peril Crop Insurance programs. For a review and analysis see the World Bank Report on Agricultural Insurance in China, 2007.

Box 2: Drought Insurance in India

In 2003, BASIX (a microfinance institution), in a partnership with ICICI Lombard (an insurer) and supported by technical assistance from the World Bank, introduced rainfall-index insurance to address high default rates and to increase lending opportunities in rural areas. BASIX conducted a pilot study that sold weather insurance to 230 farmers in Andhra Pradesh that was designed to protect against drought during the groundnut and castor bean growing season.[17]

BASIX improved its rainfall insurance program operations and extended its regional scope. It also improved accessibility by reducing costs of delivery by simplifying the underwriting process and training loan agents to sell index insurance.

Almost every season, BASIX has improved the insurance product according to farmer feedback. For example, BASIX added coverage against excess rain during the harvest season, and made their rainfall insurance policies more flexible by insuring any crop — farmers can purchase a certain level of liability and plant whatever they wish.

Due to the success of BASIX' 2003 pilot program, other insurers began selling rainfall insurance in 2004. AICI, the state-sponsored insurance company of India, has become the largest seller of weather index insurance, selling 675,000 policies in 2007/2008. One explanation for the growth of AICI is that farmers who receive loans from the state bank are required purchase agricultural insurance.

Despite the rapid expansion of weather index insurance, market penetration remains very shallow (India has 300 million farmers). Adequate meteorological infrastructure has limited further expansion. Public and private investments are being made to overcome this constraint.

Many weather index insurance programs rely on government and/or donor involvement to fund start-up costs, including technical assistance and education for the target market and facilitating new partnerships among private- and public-sector stakeholders. These include facilitating relationships between insurers, delivery agents, reinsurers, data collection offices, etc. (See Figure 1 for a schematic of key stakeholders for weather index insurance programs). For some projects, donor support has focused on developing the capacity of local stakeholders, such as insurers and delivery agents, to manage the weather index insurance program so that donor support plays a diminishing role as the program expands. For other projects, donors may have to be involved for an extended period. Prolonged donor involvement may be a consequence of low local familiarity with insurance, or it may be due to the sophistication of product design or program structure.

---

[17] Modified from GlobalAgRisk (2007); Manuamorn (2007) provides much of the detail for this case study and is an excellent source for additional information.

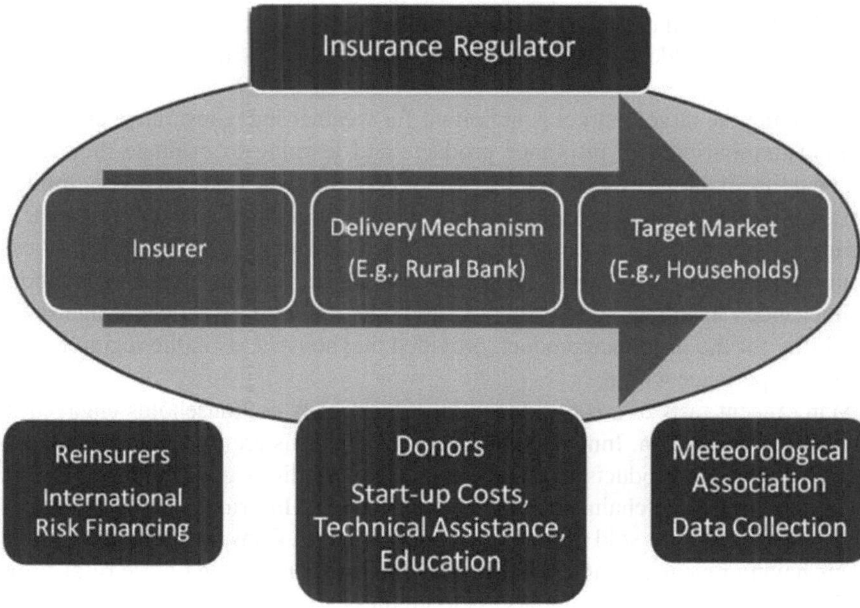

Fig. 1. Stakeholders for Weather Index Insurance
Source: Authors

The World Bank and the governments of Mexico and India have been the largest supporters of weather index insurance. The World Bank typically engages in a weather risk assessment to determine if insurance is a suitable solution, and if the partner is a local insurer with the potential capacity to manage the program. These programs often require establishing delivery channels, improving insurance laws and regulations,[18] and establishing risk financing through international reinsur-

[18] Most often, the largest legal and regulatory constraints are to persuade a country's insurance regulator that weather index insurance is a legitimate form of insurance. Two issues that are often of concern for regulators are 1) that insureds receive payouts corresponding to the loss, and 2) that individuals purchasing the insurance have an "insurable interest." Regarding the former, basis risk does create the possibility that the insured may suffer a loss and receive no payout; however, other forms of insurance (e.g., traditional crop insurance) also have basis risk. The important point for regulators is that they be able to evaluate whether the index on which payouts are made is a suitable proxy for the losses the insurance contract is meant to cover. Regulators could benefit from the development of international guidelines to enhance their ability to make this assessment (Carpenter and Skees, 2005).

Regarding the latter, "insurable interest" standards are meant to ensure that people purchasing the insurance are managing risk rather than engaging in speculation. Regulators are better able to assess that the target market has an insurable interest if it can be shown through historical data that the weather index is correlated with revenues for the target market.

ance. Marketing and educational requirements for the target market, which is typically rural smallholders who have little or no experience with insurance, are also significant.

Educating the target market is important for weather index insurance programs. Gaining familiarity with insurance products and learning to evaluate their costs and benefits take time. Where training and marketing were done on a very limited basis, sales were so low that pilot projects were discontinued after the first year.[19] Weather index insurance programs have used townhall-style meetings, focus groups, advertising, and individualized training to inform households about weather index insurance. Pilot programs provide important experiences that build credibility for the insurance product, provided that households in the region have a positive experience with it.

Many recent tests of weather index insurance focus on households engaged in agricultural production. Innovative delivery mechanisms are also being tested, including composite products that link insurance to credit or goods and services in the agricultural value chain, such as seed or fertilizer. In principal, weather index insurance can also be sold directly to lenders or rural firms in agricultural value chains having revenues that are affected by the weather. Helping these rural firms can help the poor by increasing access to credit or to the agricultural value chain. Governments and donors can also purchase weather index insurance to support relief efforts for natural disasters. For example, Mexico has a weather index insurance program that funds state-level relief efforts when drought occurs.

This flexibility results in many innovative approaches and promising market growth, as decision makers continue to explore how weather index insurance can best be used to address weather risk in developing countries. Our work has evolved to focus on designing weather index insurance products for rural firms, which we have done in Peru and Vietnam (Skees, Hartell, and Murphy, 2007). Targeting these firms creates opportunities for weather index insurance coverage in areas where it is too difficult and costly to target households. Weather index insurance products for firms should establish a market that can expand to include more rural stakeholders, including households.[20] Almost thirty pilot tests for weather index insurance have occurred in developing and transitioning countries (see Appendix A). Initial experiences with weather index insurance indicate that these products have the potential to create access to insurance in developing countries where it has not previously been available (see Skees et al., 2007).

Other legal and regulatory conditions are also important to the long-term sustainability of weather index insurance markets (e.g., risk financing and marketing standards). Because several weather index insurance programs exist, some important legal and regulatory precedents are in place and may be helpful for stakeholders interested in developing weather index insurance markets.

[19] See a previous paper prepared for KfW (Skees et al., 2007) for further description of weather index insurance markets.

[20] See Skees, Hartell, and Murphy (2007) for more on this approach.

Challenges for Weather Index Insurance

Although weather index insurance shows promise, many challenges remain in the scalability of these programs. These include delivering products to remote households, informing the target market, establishing appropriate legal and regulatory standards, and the availability of appropriate weather data.[21] Although the transaction costs of weather index insurance are usually lower than those of traditional forms of agricultural insurance, insuring weather risk for the poor in developing countries is not straightforward. Product affordability is a constant concern. Even when poor households recognize the serious weather risks they face, their opportunity cost of purchasing insurance is high. Many of the innovations in this market therefore involve efforts to reduce the premium cost. As experience with weather index insurance increases, some of these costs will decrease. In the meantime, governments and donors will continue to support weather index insurance programs, financing start-up costs and designing products that work within the constraints in areas where the risk can be insured at prices affordable to the target market. Two challenges are discussed in more detail below.

First, large R&D costs are required to create weather index insurance. Since these products must be highly tailored to local conditions, R&D costs cannot be spread across large areas. Two major components of R&D costs are finding sufficient weather and loss data and analyzing those data to determine the structure and pricing of the insurance product. Tailoring weather index insurance to local conditions constrains their scalability. Unlike microfinance, which has relied on a handful of business models to dramatically expand access to credit and savings on a global scale, weather index insurance requires a much greater variety of product and program structures to address the myriad weather risks and their consequences. There are also a number of regions where weather index insurance programs would be relatively ineffective, as in mountainous areas where the major weather risks are not highly correlated across the target market.

As a result of these limitations, institutions interested in implementing weather index insurance programs[22] need professionals with a variety of specialized training, including training in risk assessment, product design and risk financing. Private-sector stakeholders in developing countries can and are learning these skills,

---

[21] For a more comprehensive review of these challenges see Skees (2008).

[22] Legal and regulatory standards often prevent microfinance institutions and other organizations that offer savings and credit from underwriting weather index insurance contracts. When a weather shock occurs, these institutions experience capital shortages due to loan defaults and savings withdrawals, putting them in a poor position to make insurance payouts. Thus, these rural financial institutions cannot simply expand their business to underwrite weather risk as well. In contrast, these financial institutions may be able to sell weather index insurance as a delivery agent for an insurer. In this capacity an insurer, not the credit/savings financial institution, underwrites the insurance product. The bank can bundle weather index insurance with credit or savings products. This is the generalized case: such product linkages ultimately depend on local legal and regulatory standards.

often with technical assistance from donors. These capacity building investments should benefit many households as insurers are able to expand the variety of insurance products offered.

Second, weather index insurance products require international risk financing. Weather index insurance insures spatially correlated risk — everyone in the region may suffer from the same loss event. Insurers selling weather index insurance therefore require careful financing.

Risk financing typically comes from reinsurers in international risk transfer markets. Reinsurers create tailored — over-the-counter (OTC) — contracts for each insurance program. Such OTC contracts are expensive to create and pose obstacles for reinsurers who must still understand the weather risk and local market in the developing country, often with limited historical data and inadequate regulation governing insurance markets. From the perspective of insurers, reinsurers writing OTC contracts have significant control over the price of the product the insurer wants to sell; if no suitable reinsurance agreement can be made, the insurer may not be able to market the product. OTC reinsurance contracts for catastrophic risks have well-documented limitations that include the lack of transparent pricing and cycles in insurance pricing that follow major catastrophic events (Jaffee and Russell, 1997). As a result, alternative risk financing structures would be required. Progress in alternative risk financing has occurred in another part of weather markets — weather derivative markets.

Weather Derivative Markets and Their Relevance for Developing Countries

Actively traded weather derivative markets emerged in the United States in the late 1990s following deregulation of energy markets (Brockett, Wang, and Yang, 2005). Energy companies wanted to manage the risk of extreme temperatures that could adversely affect their profits (Russ, 2004). (For example, a heating oil distributor in the northeast US will lose revenues if winter temperatures are warmer than normal for an extended period.[23]) Extreme patterns of either cold or hot temperatures were calibrated into an index of heating or cooling degree days and packaged into financial instruments — weather derivatives — that offset the reduced revenue or increased costs of energy that accompanied outliers in weather patterns. Weather derivative markets continue to grow quickly — in 2007/2008 the notional value of contracts traded in weather derivative markets was USD 32 billion, a 76 percent increase over the previous year (WRMA, 2008).

Weather derivatives are best suited for large and sophisticated firms in developed countries. They are poorly suited to the smallholders and rural businesses common in developing countries. Issues of regulation, market volume, and transaction costs constrain the use of weather derivatives in this context (Skees et al., 2007; Skees and Collier, 2008).

---

[23] See Russ (2004) for a more specific example.

But weather derivative markets are relevant to our discussion in two ways. First, reinsurers are key stakeholders in these markets, which allow reinsurers to leverage innovations that would improve the weather index insurance market. In the fall of 1997, the first weather derivative OTC contracts were traded by large energy firms (Brockett, Wang, and Yang, 2005). However, the management experts designing these contracts were soon hired by reinsurance firms wanting a larger stake in weather markets. Reinsurers are actively engaged in weather index insurance and weather derivatives.

Second, weather derivative markets quickly expanded to include standardized exchange-traded products on capital markets,[24] providing valuable lessons in potential alternative risk financing structures for weather index insurance.[25] Because obtaining affordable risk financing remains a challenge for weather index insurance programs, such advancements could be important for increasing access to weather index insurance. As with weather index insurance products, creating OTC weather derivative products is expensive, because the index and associated pricing model have to be developed or at least adapted for the circumstances of the buyer. To reduce these costs and expand the market to smaller firms, the Chicago Mercantile Exchange initiated futures and options contracts in 1999 based on temperature indexes, which has expanded to financial exchange markets for major cities in the United States and Europe (Brockett, Wang, and Yang, 2005).

Bringing natural disaster risks into capital markets creates the opportunity to trade or securitize the risks with many buyers (Doherty, 1997; Skees, 1999). When exchange-traded securities can generate sufficient market volume, more efficient price discovery occurs. Additionally, exchange-traded products are dynamically priced, meaning that the value of the security can fluctuate as new information emerges.

Capital markets could create more efficient financing of weather index insurance in developing countries. However, the tailoring required for a weather index insurance product would probably not generate sufficient market volume to trade on an exchange. Financing weather index insurance through exchange-traded securities is not currently practicable for developing countries. Furthermore, in areas with underdeveloped financial sectors, the infrastructure, regulatory environment, and experience with exchange markets are all likely to be inadequate to support exchange-traded instruments.

---

[24] "Capital markets" generally covers a wide range of activities. It is used here to recognize that catastrophic risk products could take a variety of forms including derivatives, securities, or catastrophe bonds. The focus in this chapter is on standardized products that can be traded on an exchange market (e.g., the Chicago Mercantile Exchange). OTC products may look very similar to exchange traded products. However, they are not as well regulated and the price is negotiated, rather than being the result of the bids of many buyers and sellers.

[25] We discuss a possible convergence for exchange-traded products and weather index insurance in Section 4 of this chapter. Exchange trading may help weather index insurance overcome some of the problems that climate change creates for these insurance products discussed in Section 3.3.

The potentially important role of reinsurers and capital markets in weather markets in both developed and developing countries should not be underrated. Reinsurers continue to advance innovative financing structures for natural disaster risk transfer products, such as securitization of natural disaster risks (Swiss Re, 2006).[26] Among these activities, reinsurers help to establish a financial architecture in developing countries that can facilitate a future convergence of weather and capital market innovations.[27]

4.3 Climate Change and Weather Index Insurance

The previous section described weather index insurance and outlined the potential benefits of insurance to facilitate adaptation. In this section, we discuss specific challenges for implementing weather index insurance programs in the context of increasing weather risk due to climate change. This discussion is based on the following: 1) in principal, weather markets can protect against increasing weather risk; 2) with increasing weather risk comes higher premium costs; 3) some policy responses to higher premium costs (such as premium subsidy) can undermine the primary advantage of weather markets, which is pricing the risk; and 4) weather markets cannot protect against long-term climate change trends. Here it is important to note that weather index insurance protects against correlated risks: even small losses can create large insurer liabilities because many insured households will require payment at the same time. As a result, insurers must be very careful when evaluating the risks that they are insuring in order to organize appropriate financing.

If climate change increases weather risk, the price of weather index insurance will increase, significantly affecting the ability of poor households to buy these products. The price of insurance will increase for three primary reasons: increases in pure risk, the potential size of losses, and the ambiguity of the risk.

Increasing Pure Risk

The fundamental element in the price of insurance is the expected losses the insurer is likely to pay. Insurers use historical data to develop probability distributions that predict the likely frequency and severity of future losses — also called the *pure risk.* For weather index insurance, the pure risk is the weather risk for which the insurer is liable. When insurers find trends of increasing weather risk in historic data, such as would occur with climate change, they project these trends to devise their estimates of pure risk for the period they are about to insure. Climate change can affect two aspects of the pure risk.

---

[26] Catastrophe (CAT) bonds are another example (Doherty, 1997).

[27] Interestingly, WRMA (2008) notes the expansion of the weather derivatives market in India, Latin America, and Southeast Asia in 2007/2008, which provides some anecdotal evidence of how weather markets already converge.

First, if the frequency of catastrophic weather risks is increasing, the variance of the probability distribution will increase. Because insurance underwrites extreme events, the expected losses will increase. To accommodate this, insurers must raise the price of insurance.

Second, if average weather conditions become riskier (e.g., a decline in average rainfall), the central tendency or median of the probability distribution will shift toward the events of concern. Because the majority of events occur around this central tendency, this shift implies a fundamental change in the weather risk and significantly increases the expected losses of the insurer. Failure to estimate the central tendency can quickly put an insurer out of business. As a result, insurers must raise the price of insurance substantially to accommodate this change — noticeably more than in the case of increasing variance.

Increasing the Potential Size of Losses

Whether the central tendency is shifting toward more risk or if the variance of the distribution is increasing, insurers worry that losses may be more severe than in the past. In this case insurers increased the catastrophe load — a component in the price of insurance that allows insurers to build reserves quickly to cover large losses.

Increasing the Ambiguity of the Risk

Beyond adjusting the pure risk and increasing catastrophe loads, insurers charge "ambiguity loads." These are an additional cost added to the premium to reflect the possibility that insurers may underestimate future losses. For example, climate change could affect weather risk in a particular region, causing an insurer to misestimate the weather risk. When the risk is changing, the likelihood of misestimating the central tendency increases; thus, if insurers expect that the effect of climate change in a region is increasing the weather risk, they are likely to raise ambiguity loads greatly.

At any given time it is extremely difficult to determine if risk is changing. For example, consider an insurer who experiences an extreme loss or a series of extreme losses in a single year. This loss could indicate that weather risk is changing (e.g., that the variance of the distribution is increasing) or it could simply be the type of low frequency, high severity event accounted for in the probability distribution (e.g., a 1-in-100 year flood).

While our focus on climate change has been in the context of anthropogenic contributions, there are also natural phenomena that contribute to changing weather patterns. When insurers examine historical data, they must make assumptions regarding the distribution of past weather events — are extreme events explained by the probability distribution? Is climate change affecting the probability of losses? Is this change part of natural oscillations in the climate, or do any or all of these changes indicate longer-term, more permanent anthropogenic climate change? Insurers' conclusions will affect the price of insurance. For example, from the insurer's perspective, either cause of changing weather patterns will be ambiguous regarding the assessment and pricing of the underlying risks. Still, the uncertainty of potential anthropogenic climate change is likely to be greater than that of historic climate patterns and can translate into higher ambiguity loads. Thus, different insurers may price the risk differently, based on their assumptions.

Summary

As scientific understanding of the impacts of climate change progresses, especially the impacts at regional and sub-regional levels, insurers should be able to leverage this information to improve their estimates of pure risk and to minimize ambiguity loads.

Providing insurance products for the poor at prices they can pay is very difficult because of the constraints of accessibility and market failure. It should therefore be obvious that climate change poses a significant challenge to creating sustainable weather index insurance products for the poor.

4.4 Climate Change, Weather Index Insurance, and Subsidies

This challenge and the potentially significant advantages of introducing weather index insurance in areas where adaptation is warranted have led some observers to suggest subsidies. However, experience with insurance indicates that unless subsidies are carefully planned, they can reduce incentives to adapt.[28]

To illustrate, consider the effects of a crop-specific insurance subsidy on household incentives. In general, households recognize when their risks are increasing, especially if the central tendency is shifting. These conditions create incentives to adapt in order to preserve income. Yet when governments or donors subsidize premiums for an increasingly risky livelihood (e.g., cotton farming in a region with insufficient and declining rainfall), it can distort the price signal generated by insurance. As a result, households may try to maximize their income by receiving government subsidies and remaining in an unsustainable livelihood rather than making the difficult transition to a more sustainable livelihood. Thus, household adaptations are delayed; this is ultimately likely to be at great costs to governments or donors.[29]

Other, more carefully-planned, subsidies — such as subsidizing coverage of the most extreme risk — may be less likely to distort adaptation incentives, but these measures are largely untested. Instead, governments and donors can make signifi-

[28] Many lessons can be learned from poorly planned agricultural insurance subsidies in developing countries. A hallmark of these programs is that they provide incentives to take more risks at the expense of the government. For more on this subject, see Goodwin, Vandeveer, and Deal (2004) or Skees (2001).

[29] Experience with subsidizing insurance premiums indicates that the total cost of these subsidies tends to grow over time with high opportunity costs for developing countries.

cant contributions in public investments that facilitate the development of weather index insurance. Other market solutions are also possible, such as promoting insurance regulation that expands the range of insurance products. Good public investments that facilitate weather index insurance, such as improving weather station infrastructure and the availability of weather data, may also have significant advantages in addressing climate change by improving information systems that enhance public and private adaptation planning.

5 Are Climate Markets Possible?

Thus far, we have provided context for the importance of weather insurance as a tool for adaptation in developing countries. We have also made a distinction between weather risks and climate risks — weather risk being year-to-year variability and climate risk being the risk of significant changes in weather patterns. Generally, weather products are available only for events one year in advance, yet even these products must be priced using the best estimates of climate change effects on the pure risk (Skees, Barnett, and Collier, 2008). No markets yet exist to trade climate risk, i.e., the longer-term expectations regarding important weather variables.

This section makes the case for markets trading climate risk, and provides basic concepts for creating climate markets. Stakeholders still have to pay for the expected losses associated with climate change impacts which are included in the premiums for products sold on climate markets. Moreover, climate markets will provide a hedge against the risk that losses will be greater than expected. Climate markets are relevant to adaptation efforts for the poor in developing countries because they could 1) provide useful hedging mechanisms that allow insurers and reinsurers supplying weather index insurance to reduce ambiguity loads; 2) serve decision makers planning longer-term adaptation investments who want to hedge against extreme scenarios in future climate change effects; 3) improve pricing signals for public and private decision makers planning longer-term projects (e.g., infrastructure investments); and 4) provide additional, immediate economic incentives for research to improve the measurement and the ability to forecast and model climate change. We describe how creating a market that can hedge against climate change for short-term weather risks is a necessary first step toward creating a market to hedge against longer-term climate change effects. We also suggest creation of such a market based on ENSO (El Niño Southern Oscillation).[30]

---

[30] ENSO cycles include warming (El Niño), cooling (La Niña), and neutral southern Pacific conditions (McPhaden, 2003).

5.1 Short-Term Climate Markets

Section 3.3 describes how insurance suppliers set insurance prices, based in part on their assumptions about the effects of climate change on the insured risk. Instead, if important risks thought to be affected by climate change could be traded on an exchange market, the interaction of buyers and sellers having their own views about weather patterns would converge on a price for weather risk.

Moving from an abstract "climate market" to the actual steps to create such a market is daunting and beyond the scope of this paper. Some basic preconditions for a climate market are that 1) there is a standardized index to be traded; 2) that the index has both negative and positive effects (e.g., in the vernacular of futures markets — that there are natural long and short positions); and 3) that there is enough volatility in the index to stimulate participation in the market among those exposed to the risks and speculators who provide liquidity in futures markets.[31] An ENSO index potentially meets all these conditions.

Trading ENSO

El Niño — the part of the ENSO cycle with the highest impact — is a climatic event that affects weather conditions on a global scale. El Niño events occur roughly every three to seven years and last for twelve to eighteen months. El Niño results from the complex interaction of trade winds, atmospheric pressure, and sea surface temperatures (SSTs). It impacts global circulation patterns, resulting in a variety of effects including drought in Australia, Indonesia, southern Africa; heavy rains in Peru and equatorial East Africa; warmer temperatures in Canada, the U.S. Northeast and southern Brazil; and a reduced incidence of Atlantic hurricanes (McPhaden, 2003).

As expected, these changes have many economic consequences. Perhaps the impacts are most widespread in agricultural production, due to rainfall and temperature changes. Torrential rain destroys property and infrastructure and results in loss of life in northwestern South America (e.g., Peru and Ecuador). Pacific Ocean swells, sea surges, and intense rain cause significant property damage in highly-developed coastal regions of southern California. Additionally, fisheries in the equatorial Pacific are affected by rising SSTs — the Peruvian anchovy industry collapsed due to the 1972–1973 El Niño (McPhaden, 2003). By contrast, the likelihood of hurricanes off the eastern seaboard of the United States declines as ENSO measures increase (AIR, 2008; McPhaden, 2003). Additionally, the fact that winters are warmer in North America and some other regions provides a benefit to offset many of the negative effects from strong El Niño events (McPhaden, 2003). Much uncertainty remains regarding the climate risk of ENSO patterns, which is of great significance given the importance of the ENSO cycle to climate change effects and the substantial economic costs of El Niño events (see Box 3).

---

[31] In a futures market this volatility can be framed as uncertainty regarding the outcome of the index. In a context of climate risk and uncertainty, the critical variables are those where information is available about the underlying risk. However, some uncertainty remains.

Box 3: Is Climate Change Affecting ENSO?

Because the occurrence of El Niño depends on SSTs and other climatological factors that are changing with much certainty due to climate change, the effects of climate change on ENSO cycles has been of some concern to researchers (Stevenson et al., 2005). However, the complexity of the ENSO cycle has limited researchers' understanding of the effects of climate change on ENSO patterns (Merryfield, 2006). Additionally, because ENSO is a leading source of climate variability, understanding ENSO patterns and how they might be affected by GHG emissions is very important for assessing climate change effects more generally (Guilyardi, 2006; Hulme et al., 2001).

Global circulation models produce differing conclusions regarding the effects of GHG emissions on ENSO: some project that ENSO patterns will remain the same over the next century, while others project a variety of changes in severity and/or frequency (Collins and CMIP Modelling Groups, 2005; Guilyardi, 2006; Merryfield, 2006; van Oldenborgh, Phillip, and Collins, 2005; Zelle et al., 2005). Differences in model outcomes depend on the many assumptions researchers must make regarding ENSO patterns and climate change. The ambiguity regarding ENSO redfuces the precision of global circulation models (Hulme et al. 2001; Merryfield, 2006; van Oldenborgh, Phillip, and Collins, 2005; Zelle et al., 2006)

ENSO insurance could have a variety of applications and has already moved beyond the conceptual stages. Khalil et al. (2007) demonstrate how and why an ENSO insurance product could be useful for the northern regions of Peru. The insurance regulator of Peru approved the use of ENSO index insurance as a result of some of our work in 2006 (Skees, Hartell, and Murphy, 2007). Osgood et al. (2007) also demonstrate how ENSO-based seasonal forecasting could be incorporated into weather insurance for farmers in Malawi.

ENSO indexes are available in the form of Pacific SST data dating back to 1856. These are compiled and published monthly by the US National Oceanographic and Atmospheric Administration (NOAA). ENSO 1.2 is an index published by NOAA that measures SSTs off the coast of Peru, a particularly important location in ENSO patterns. Figure 2 plots a composite index of ENSO 1.2 anomalies from 1856 to 2005. Clearly, positive anomalies (El Niño) occur more frequently and are more severe than negative anomalies (La Niña). The El Niño events of 1983 and 1998 stand out as the strongest events in the last 150 years.

An active exchange market could trade the composite ENSO 1.2 index in a number of ways. For example, the index could be the three-month moving average as presented in Figure 2. Traders actively engaged in the market would bet on the index. Any active exchange market on such an index, either increasing or decreasing contracts, would converge on an aggregated market forecast of future

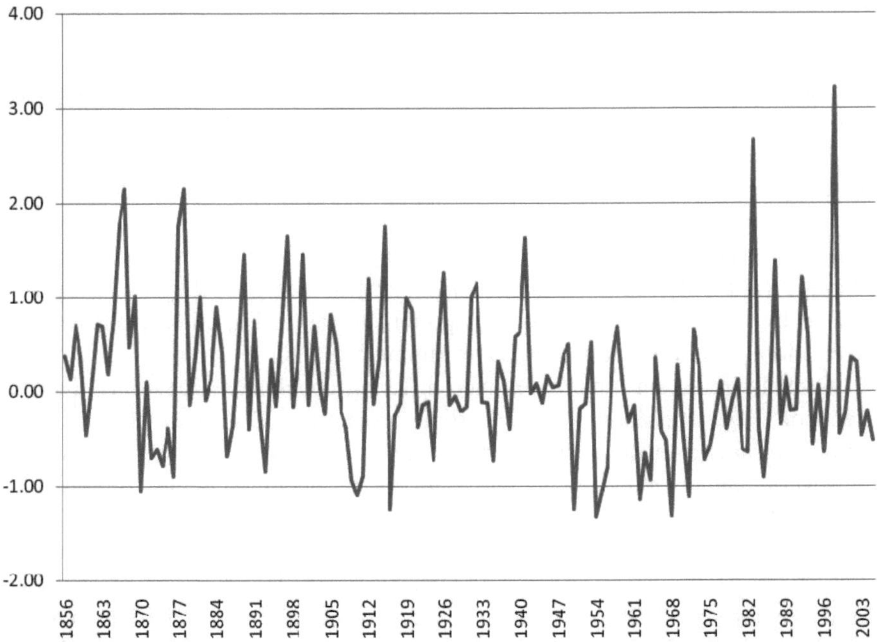

Fig. 2. Composite ENSO 1.2 Index from 1905–2004 [Refer Dates to Authors]

Source: Authors; based on NOAA data

conditions. This price would incorporate information from myriad sources including the effects of anthropogenic climate change on ENSO patterns over the life of the short-term (e.g., three-month) contract.[32] Thus, an implicit market estimate of the climate risk for ENSO would "naturally" emerge. Such pricing would reduce the climate change ambiguity regarding ENSO. This is achieved by insurers by spreading the risk among the stakeholders taking different positions in the market. In this manner, climate markets are immediately relevant for hedging against current climate change effects.

Short-term markets act as the foundation for a longer-term climate market because they create volume and familiarity with the risk being traded. For longer-term products, the climate risk becomes a larger determinant of the price of the risk management product.

---

[32] Roll (1984) found that the pricing of orange juice futures outperformed the US National Weather Service in predicting short-term Florida temperatures. Roll describes how orange juice futures pricing integrates many sources of information, including short- and long-term temperature forecasts from the National Weather Service.

5.2 Toward a Longer-Term Climate Market

A short-term ENSO index market may be adequate for improved pricing of weather insurance products. However, creating complementary exchange-traded ENSO contracts could provide even more impetus for improved information about longer-term ENSO trends. For example, trading a ten-year moving average ENSO 1.2 index could have many benefits and may be possible after a short-term market develops. The trades could be actively rolled into the future and arbitraged with the short-term ENSO market to protect longer-term positions.

Improvements in our ability to forecast changing climate and the associated effects on economic activity are likely to create exchange markets such as this hypothetical ENSO market. It may also be possible to create climate markets for other regional sea surface oscillations. Active trading of global warming forecasts or possibly even sea levels may someday be possible.

6 Conclusions

Carbon and weather markets comprise a portfolio of mechanisms that address climate change. As carbon and weather market activity increases in developing countries, a key question remains: to what extent will the poor be included in these markets? Following is a summary and a look ahead examining several important factors that will affect how the poor can participate in these markets. This occurs as costs are redcuced and as coverage is increased.

6.1 Improving Incentives to Mitigate Emissions

The logical priority for mitigation efforts is to motivate big polluters in developed countries and large firms in developing countries to reduce emissions through emissions taxes, emissions allowances, etc. But the aggregated emissions produced by the poor — through inefficient energy practices, deforestation, etc. — are also significant. With a troubled world economy and over 2 billion of the world's poor living on less than USD 2 a day (World Bank, 2007), it is also important to provide incentives for the poor to mitigate these effects, which should be designed to create new revenue and improve the quality of life for poor households. Efforts of UNFCCC and others are consistent with these conclusions.

Additional R&D investments in small-scale technology, especially in agriculture, would create more opportunities for the participation of the poor. The participation of donors and governments interested in improving incentives for the poor to mitigate emissions should 1) promote increased opportunities for the poor to participate in carbon offset projects, (perhaps through a streamlined CDM review process for carbon offset projects in the least developed countries; 2) advance new methodologies through the CDM approval process that are relevant to the poor (Chapple, 2008); and 3) invest in the development of emission-reducing technologies designed for poor households.

The price of carbon set by carbon markets is a critical factor in determining how the poor could actively participate in mitigation efforts. The successes of mitigation projects designed for the poor[33] provide anecdotal evidence that they can benefit from these markets at current prices when these efforts are supported by donor coordination. Future demand for carbon offsets depends on the level of growth in the world economy and political outcomes. Of special importance is whether the United States will develop a mandatory carbon trading market and the carbon regulation standards of the EU after Kyoto expires in 2012 (Capoor and Ambrosi, 2008). Higher carbon prices are more likely to attract finance and expand opportunities for the poor.

6.2 Seeding Credit for Mitigation and Adaptation

For mitigation and adaptation, credit is crucial for households in developing countries. Mitigation and adaptation funding to seed environmental credit markets for the poor could advance efforts to increase their participation. If new livelihood strategies can improve their income, the poor would have natural incentives to adapt. Likewise, if carbon offsets can create a new income source or contribute to their economic development, the poor would have incentives to mitigate. Information about climate change and mitigation and adaptation opportunities would improve household choices and increase participation.

A link between carbon markets and adaptation exists: two percent of payments for carbon offsets are paid into an Adaptation Fund. The intermediaries working between the poor and the carbon market have a strategic position to provide credit for mitigation and adaptation projects. Additionally, adaptation funds could foster weather index insurance markets by funding the start-up costs of offering access to data, financing product development research, etc. Donors and governments could provide seed funds designed to increase access to credit for these purposes.

6.3 Transferring Intermediation to the Private Sector

Because carbon and weather markets are organized on a global scale, the poor tend not to have access to these markets without an intermediary that can, for example, leverage carbon market funds to finance loans for household mitigation investments. Governments and donor organizations currently act as this intermediary (Chapple, 2008). In the future, private-sector intermediaries could emerge and improve the scalability and sustainability of these markets in developing countries. Profitable private sector services to the poor can be extended more expeditiously than those dependent on the relatively limited budgets of donor organizations. Microfinance is a powerful example.

---

[33] For examples, see 2.1. Clean Development Mechanisms: The Potential for Developing Countries.

Education and capacity building are central to the creation of suitable intermediaries in the private sector. In carbon markets, multilateral organizations (e.g., the UNFCCC, World Bank) are already engaged in capacity building and carbon offset projects in developing countries (UNFCCC, 2007). As local stakeholders gain increased experience with carbon markets through donor- and government-supported projects, the private sector is likely to play a larger intermediary role, organizing families for mitigation projects and packaging these projects for carbon markets. Some of this is already occurring. Education for carbon market opportunities to help the environment, improve the quality of life, and/or earn additional income are likely to increase demand and energize the private sector. Educating households and building private sector capacity to manage carbon offset projects could be effective for governments and donors interested in increasing the participation of the poor in carbon markets.

Increasing the links among the poor in weather markets is more complex. It is a goal of reinsurers, governments, multilateral organizations, and donors. Many insurers in developing countries lack the technical capacity to design these complex programs. Strategies that simplify the design process — such as more generic weather index insurance contracts — may be effective in transferring the ownership of weather index insurance programs from governments and donors to the private sector.

The complexities created by climate change may discourage insurers. Insurers understand that climate change increases risk in a general sense, while pricing the effects of climate change on a specific weather risk in a specific region is more difficult. Climate change research does not currently provide sub-regional and local projections that are satisfactory to insurers. But even as climate change projections improve, insurers are not generally trained to evaluate new findings and their design implications. Climate markets can help address this constraint by pricing major climate risks.

Donors and governments interested in increasing the scalability and sustainability of mitigation and adaptation efforts for the poor should consider capacity building among private-sector stakeholders. Experience with weather index insurance shows that capacity building can lead to local ownership of these projects and to market competition as successful programs expand over time in ways that help the poor can gain access to these markets.

6.4 Creating Climate Markets to Facilitate Adaptation

Short- and longer-term climate markets could address the capacity constraints of insurers planning for climate change, improving the competitiveness of their pricing. While we have puzzled through an example of a short-term climate market for ENSO, it would be significantly more difficult to create longer-term climate markets. The motivation for creating active trading of important climate variables is to lower the price of weather insurance via more efficient and competitive price discovery that would improve access by the poor. Donors, governments, and the private sector could use climate markets to hedge against large climate change effects. If these impacts were to occur, climate market payouts could fund investments to adapt to large climate change effects. Donors and governments interested in facilitating adaptation through climate market development can invest in R&D for products such as financial-exchange traded ENSO insurance. This would increase access to weather insurance and improve the capacity of governments and donors to manage longer-term climate risks. These products insure against potential climate risks that would have significant impacts on the poor

The activities we describe include increasing household access and incentives to participate in carbon markets, creating weather markets in developing countries, increasing the role of private sector intermediaries, and potentially creating both short-term and long-term climate markets. These factors should increase the participation of the poor in carbon and weather markets and improve their ability to address climate change.

APPENDIX: Summary of Index-Based Risk Transfer Products in Developing Countries

Country	Risk Event	Contract Structure	Index Measure	Target User	Status	Source
Bangladesh	Drought	Index insurance linked to lending	Rainfall	Smallholder rice farmers	In development; pilot launch planned for 2008	Barnett and Mahul 2007
Caribbean Catastrophe Risk Insurance Facility	Hurricanes and earthquakes	Index insurance contracts with risk pooling	Indexed data from NOAA and USGS	Caribbean country governments	Implemented in 2007	Barnett and Mahul 2007 Isom 2007
China	Low, intermittent rainfall	Index insurance	Rainfall and storm day count	Smallholder watermelon farmers	Implemented June 2007 in Shanghai only; includes a 40% premium subsidy	Barnett and Mahul 2007
Ethiopia	Drought	Index insurance	Rainfall	WFP operations in Ethiopia	USD 7 million insured for 2006; policy not renewed for 2007 due to lack of donor support	Skees et al. 2006, Syroka and Wilcox 2006

Country	Risk Event	Contract Structure	Index Measure	Target User	Status	Source
Ethiopia	Drought	Index insurance	Rainfall	Smallholder grain farmers	2006 pilot; Implemented 2008, sold by private insurer	Barnett, Barrett, and Skees 2008, Ethiopian Insurance Corporation 2008, Shewareged 2008
	Drought	Weather derivative	Satellite and weather data	NGO	Implemented in 2007	Swiss Re 2007
Honduras	Drought		Rainfall		In development	Syroka 2007
India	Drought and flood	Index insurance linked to lending; offered directly to farmers	Rainfall	Smallholder farmers	Began with pilot in 2003; index insurance products now offered by private sector and government; As of March 2008, close to 1 million contracts were sold[34]	Manuamorn 2007, Ibarra and Syroka 2006
Kazakhstan	Drought	Index insurance linked to MPCI program	Rainfall	Medium and large farms	In development	Barnett and Mahul 2007
Kenya	Drought	Weather derivative	Satellite and weather data	NGO	Implemented in 2007	O'Hearne 2007
Mali	Drought	Weather derivative	Satellite and weather data	NGO	Implemented in 2007	Swiss Re 2007
Malawi	Drought	Index insurance linked to lending	Rainfall	Groundnut and maize farmers who are members of NASFAM	Pilot began in 2005; 1710 policies sold in 2006/2007 pilot season; USD5238 premium volume	Alderman and Haque 2007, Leftley and Mapfumo 2006, Micro Insurance Agency 2008

34 Estimate based on Manuamorn (2007) and personal communication between Jerry Skees and Kolli Rao of AICI, 29 March 2008.

Country	Risk Event	Contract Structure	Index Measure	Target User	Status	Source
Mexico	Natural disasters impacting smallholder farmers, primarily drought	Index insurance	Rainfall, windspeed, and temperature	State governments for disaster relief; Supports the FONDEN program	Pilot began in 2002; available in 26 of 32 states; currently 28% (2.3 million ha) of dryland cropland is covered	Agroasemex 2006a, Skees et al. 2006
	Major earthquakes	Index-linked CAT bond and index insurance contracts	Richter scale readings	Mexican government to support FONDEN	Introduced in 2006; CAT bond provides up to USD 160 million; index insurance coverage up to USD 290 million	Wenner 2007, Cárdenas 2006
	Drought affecting livestock	Index insurance	Normalized Difference Vegetation Index	Livestock breeders	Launched in 2007, sum insured USD 22.5 million across 7 states, insured 913,000 cattle	Agroasemex 2006b
	Insufficient irrigation supply	Index insurance	Reservoir levels	Water user groups in the Rio Mayo area	Feasibility assessment conducted	Skees and Leiva 2005
Mongolia	Large livestock losses due to severe weather	Index insurance with direct sales to herders	Area livestock mortality rate	Nomadic herders	Third sales season of pilot completed in 2008; offered in 3 provinces; 17% of eligible herders participated; about 4,000 policies sold	Mahul and Skees 2005, Skees and Enkh-Amgalan 2002
Morocco	Drought	Index insurance	Rainfall	Smallholder farmers	No interest from market due to declining trend in rainfall	Barnett and Mahul 2007, Skees et al. 2001, Stoppa and Hess 2003

Country	Risk Event	Contract Structure	Index Measure	Target User	Status	Source
Nicaragua	Drought, excess rain, and excess humidity	Index insurance	Rainfall	Groundnut farmers	Launched in 2006	Barnett and Mahul 2007, Syroka 2007
Peru	Flooding, torrential rainfall from El Niño	Index insurance	ENSO anomalies in Pacific Ocean	Rural financial institutions	Feasibility assessment and preliminary market development work conducted	USAID 2006 Skees, Hartell, and Murphy 2007
	Drought	Index insurance linked to lending	Area-yield production index	Cotton farmers	First sales season launched in 2008	Carter, Boucher, and Trivelli 2007.
Senegal	Drought	Index insurance linked to area-yield insurance	Rainfall and crop yield	Smallholder farmers	Proposed	Barnett and Mahul 2007 Swiss Re 2007
Tanzania	Drought	Index insurance linked to lending	Rainfall	Smallholder maize farmers	Pilot implementation in 2007	Barnett and Mahul 2007, Swiss Re 2007
Thailand	Drought	Index insurance linked to lending	Rainfall	Smallholder maize farmers	Pilot implementation in 2007	Barnett and Mahul 2007, Manuamorn 2006
	Flood	Index insurance	River level or rainfall	Smallholder rice farmers	Proposed	Manuamorn 2006
Ukraine	Drought	Index insurance	Rainfall	Smallholders	Implemented in 2005; currently closed due to limited sales	Barnett and Mahul 2007, Skees, Hess, and Ibarra 2002
Vietnam	Flooding during rice harvest	Index insurance linked to lending	River level	The state agricultural bank and, ultimately, smallholder rice farmers	In development; a draft business interruption insurance contract is being considered by the state agricultural bank	Skees, Hartell, and Murphy 2007

Source: Authors (updated from Barnett, Barrett, and Skees, 2008)

Sources for Summary Table

Agroasemex (2006a) The Mexican Experience in the Development and Operation of Parametric Insurances Applied to Agriculture. Working Paper.

Agroasemex (2006b) The Mexican Experience in the Development and Operation of Parametric Insurance Oriented to Livestock. Working Paper.

Alderman, H., Haque, T. (2007) Insurance against Covariate Shocks: The Role of Index-based Insurance in Social Protection in Low-Income Countries of Africa. Working Paper 95, Africa Region Human Development Department. Washington, DC: The World Bank, March 2007.

Barnett, B.J., Mahul, O. (2007) Weather Index Insurance for Agriculture. American Journal of Agricultural Economics 89:1241–1247.

Barnett, B.J., Barrett, C.B., Skees, J.R. (2008) Poverty Traps and Index-Based Risk Transfer Products. World Development 2008, doi:10.1016/j.worlddev. 2007.10.016.

Cárdenas, V.S. (2006) Developmental Challenges in Using Catastrophic Bonds for Disaster Risk Management: The Mexican Experience. Presented at the Sixth DPRI-IIASA Forum on Integrated Disaster Risk Management, Istanbul, Turkey, August 13–17, 2006.

Carter, M.R., Boucher, S.R., Trivelli, C. (2007) Concept Note: Area-Based Yield Insurance Pilot Project for Peruvian Coastal Agriculture. BASIS Collaborative Research Support Program (CRSP), Department of Agricultural and Applied Economics, University of Wisconsin, Madison, WI, December, 2007.

Ethiopian Insurance Corporation: Retrieved September 11, 2008 from http://www.eic.com.et/.

Ibarra, H., Syroka, J. (2006) Case Studies for Agricultural Weather Risk Management. In: Risk Management in Agriculture for Natural Hazards. Rome: ISMEA.

Isom, W.R. (2007) Traditional Catstrophic Reinsurance and CAT Bonds. Presented at Expert Meetings of the Catastrophe Insurance and Weather Risk Management Markets for National Meteorological and Hydrological Services, WMO Headquarters, Geneva, Switzerland, December 5–7, 2007.

Leftley, R., Mapfumo, S. (2006) Effective Micro-Insurance Programs to Reduce Vulnerability. Paper commissioned for the Global Microcredit Summit Campaign, Nova Scotia, Canada, November 12–16, 2006, http://www.opportunity.net/publications/pub.reduceVulnerability.asp.

Mahul, O., Skees, J.R. (2005) Managing Agricultural Catastrophic Risk at the Country Level: The Case of Livestock Mortality Risk in Mongolia. Working Paper. The World Bank, April 2005.

Micro Insurance Agency: Malawi Index Linked Crop Insurance Project. Retrieved September 11, 2008 from http://www.microinsurancecentre.org/UploadDocuments/Malawi%20Index%20linked%20crop%20insurance%20project1.pdf.

Manuamorn, O.P. (2007) Scaling Up Microinsurance: The Case of Weather Insurance for Smallholders in India. Agriculture and Rural Development Discussion Paper 36. Washington, DC: The World Bank, 2007.

Manuamorn, O.P. (2006) Review of Weather Index Insurance Project Developments in Thailand. Presentation at the seminar, Weather Index Insurance: Weather Risk Management for Agriculture in Thailand, organized by the World Bank Office Bangkok and the Commodity Risk Management Group (CRMG) of the World Bank, Bangkok, Thailand, October 13, 2006.

O'Hearne, B. (2007) Case Study No. 3: Millennium Village Project. Presented at Expert Meetings of the Catastrophe Insurance and Weather Risk Management Markets for National Meteorological and Hydrological Services, WMO Headquarters, Geneva, Switzerland, December 5–7, 2007.

Shewareged, B. (2008) Insurance Company to Sell New Policies. The Reporter (February 4, 2008). Retrieved September 11, 2008 from http://ov.ethiopianreporter.com/modules.php?name=News&file=article&sid=2901.

Skees, J.R., Leiva, A.J. (2005) Analysis of Risk Instruments in an Irrigation Sub-Sector in Mexico. Report prepared for the Inter-American Development Bank Technical Cooperation Program and IDB-Netherlands Water Partnership Program, June 30, 2005.

Skees, J.R., Enkh-Amgalan, A. (2002) Examining the Feasibility of Livestock Insurance in Mongolia. Policy Research Working Paper 2886, Rural Development and Natural Resources Sector Unit East Asia and Pacific Region. Washington, DC: The World Bank, September 17, 2002.

Skees, J.R., Hartell, J., Murphy, A.G. (2007) Using Index-Based Risk Transfer Products to Facilitate Micro Lending in Peru and Vietnam. American Journal of Agricultural Economics 89:1255–1261.

Skees, J.R., Hess, U., Ibarra, H. (2002) Crop Disaster Assistance in Ukraine: Issues, Alternatives, and Consequences. Rural Finance Project P076553. Washington, DC: The World Bank, December 2002.

Skees, J.R., Gober, S., Varangis, P., Lester, R., Kalavokonda, V. (2001) Developing Rainfall-Based Index Insurance in Morocco. Policy Research Working Paper 2577. Washington, DC: The World Bank, April 2001.

Skees, J.R., Goes, A., Sullivan, C., Carpenter, R., Miranda, M.J., Barnett, B.J. (2006) Index Insurance for Weather Risk in Low Income Countries. USAID Microenterprise Development (MD) Office, USAID/DAI Prime Contract LAG-I-00-98-0026-00 BASIS Task Order 8, Rural Finance Market Development.

Stoppa, A., Hess, U. (2003) Design and Use of Weather Derivatives in Agricultural Policies: The Case of Rainfall Index Insurance in Morocco. Paper presented at the international conference: "Agricultural Policy Reform and the WTO: Where Are We Heading?" Capri, Italy, June 23–26, 2003.

Swiss Re (2007) Swiss Re Launches Climate Adaptation Development Program Providing Financial Protection Against Weather Risk in Emerging Countries. Press release, September 27, 2007.

Syroka, J. (2007) Weather Insurance for Small and Medium Farmers: Building a Weather Risk Market in Central America. WRMA Annual Meeting, Miami, FL, May 9–11, 2007.

Syroka, J., Wilcox, R. (2006) Rethinking International Disaster Aid Finance. Journal of International Affairs 59:197–214.

USAID (United States Agency for International Development) (2006) Hedging Weather Risk for Microfinance Institutions in Peru. Report prepared by GlobalAgRisk, Inc., under USAID/DAI Prime Contract LAG-I-00-98-0026-00 BASIS Task Order 8, Rural Finance Market Development, November 2006.

Wenner, M. (2007) New Developments in Agricultural Insurance: A Latin American and Caribbean Perspective. Presented at Third Annual Microinsurance International Conference, Mumbai, India, November 13–15, 2007.

Glossary

Adaptation	Efforts to adjust to the physical impacts of climate change, as related to increasing weather risk affecting agriculture, behavioral changes that reduce household vulnerability and/or exposure resulting in fewer farm losses.
Adverse Selection	Occurs when potential insurance purchasers know more about their risk exposure than the insurer, leading to participation by high-risk individuals and non-participation by low-risk individuals. Insurers react either by charging higher premiums or not insuring at all, as in the case of floods. Adverse selection is also referred to as anti-selection. *See also Asymmetric Information.*
Ambiguity Loads	An additional cost added to the premium to reflect the possibility that insurers may underestimate future losses.
Basis Risk	A term generally used to reflect variance around a futures exchange price and a local cash price. In the context of index insurance, it refers to the difference between the loss as reflected

in the index versus the individual loss. Indexes rarely perfectly match individual losses. Some households experiencing loss do not receive indemnity payments and/or households that experience no loss receive indemnity payments. Basis risk increases as the geographical area covered by the index expands.

Asymmetric Information	An information imbalance in a transaction in which one party possesses more or better information than another party or parties, such as knowledge of hidden costs or risky behavior. Buyers of insurance products typically have better information about their level of risk exposure than do the sellers of insurance. Thus these buyers have incentives to hide information to gain better terms for insurance in a way that will increase the probability of payout. *See also Adverse Selection and Moral Hazard.*
Catastrophe Loading	A component of the price of weather index insurance that accounts for the possibility of an extreme weather event occurring in the early years in which the product is offered.
Central Tendency	The median or most frequently occurring value used by term insurers to describe a weather event.
Climate Change	Theory that overall weather patterns are changing on a global scale for the long-term due to human contributions to greenhouse gases.
Correlated Risk	A risk or risks affecting many individuals or households in the same area at the same time, such as drought, which can damage agricultural production over an entire region, or a fall in a commodity price that simultaneously affects all producers of the commodity within the same market. Correlated risk is also referred to as covariant risk and systemic risk.
Derivative	A financial instrument, traded on or off an exchange, having a price that is directly dependent upon or "derived" from the value of one or more underlying instruments. Examples include debt instruments, commodities, or any established pricing index. Derivatives involve the trading of rights or obligations based on an underlying product, but they do not directly transfer underlying property. The derivative is merely a contract between two or more parties. Its value is determined by fluctuations in the underlying asset. Derivatives can hedge risk or lock in a fixed rate of return. Derivatives are generally used to hedge risk, but they may be used for speculative purposes. *See also Hedging.*

El Niño	A warming of sea surface temperatures in the equatorial Pacific Ocean associated with dramatic changes in the weather patterns of the region and worldwide.
El Niño Southern Oscillation (ENSO)	ENSO is an oceanic-atmospheric process that results from interaction between the temperature of the equatorial Pacific Ocean and the atmosphere. Changes in the ocean affect the atmosphere and climate patterns around the globe. In turn, changes in the atmosphere impact the ocean temperatures and currents. The system oscillates between warmer than average (El Niño) and cooler than average (La Niña) conditions.
Futures Contract	A standardized agreement or the deferred delivery of a commodity, or its equivalent, traded through organized futures exchanges. The holder of the contract has the right and obligation to buy or sell a commodity at a certain date for a price determined in advance. Most agricultural futures contracts require physical delivery, but some contracts such as feeder cattle futures contracts call for cash settlement at contract maturity. In fact, contracts are usually liquidated before delivery. Traders are classified as hedgers or speculators. Futures contracts have standard delivery dates, trading units, terms, and conditions.
Index Insurance	Index insurance makes indemnity payments that are not based on an assessment of the policyholder's individual loss, but rather on measures of an index that is correlated with losses and serves as a proxy for actual losses. Agricultural index insurance products are based on area yields (where the area is some unit of geographical aggregation larger than the farm) and on products based on measurable weather events. *See also Weather Index Insurance.*
Loss Adjustment	The process of estimating actual losses after an insured party has filed a claim.
Mitigation	Efforts aimed at reducing anthropogenic contributions to climate change.
Moral Hazard	A change of behavior that increases the chance of loss because of the existence of insurance. Examples of moral hazard can range from poor management or carelessness to fraud, in the latter case specifically targeted at creating losses and collecting the insurance. *See also Asymmetric Information.*

Multiple Peril Crop Insurance	MPCI is a form of traditional agricultural insurance, designed to insure against multiple crop perils. Most of the risks covered are weather perils (excess moisture, drought, freeze, etc.), and other perils such as fire can be included. Two forms of MPCI are dominant: 1) coverage is set based on expectations of the average farm yield, and payments are made if the individual farm yield falls below some percentage of that average farm yield; and 2) losses are established based on an assessment of the portion of damage to the crop. In either case, it is difficult to prove whether losses are from an insured weather peril or if they are the result of poor farm management practices. *See also Traditional Agricultural Insurance.*
Over-the-Counter (OTC)	The trading of financial instruments such as securities or derivatives directly between dealers or their counterparties. OTC trading operates outside organized market exchanges.
Premium	The monetary sum payable by the insured to the insurer for the period (or term) of insurance granted by the policy.
Probability Distribution	(i) A function of a discrete random variable yielding the probability that the variable will have a given value. (ii) Outcomes of an experiment and their probabilities of occurrence. If the experiment were repeated a large number of times, the same probabilities should also repeat. (iii) A statistical function that describes all the possible values and likelihoods that a random variable can take within a given range. This range will be between the minimum and maximum statistically possible values, but where the possible value is likely to be plotted on the probability distribution depends on a number of factors, including the distribution's mean, standard deviation, skewness, and kurtosis.
Pure Risk	A component of the price of weather index insurance that estimates weather risk based upon the probability distribution.
Reinsurance	The shifting of part or all of the insurance originally written by one insurer to another insurer who is known as a reinsurer. When the total exposure of a risk or group of risks presents the potential for losses beyond a limit that is prudent for an insurance company to carry, the insurance company may purchase reinsurance, i.e., insurance of the insurance. Reinsurance has many advantages, including (i) stabilizing

	or evening out the financial performance of the insurance company over a period of time; (ii) limiting the exposure of individual risks and restricting or reducing losses paid out by the insurance company; (iii) the possibility of increasing an insurance company's solvency margin (percent of capital and reserves to net premium income) and hence the company's financial strength.
Reinsurer	A company that sells reinsurance. Commercial reinsurers often operate on a global scale, making them able to pool a diverse portfolio of large risks to reduce their overall risk exposure. *See also Reinsurance.*
Risk Financing	The process of managing the financial consequences of risk through instruments such as insurance contracts, CAT (catastrophe) bonds, reinsurance, or options contracts. In this context the authors use risk financing to describe the methods insurers must use to manage correlated risk in their insurance portfolio.
Sea Surface Temperature	The surface temperature of the ocean. These temperature readings are predictive of atmospheric pressure patterns. For example, El Niño Southern Oscillation is associated with increasing sea surface temperatures in Peru several months prior to the atmospheric change.
Stakeholder	A party who has a vested interest in the topic being discussed. For example, insurers, reinsurers, insurance regulators, delivery agents, households, etc., involved in an insurance program are stakeholders.
Subsidy	A direct or indirect benefit granted by a government (or donor) for the production or distribution of a good or to supplement other services. Thus, the term has a wide range of applications. In insurance for agriculture, premium subsidies occur when a government pays a portion of insurance premiums for farmers. Premium subsidies, for example, often have unintended consequences, motivating farmers to take more risk at the government's expense, resulting in larger and larger losses by the government.
Traditional Agricultural Insurance	Insurance in agriculture has historically underwritten a specific crop on a specific plot of land. This insurance is priced by using historical farm yield data. In the event of a loss from an insured event, a trained claim agent will visit the

	plot of land and assess the amount of damage incurred. One of the most common forms of traditional agricultural insurance is multiple peril crop insurance. *See also Multiple Peril Crop Insurance.*
Transaction Costs	The financial or in-kind costs of business transactions, such as the cost or time spent obtaining information or permits. Transaction costs associated with insurance include those associated with underwriting, contract design, rate making, and monitoring to control adverse selection and moral hazard.
Underwriting	Process of selecting risks for insurance and determining the amounts and terms the insurance company (the underwriter) will accept the risk.
Weather Index Insurance	Contingent claims contracts for which payouts are determined by an objective weather parameter that is highly correlated with farm-level yields or revenue outcomes, such as rainfall levels, temperature, or soil moisture. *See also Index Insurance.*

References

AIR (AIR Worldwide Corporation) (2008) Climatalogical Influences on Hurricane Activity: The Air Warm SST Conditioned Catalog. Boston, MA: AIR Worldwide Corporation.

Anderson, J.R. (2002) Risk Management in Rural Development: A Review. Agriculture and Rural Development (ARD). Strategy Background Paper 7. Washington, DC: The World Bank.

Alderman, H., Haque, T. (2007) Insurance against Covariate Shocks: The Role of Index-Based Insurance in Social Protection in Low-Income Countries of Africa. Working Paper 95. Washington, DC: Africa Region Human Development Department, The World Bank

Barnett, B.J., Barrett, C.B., Skees, J.R. (2008) Poverty Traps and Index-Based Risk Transfer Products. World Development 36(10), 1766–1785.

Bindoff, N.L., Willebrand, J., Artale, V.A.C., Gregory, J., Gulev., S., Hanawa, K., Quéré, C.L., Levitus, S., Nojiri, Y., Shum, C.K., Talley, L.D., Unnikrishnan, A. (2007) Observations: Oceanic Climate Change and Sea Level. In: Solomon, S., Qin, D., Manning, M., Chen, Z., Marquis, M., Averyt, K.B., Tignor, M., Miller, H.L. (Eds.) Climate Change 2007: The Physical Science Basis, Working Group I Contribution to the Fourth Assessment Report of the Intergovernmental Panel on Climate Change (IPCC). Cambridge, UK, and New York, NY: Cambridge University Press.

Bozmoski, A., Lemos, M.C., Boyd, E. (2008) Prosperous Negligence: Governing the Clean Development Mechanism for Markets and Development. Environment 50:18–30.

Brockett, P.L., Wang, M., Yang, C.C. (2005) Weather Derivatives and Weather Risk Management. Risk Management and Insurance Review 8:127–140.

Capoor, K., Ambrosi, P. (2008) State and Trends of the Carbon Market 2008. Report funded by the CF-Assist Program. Washington, DC: The World Bank Institute.

Carpenter, R., Skees, J.R. (2005) Index-based Insurance Products: Regulatory and Legal Issues. Unpublished Report. Washington, DC: The World Bank.

Carter, T.R., Jones, R.N., Lu, X., Bhadwal, S., Conde, C., Mearns, L.O., O'Neill, B.C., Rounsevell, M.D.A., Zurek, M.B. (2007) New Assessment Methods and the Characterisation of Future Conditions. In: Parry, M.L., Canziani, O.F., Palutikof, J.P., van der Linden, P.J., Hanson, C.E. (Eds.) Climate Change 2007: Impacts, Adaptation, and Vulnerability, Working Group II Contribution to the Fourth Assessment Report of the Intergovernmental Panel on Climate Change (IPCC). Cambridge, UK, and New York, NY: Cambridge University Press.

CCX (Chicago Climate Exchange) (2007) The Andhyodaya Joins Chicago Climate Exchange as an Offset Aggregator First Indian Offset Credits Approved for Trading in the Exchange. Press release. Chicago, IL: Chicago Climate Exchange.

CDM (Clean Development Mechanism) Executive Board. (2005) Biogas Support Program — Nepal (BSP-Nepal) Activity 1. Clean Development Mechanism Simplified Project Design Document for Small-Scale Project Activities, Version 02. United Nations Framework Convention on Climate Change. Retrieved November 14, 2008 from http://cdm.unfccc.int/UserManagement/FileStorage/A4NYD8EXQY928HD61LHWHEIM82MBIN.

Chapple, A. (2008) Making the Voluntary Carbon Market Work for the Poor: Current and Future Roles. Forum for the Future: Action for a Sustainable World. Report commissioned by the Department for International Development. London: Forum for the Future.

Chhabara, R. (2008) Gameen's World Bank Deal Brings Solar Power to Bangladesh. Climate Change Corp.com/Markets Report, April 23. Retrieved November 14, 2008 from http://www.climatechangecorp.com/content_print.asp?ContentID=5283.

CFU (The World Bank Carbon Finance Unit) (2008) Peoples Republic of Bangladesh: Instillation of Solar Home Systems in Bangladesh. Project Description. Retrieved November 14, 2008 from http://wbcarbonfinance.org/Router.cfm?Page=Projport&ProjID=37262.

CFU (The World Bank Carbon Finance Unit) (2006) Mali: Acacia Senegal Plantation Project (BioCarbon Fund). Project Description. Retrieved August 7, 2008 from http://carbonfinance.org/Router.cfm?Page=Projport&ProjID=24878.

CIA (Central Intelligence Agency) (2008) The World Factbook: Nepal. Retrieved November 18, 2008 from https://www.cia.gov/library/publications/the-world-factbook/geos/np.html.

Collins, M., and CMIP Modelling Groups (2005) El Niño- or La Niña-Like Climate Change? Climate Dynamics 24:89–104.

Corbera, E., Conway, D., Goulden, M., Vincent, K. (2006) Climate Change in Africa: Linking Science and Policy for Adaptation. Royal Society Workshop Report G00022. Norwich and London: The Tyndall Centre and International Institute for Environment and Development (IIED).

den Elzen, M.G.J., Lucas, P.L., van Vuuren, D.P. (2008) Regional Abatement Action and Costs Under Allocation Schemes for Emissions Allowances for Achieving Low CO_2-Equivalent Concentrations. Climatic Change 90:243–268.

Doherty, N.A. (1997) Innovations in Managing Catastrophe Risk. Journal of Risk and Insurance 64:713–718.

Fankhauser, S., Argawala, S., Hanharan, D., Pope, G., Skees, J.R., Stephens, C., Yasmine, S. (2008) Economic Policy Instruments to Promote Adaptation. In: Argawala, S., Fankhauser, S. (Eds.) Economic Aspects of Adaptation to Climate Change: Costs Benefits and Policy Instruments. Paris: Organisation for Economic Cooperation and Development.

GEF (Global Environment Facility) (2008) The GEF Small Grants Programme. Retrieved November 6, 2008 from http://sgp.undp.org/index.cfm.

Goodwin, B.K., Vandeveer, M., Deal, J. (2004) An Empirical Analysis of Acreage Distortions and Participation in the Federal Crop Insurance Program. American Journal of Agricultural Economics 86:1058–1077.

Grameen Shakti (2007) Grameen Shakti Homepage. Retrieved November 14, 2008 from http://www.gshakti.org/index.html.

Guilyardi, E. (2006) El Niño-Mean State-Seasonal Cycle in a Multi-Model Ensemble. Climate Dynamics 26:329–348.

Hare, B., Meinhausen, M. (2006) How Much Warming Are We Committed to and How Much Can Be Avoided? Climate Change 75:111–149.

Hazell, P.B.R. (1992) The Appropriate Role of Agricultural Insurance in Developing Countries. Journal of International Development 4:567–581.

Hess, U., Syroka, J. (2005) Weather-Based Insurance in Southern Africa: The Case of Malawi. Agriculture and Rural Development (ARD) Department Discussion Paper 13. Washington, DC: The World Bank.

Hulme, M., Doherty, R. Ngara, T. New, M., Lister, D. (2001) African Climate Change. Climate Research 17 145–168.

IIED (International Institute for Environment Development) (2008) Scaling up Low Carbon Energy for the Poor: Learning from the Ashden Awards for Sustainable Energy. Summary of a review of Ashden Award-winners, commissioned by the Department for International Development (DFID) and carried out by the International Institute for Environment and Development. Retrieved November 18, 2008 from http://www.ashdenawards.org/files/reports/DFID_summary.pdf.

IPCC (International Panel for Climate Change) (2007a) Climate Change 2007: Synthesis Report. Intergovernmental Panel on Climate Change Fourth Assessment Report. Geneva, Switzerland: IPCC Secretariat.

IPCC (International Panel for Climate Change) (2007b) Impacts, Adaptation, and Vulnerability, Appendix I: Glossary. Intergovernmental Panel on Climate Change Working Group II Report. Geneva, Switzerland: IPCC Secretariat.

Jaffee, D.M., Russell, R. (1997) Catastrophe Insurance, Capital Markets, and Uninsurable Risks. Journal of Risk and Insurance 64:205–230.

Khalil, A.F., Kwon, H.H., Lall, U., Miranda, M.J., Skees, J.R. (2007) El Niño–Southern Oscillation-Based Index Insurance for Floods: Statistical Risk Analyses and Application to Peru. Water Resources Research 43(10), Manuscript #2006WR005281.

Kundzewicz, Z.W., Mata, L.J., Arnell, N.W., Döll, P., Kabat, P., Jiménez, B., Miller, K.A., Oki, T., Sen, Z., Shiklomanov, I.A. (2007) Freshwater Resources and Their Management. In: Parry, M.L., Canziani, O.F., Palutikof, J.P., van der Linden, P.J., Hanson, C.E. (Eds.) Climate Change 2007: Impacts, Adaptation and Vulnerability. Contribution of Working Group II to the Fourth Assessment Report of the Intergovernmental Panel on Climate Change. Cambridge, UK: Cambridge University Press.

Leiva, A.J., Skees, J.R. (2008), Using Irrigation Insurance to Improve Water Usage in the Rio Mayo System of Northwest Mexico. World Development 36(12): 2663–2678.

Lecocq, F., Shalizi, Z. (2007) Balancing Expenditures in Mitigation and Adaptation to Climate Change: An Exploration of Issues Relevant to Developing Countries. Policy Research Working Paper 4299. Washington, DC: Sustainable Rural and Urban Development Team, The World Bank.

Lobell, D.B., Marshall, B.B., Tebaldi, B.C., Mastrandrea, M.D., Falcon, W.P., Naylor, R. (2008) Prioritizing Climate Change Adaptation Needs for Food Security in 2030. Science 319:607–610.

Mahul, O., Skees, J.R. (2007) Managing Agricultural Risk at the Country Level: The Case of Index-Based Livestock Insurance in Mongolia. Policy Research Working Paper WPS4325. Washington, DC: The World Bank.

Manuamorn, O.P. (2007) Scaling up Microinsurance: The Case of Weather Insurance for Smallholders in India. Agriculture and Rural Development Discussion Paper 36. Washington, DC: The World Bank.

McPhaden, M.J. (2003) El Niño and La Niña: Causes and Global Consequences. In: MacCracken, M.M., Perry, J.S. (Eds.) and Munn, T. (Editor-in-Chief) Encyclopedia of Global Environmental Change, Volume 1: The Earth System: Physical and Chemical Dimensions of Global Environmental Change. Hoboken, NJ: Wiley.

Merryfield, W.J. (2006) Changes to ENSO Under CO_2 Doubling in a Multimodal Ensemble. Journal of Climate 19:4009–4027.

Morton, J.F. (2007) The Impact of Climate Change on Smallholder and Subsistence Agriculture. Proceedings of the National Academies of Sciences 104(50):19680–19685.

Müller, B. (2008) International Adaptation Finance: The Need for an Innovative and Strategic Approach. Working Paper EV42. Oxford: Oxford Institute for Energy Studies.

Nicholls, R.J., Wong, P.P., Burkett, V.R., Codignotto, J.O., Hay, J.E., McLean, R.E., Ragoonaden, S., Woodroffe, C.D. (2007) Coastal Systems and Low-lying Areas. In: Parry, M.L., Canziani, O.F., Palutikof, J.P., van der Linden, P.J., Hanson, C.E. (Eds.) Climate Change 2007: Impacts, Adaptation and Vulnerability. Contribution of Working Group II to the Fourth Assessment Report of the Intergovernmental Panel on Climate Change. Cambridge, UK: Cambridge University Press.

Osgood, D.E., McLaurin, M., Carriquiry, M., Mishra, A., Fiondella, F., Hansen, J., Peterson, N., Ward, N. (2007) Designing Weather Insurance Contracts for Farmers in Malawi, Tanzania, and Kenya. Final Report to the Commodity Risk Management Group (CRMG). Washington, DC: The World Bank, and the International Research Institute for Climate and Society (IRI), Columbia University.

Perkins, R. (2008) Incentivizing Climate Mitigation: Engaging Developing Countries. Harvard International Review, Summer, 42–47.

Roll, R. (1984) Orange Juice and Weather. American Economic Review 74:861–880.

Russ, R. (2004) Weather Derivatives: Global Hedging Against the Weather. Derivatives Use, Trading and Regulation 9:293–301.

Skees, J.R. (2008) Challenges for Use of Index-Based Weather Insurance in Lower Income Countries. Agricultural Finance Review 68:197–217.

Skees, J.R. (2001) The Bad Harvest: More Crop Insurance Reform: A Good Idea Gone Awry. Regulation: The CATO Review of Business and Government 24:16–21.

Skees, J.R. (1999) Opportunities for Improved Efficiency in Risk Sharing Using Capital Markets. American Journal of Agricultural Economics 81:1228–1233.

Skees, J.R., Collier, B. (2008) The Potential of Weather Index Insurance for Spurring a Green Revolution in Africa. Presentation to the Alliance for a Green Revolution in Africa Policy Makers' and Private Sector Convening, Nairobi, Kenya, June 23–25.

Skees, J.R., Barnett, B.J., Collier, B. (2008) Agricultural Insurance: Background and Context for Climate Adaptation Discussions. Presentation to the OECD, Paris, France, April 7–8.

Skees, J.R., Hartell, J., Murphy, A.G. (2007) Using Index-Based Risk Transfer Products to Facilitate Micro Lending in Peru and Vietnam. American Journal of Agricultural Economics 89:1255–1261.

Skees, J.R., Murphy, A.G., Collier, B., Roth, J. (2007) Scaling Up Index Insurance: What Is Needed for the Next Big Leap Forward? Weather insurance review prepared by the MicroInsurance Centre and GlobalAgRisk for Kreditanstalt für Wiederaufbau (KfW).

Stern, N. (2006) Stern Review Report on the Economics of Climate Change. Cambridge: Cambridge University Press.

Stevenson, D., Doherty, R., Sanderson, M., Johnson, C., Collins, B., Derwent, D. (2005) Impacts of Climate Change and Variability on Tropospheric Ozone and Its Precursors. Faraday Discussion 130:41–57.

Swiss Re (Swiss Reinsurance Company) (2006) Securitization – New Opportunities for Insurers and Investors. Sigma 7.

UNFCCC (United Nations Framework Convention for Climate Change) (2007) Uniting on Climate: A Guide to the Climate Change Convention and the Kyoto Protocol. Bonn, Germany: Climate Change Secretariat (UNFCCC).

van Oldenborgh, G.J., Phillip, S.Y., Collins, M. (2005) El Niño in a Changing Climate: A Multi-Model Study. Ocean Science 1:81–95.

World Bank (2007) World Development Report 2008: Agriculture for Development. Washington, DC: The World Bank.

WRMA (Weather Risk Management Association) (2008) Weather Market Shows Robust 35% Increase in Trades for 2007–2008: Market Reach Is Expanded into India, Latin America, Southeast Asia. Press Release.

Yohe, G.W. (2006) Representing Dynamic Uncertainty in Climate Policy Deliberations. Ambio 35:89–91.

Zelle, H., van Oldenborgh, G.J., Burgers, G., Dijkstra, H. (2005) El Niño and Greenhouse Warming: Results from Ensemble Simulations with the NCAR CCSM. Journal of Climate 18:4669–4683.

CHAPTER 5

Mainstreaming Impact over Time – Who Measures What for Whom?

Renate Schubert[*], *Markus Ohndorf*[**], *and Moritz Rohling*[***]

Abstract

Within environmental finance, the guiding question of "who measures what for whom" can be examined from different angles. In this paper the authors argue that, provided environmental markets are well-designed, measuring environmental performance is very closely related to measuring financial success for the primary actors on the market. Hence, at the aggregate level, market volume can be used as a highly correlated proxy for environmental success. In a second-order interpretation of the guiding question it is, however, revealed that information-related concerns need to go beyond simple measurement issues. It is argued here that transaction costs in the form of information barriers mainly account for inefficiently low levels of environmental finance. The authors explore this information-finance nexus on a actor-by-actor basis in order to identify the general nature of these barriers. From these general considerations, the authors deduce that a part of these transaction costs could be reduced through enabling actors to scale-up overall investments by pooling small-scale projects. In fact, different actors could assume the role of an Information & Technology Broker. Due to limitations in scope, the authors focus their analysis on two of these actors: the Clean Development Mechanism project developers and energy services companies. As it turns out, while seeking to secure project financing, these actors face information related barriers on the supply side. Commercial finance institutions apparently have difficulties to assess the risks associated with environmental small-scale projects, which is due to the lack of an established credit history as well as a deficit in banking expertise for these markets. To overcome such information related barriers, a case for intervention by governments or development finance institutions definitely exists. In this context, all measures fostering a "risk-reduced learning by doing" seem to be particularly promising.

---

[*] Head of Chair, Institute for Environmental Decisions, ETH Zurich.

[**] Senior Researcher and Lecturer, Institute for Environmental Decisions, ETH Zurich.

[***] Research Assistant, Institute for Environmental Decisions, ETH Zurich.

D. Köhn (ed.), *Greening the Financial Sector: How to Mainstream Environmental Finance in Developing Countries*, DOI 10.1007/978-3-642-05087-9_5,

1 Introduction

According to many scientific sources, it seems quite obvious that global climate change is advancing and that mitigation and adaptation measures are needed in industrialized as well as in developing countries. Necessarily, an increase in energy efficiency (EE) and an increasing share of renewable energies (RE) are the key mitigation measures. Furthermore, it is commonly recognized that these technologies also generate beneficial environmental effects beyond climate change mitigation. Within each category a plethora of technologies is available. However, few of these measures are implemented, which is partly due to a dearth of financial resources. Clearly missing financial resources affect developing countries much more than they affect industrialized countries. Since a large share of greenhouse gas (GHG) emission sources, as well as the potential to increase energy efficiency and the use of renewable energy, stems from developing countries, financing projects in environmental markets in developing countries has high priority. In many cases such projects are small-scale, which generally decreases the chances for third-party financing. In this sense, environmental or "green" finance for developing countries is a topic worthwhile to discuss in detail.

When thinking about environmental or "green" finance, it is important to note that the term does not refer to any deeds of charity by commercial banks; rather, it is clearly driven by the motive of increasing revenues and profits, at least in the longer term. In fact, as other authors in this publication point out, the demand for such financial services stems from markets that are themselves driven by the profit motives of market participants. On such *environmental markets,* environmental externalities are reduced simply because it is rational and profitable for the single actor to do so. This is most obvious on markets that are directly created through environmental regulations, like the international carbon market. This market emerged because a global public good, i.e. greenhouse gas reductions, was privatized through the allocation of tradable emission quotas. The possibility of trading securitized emission credits attributes a value to every tonne of CO_2 equivalent abated, which is referred to as carbon price. It is simply because emission reductions have a value that self-interested actors have an incentive to implement greenhouse gas reduction projects and sell the generated emission offsets on the market.

The same reasoning can be applied to the other environmental markets discussed within this publication, notably the markets for projects in the field of Energy Efficiency and Renewable Energy (EERE). Other contributors to this publication point out that activities on these markets would, in fact, generate positive cash flows and could even be very profitable. One of the major problems with financing such projects is that most investment costs are frontloaded, while returns are realized over a longer term. While this is usually not a problem if financial markets were efficient, certain characteristics of the market for green finance in developing countries significantly hamper the procurement for small-scale projects. Many of the most important market barriers that were identified within the other chapters are informational in nature. As a consequence, the question of "who measures what for whom?" is of particular importance for increasing the levels of financing for small-scale projects on environmental markets.

It is argued below that, when considering such markets, measuring environmental impacts is less of a concern, as these are closely correlated with financial success. Hence, when considering the role of information, the major challenge lies rather in overcoming the informational barriers preventing the implementation of financially viable and environmentally beneficial projects. If market participants face large information-related transaction costs, it is important to identify and strengthen actors that are able—and have an interest in—reducing these barriers. It is in this sense that the above-mentioned question will provide the most valuable answers. Therefore, the focus of the analysis lies on actors that can potentially play such a role of brokering information. As the business models of these actors usually also involve the application of knowledge on available technologies, the authors refer to them as *Information and Technology Brokers*.

This chapter is structured as follows. Following this introductory section, the authors explore the connection between the measurement of environmental improvements and financial success on environmental markets. The most important measurables for the different actors are presented. In section three, the case for enlarging the informational considerations beyond the pure measurement and evaluation concerns is established. The authors further present an overview of different information barriers on environmental markets structured by actors, which will serve as reference to the more detailed explorations that follow. The focus lies on actors that can fulfil the role of an Information and Technology Broker. In section 4, the authors present the information-finance nexus in the context of the CDM and examine to what extent the project developer could assume the brokerage role. Special emphasis is laid on small-scale and programmatic CDM. Section 5 discusses the role of energy service companies in scaling-up EERE investments. The paper concludes with section 6.

2 Measuring Environmental Impact and Financial Success

If environmental markets are to be a successful instrument for environmental policy, environmental improvements and expected gains for market participants need to be closely correlated. With respect to the markets considered by other authors within this publication, this is indeed the case. The primary focus of this publication is small-scale projects in the fields of energy Efficiency and Renewable Energy (EERE), as well as the generation of greenhouse gas offsets.

While the connection of carbon offsets to an environmental policy goal is straightforward, EERE measures might be considered as only indirectly related to environmental concerns. It is true that the motivation for fostering such markets might also be based on other policy goals, like the reduction in dependency of a country's economy on oil imports. However, insofar as EERE contributes to the reduction of fossil fuel use for energy production, such projects obviously have environmentally beneficial effects, such as reductions in emission of CO_2, NO_x, SO_2, and volatile organic compounds. In those cases where EERE projects contribute to a reduction in dependency on nuclear energy, the beneficial environmental effects are the reduction in nuclear waste and risks of radiation due to unforeseeable leakages or catastrophic events. Hence the environmental goal underlying the policies promoting EERE technologies is usually measured in energy units produced through non-renewable sources. Given this goal, the direct relationship between environmental improvements and the profit motive on this market is quite obvious. While energy savings or installation of renewable energy capacity are primarily striven for by market actors because of their financial gains, these gains translate into actions to achieve an environmental goal.

In both the EERE market and the market for carbon offsets—which are to a large extent overlapping—the connection between environmental improvements measured in KWh/GWh and tonnes of CO_2 equivalents and financial gains is very close. In fact, the financial gains of such projects are determined by multiplying the respective amounts by the market price—i.e. the price per energy unit or the price per carbon certificate—reduced by the investments costs. In fact, this close connection lies at the heart of the general idea of environmental markets. As a consequence, measuring financial success is closely correlated with measuring environmental improvements. In the logic of environmental markets the general answer to the question of "who measures what for whom" is, at least in principle, very simple: every market participant measures for himself what is in his interest to measure. As the major environmental variables on these markets are directly accounted for in the actors' calculations of expected and actual cash flows, the major case for monitoring and evaluation lies rather within a thoughtful design of environmental markets.

The problem of environmental market design is most imminent in those markets which are entirely created through regulation, like the Kyoto carbon markets. The demand for the good traded on these markets, i.e. offsets for greenhouse gas emissions, crucially depends on the stringency of the emission targets for industrialized countries which are defined within the international climate policy negotiations. The only—yet important—instrument that connects the developing countries to this market is the Clean Development Mechanism (CDM). This mechanism allows for the implementation of projects involving greenhouse gas reductions,[1] which can be sold on the carbon market in form of Certified Emission Reductions (CERs). Each of these certificates represents an offset of one metric tonne of CO_2 equivalents. On the Kyoto marketplace these certificates, and certificates stemming from other Kyoto markets, are perfectly fungible, which raises the question of how well these certificates represent *actual* emission reductions.

---

1 In fact, the CDM also allows for projects aiming for temporary absorption of CO_2 through afforestation or reforestation. The market volume of such project is, however, currently rather small.

This problem is being addressed through the Kyoto rules, which are to guarantee that the certified reductions would not have occurred without the financial leverage provided by the possibility to sell the certificates. The general principle, referred to as *additionality*, is addressed through methods applied for the calculation of overall project offsets. The project designer needs to establish a "business as usual" scenario, referred to as the baseline, depicting the emission levels that would have occurred if the project were not implemented. The number of certificates generated by a CDM project is then determined by the difference between the baseline emissions and the actual emissions still occurring under the project.

In order to reduce opportunistic misrepresentation of either the baseline or the actual project emissions, the CDM is subject to a tight regulatory framework. The project details must be thoroughly disclosed, while baseline and actual emissions are subject to third party verification. In order to reduce problems of collusion, the regulator—the role of which is mainly taken up by the CDM executive board in Bonn, Germany—is to execute regular spot checks within the set of all admitted CDM projects. The overall process for project admission is hence associated with significant transaction costs and is particularly time consuming.[2] What is important in the context addressed here, however, is the fact that all issues of measurement, monitoring and verification of carbon offsets are addressed within this CDM regulatory process. Hence, once a project is registered and certificates for greenhouse gas reductions are issued, the CDM market is not different from any other market on which standardized goods are traded.

In summary, the answer to the question of "who measures what for whom" is, as far as the CDM is concerned, meticulously defined within the Kyoto rules. As a legal claim for CDM certificates can only be established if these rules are followed, the general logic laid out above should apply: Every actor measures what is in his interest to measure. It is to note, however, that the CDM is a market entirely built from scratch. This means that all actors involved, particularly the regulators, need to learn how to best operationalize this general logic within the implementation of the mechanism. Addressing these issues would, however, require going into a level of detail which is beyond the scope of this paper.

The general statement that on environmental markets, every actor only measures those variables that are important for his own decision making raises the question of what in fact those objective variables might be. As to the primary market participants, the answer is straightforward. Provided an appropriate market design, buyers and sellers of privatized environmental goods only need to measure their own financial performance in order to foster environmental improvements. The same argument can be applied to commercial finance institutions that are to provide financing vehicles to these markets. Actors like governments or development finance institutions (DFIs), however, first need to define an objective to be achieved through potential interventions. In general, it can be rightfully assumed

2 According to Fenhann (2008a), depending on the ex ante verification cycle it may take up to three years or more until a CDM project is registered.

that these institutions want to foster environmental improvements. The measurement of success for such intervention intended to achieve this goal is rather unproblematic. Due to the close relationship between such improvements and overall market volume, the latter can easily be used as a signal for the former.

An example of this reasoning is depicted in Figure 1, representing the results from the Hungary Energy Efficiency Co-Finance Program (HEECP). This programme was headed by the IFC using GEF and IFC funds. The basic instrument used was a financial guarantee mechanism that, in cooperation with local finance institutions, aimed at building up sustainable commercial lending business for energy efficiency investment across a range of sectors. The graphic showcases that, in principle, measurement of DFI's impact on environmental finance markets is straightforward. The measurement variable of interest is, given the aim of increase in overall credit, the amount of investment triggered by the guarantee programme. The figure shows that the programme yielded a significant leverage effect, which should be at the basis of any guarantee instrument.[3]

Concluding these considerations, it can be stated that carefully designed environmental markets render the measurement of environmental improvements rather unproblematic. The problems here lie rather in the actual design of the regulatory framework than in the measurement itself, as the publicly observable data on market volumes are closely correlated with environmental improvements. If the logic

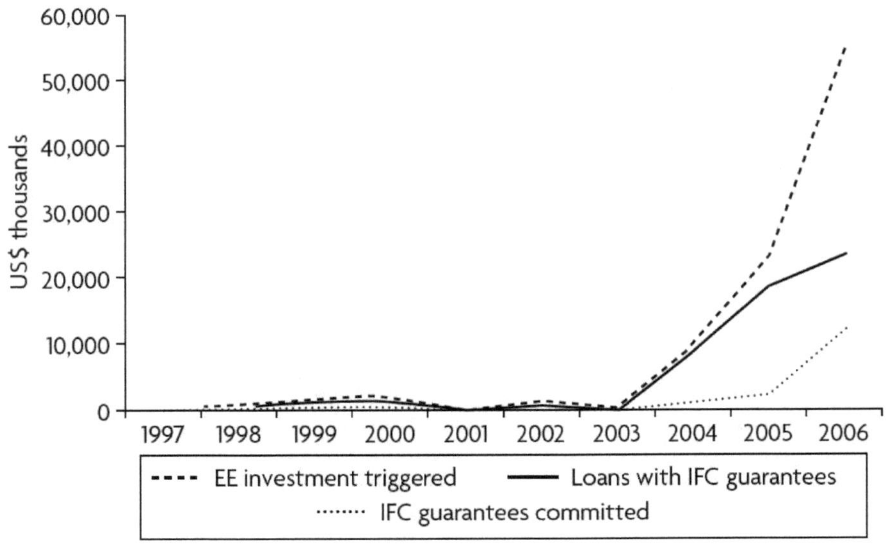

Fig. 1. Results from the HEEPC, 1997–2006
Source: World Bank (2008)

[3] World Bank (2008).

of environmental markets applies, it is sufficient that every actor evaluates those data that are needed to measure and improve his financial performance. This, in turn, facilitates the measurement of success for institutions interested in further developing markets, like governments or development banks. The base variable of evaluation for these actors is the increase in market volume that is attributable to the measure applied.

However, the question of "who measures what for whom" goes in fact deeper than a simple identification of measurables for success with respect to these markets. In fact, the question addresses, at least implicitly, the fact that one of the major areas of necessary intervention lies within the area of information flows. In the following, the implications of such a "second-degree" interpretation of the guiding question will be addressed in more detail.

3 Information and Green Markets – An Overview

Any sensible use of the term environmental finance, in its meaning of a market for financial services related to markets for environmental goods, presupposes that the latter already exist. Hence, considering financing for environmental markets that might be created in the future, for example a market for biodiversity, might be interesting but is beyond the scope of the topic discussed here. It goes without saying that the creation of such markets is not within the responsibility of financial institutions, but—insofar as they result from regulation—a task for countries' sovereigns. Any other actor on potential or actual environmental markets has to take the regulatory framework as given. The following considerations are therefore limited to the markets that were already introduced, notably the carbon market, and markets for energy efficiency and renewable energy (EERE). The discussion is further restricted here to what is generally referred to as small-scale projects in developing countries, which are usually associated with households, SMEs, and municipalities.

It has been emphasized within the other chapters that lack of knowledge and other informational barriers are among the key problems in environmental finance markets. These barriers represent simply the costs of collecting and processing the information required to take an objectively rational investment decision. As many actors perceive—rightfully or not—these costs as being too high, the level of small-scale projects on environmental markets is inefficiently low. Reducing these costs would surely not solve all problems present on the market for environmental finance,[4] but most likely result in a significant increase in investment.

When considering the role of information on environmental finance markets, it is necessary to recognise that the information-related challenges vary among the

[4] Clearly, if inefficiencies on financial markets hamper the financing of lucrative projects, measures for general financial market development will also increase the availability of financial vehicles for activities on green markets.

key actors on these markets. The relative underinvestment on environmental markets is also a result of the interaction of all these informational shortcomings. In order to discuss the information-related barriers in these markets in a systematic manner, it is useful to reduce the complexity of these interactions in an analytical framework. A graphical representation of such a reduction is given in Figure 2. This figure represents the key actors on environmental finance markets and their most important information needs. The actors themselves are interconnected through information flows; these flows can be hampered by barriers, also indicated in the figure. Development finance institutions and entities referred to as Information & Technology Brokers can act as catalysers in order to overcome these information barriers. In the following, the information-finance nexus on environmental markets is addressed on an actor-by-actor basis.

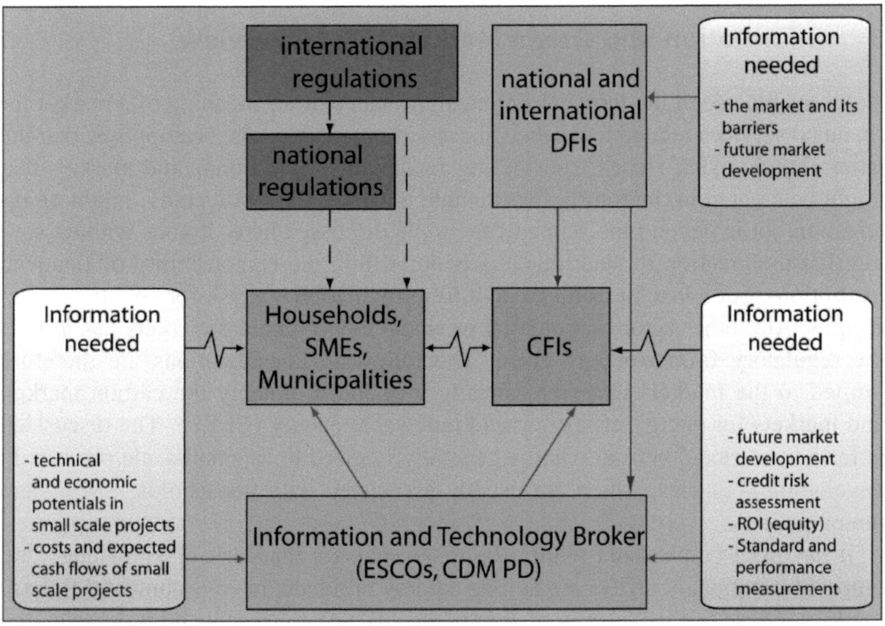

Fig. 2. Actors and Information Barriers in Environmental Markets

3.1 Households, SMEs and Municipalities

In principle, the beneficiaries from small-scale investments in environmental markets are the end-users themselves. According to the scope defined above, these consist of households, SMEs, and municipalities. In the logic of environmental markets, where actors pursuing their self-interest yield environmental improvements, these actors should have an incentive to implement such projects by themselves. As is amply discussed within the other chapters, this is apparently not the case. The fact that there still exist "big bills left on the sidewalk" is often attributed to irrational decision making. Another explanation, favoured by many economists, is the existence of information barriers. The most apparent barrier preventing investments on the markets considered here is simply a lack of awareness of the existence of potentials for savings or additional earnings. End-users are often unaware of the existence of better technologies, the associated improvements in cash flows, or the possibilities of tax rebates and subsidies that are available. The latter is of particular importance for poorer households, which are—without substantial support—rather preoccupied with improving their living conditions in the short term. A similar argument is often brought forward with respect to small enterprises, which tend to prefer investing their limited resources in upgrades of equipment which is directly related to production. But even where the existence of potential government support is known, the actual procedures of tax rebate or subsidy schemes are often considered to be too bureaucratic and time consuming. Furthermore, the energy and cost saving possibilities of a single project or site are usually small compared to the transaction costs, which are not directly related to information, like negotiation or contracting costs. This is particularly evident in the residential sector when ownership of buildings is shared by several private owners.[5]

It is probable that the persistence of end-user information barriers stems in many cases from the fact that these actors remain rationally uninformed. If the potential gains from projects are smaller than the costs for arranging government support and all other cost to be incurred prior to project implementation, it is perfectly rational to remain uninformed on these matters. The most promising way to overcome this problem is to search for potential aggregators that incur the fix cost of information gathering just once and implement a plethora of small-scale projects. This role is sometimes taken up by municipalities, which can not only implement EERE projects within their own facilities, but are also able to set up programmes for supporting small-scale projects within their constituency. This has been, for example, the case in the Kuyasa low-cost urban housing upgrade project, presented in section 4.3, where the city of Cape Town has played a vital role as intermediary.

It is often pointed out that the reluctance of implementing small-scale projects is also due to the fact that decision makers tend to apply initially very high but decreasing discount rates within individual decisions. This explanation for the lack in investment in EERE is quite plausible, as it is backed by ample evidence of such hyperbolic discounting in individual decision-making.[6] However, the existence of high discount rates alone cannot fully explain the relative lack of investment. If

---

5 WEC (2008); the shared ownership in the residential sector also features a plethora of information asymmetries that hamper investments in energy efficiency. A profound analysis of these can be found in IEA (2008).

6 See, for example, Benzion et al. (1989), or Epper et al. (2008).

end-users discount future revenues from EERE investments with rates above the interest rates, other market participants are able to yield significant gains from arbitrage. As financial institutions can refinance at market interest rates lying way below the observed individual time preferences, the overall amount of finance procured would have to be significantly larger than actually observed. This hints to the fact that not only the primary environmental markets but also the associated market for project-finance are subject to significant information barriers, as will be shortly recapitulated in the following.

3.2 Commercial Finance Institutions (CFIs)

As already pointed out in the introduction, the principles of environmental finance are not different from standard project finance. Just as any other investment project, EERE investments and greenhouse gas reduction projects are characterized by the fact that a large part of the costs are incurred in the start-up phase, while revenue streams can be only expected in the longer term. Consequently, the financing needs in environmental markets are in principle not different from what commercial finance institutions are familiar with. Environmental projects need upfront financing which—on average—can be expected to be paid back at later points in time. Still, there is a significant underprovision of environmental finance, which is the guiding theme of this publication. While the lack of demand for such services, discussed above, is a reason for low levels of project finance, a significant part of the problem can be explained by taking a closer look at the supply side.

Market observers often point out that financing environmental projects is associated with large risks, for which reason commercial banks refrain from procuring services to this market. This is not necessarily true for all cases considered here, as the revenue streams from energy savings or GHG reductions might be more secure than from other investments. It is, however, quite plausible that default risks are significantly high in the small-scale context as the collaterals procured by the end-users are limited. Still, given that the main business of CFIs consists of pooling risks over a wide customer base, a large variance alone cannot explain the general reluctance for financing potentially lucrative projects.

It is likely that the actual reason for the lack of financing lies not directly with the level of the objective risks associated with environmental projects, but rather with the difficulty to assess those risks. As the concept of environmental markets is quite new, CFIs generally lack financing expertise in this area. In order to assess the associated risks properly, a credit history would be necessary, which still needs to be generated. Under these circumstances, it is understandable that CFIs by themselves will only provide finance to customers with high levels of creditworthiness. However, if green finance is to take off in the longer term, CFIs need to build up expertise in assessing technologies used, savings and earnings that can be expected, etc. Observers also point out that CFIs lack a general understanding of the drivers of important markets in this area, such as the international carbon market.[7] As will be argued in the following sections, the additional risks associated with such projects are in general manageable if sufficient information is provided.

A specific problem in the context of environmental finance and associated transaction costs is investments of the smallest scale, like simple insulation projects in the residential sector. In such cases, it is likely that the costs of negotiating the financing terms exceed the gains from the project. Such transaction costs can, again, only be lowered through a bundling of smallest-scale projects by an institution acting as an aggregator, like the Information and Technology Brokers addressed below.

3.3 Governments and Development Finance Institutions (DFIs)

While it is within the logic of environmental markets that most actors are driven by self-interest, this should necessarily not be the case for those actors who are supposed to set the framework conditions and to facilitate the start-up phase of markets. The most important actors in this area are international regulators of the carbon market, national governments and development finance institutions. While international regulators exclusively concentrate on setting and enforcing the general rules applicable to the carbon market, governments and DFIs also interact more directly with the primary market participants.

Government policies might either increase or decrease the incentive to engage in environmental markets. A prominent example for a decrease in incentives is the case of the often-quoted "perverse" subsidies for carbon- and energy-intensive technologies. In general, however, national governments seem to have an interest in fostering environmental markets. Many countries have implemented tax rebates or subsidy schemes for EERE measures. Further instruments that are applied are grants for R&D, the implementation of pilot projects, and the procurement of soft loan schemes. An important tool for reducing information barriers is, for example, the introduction of an energy audit scheme. Important information on the average benefits and costs of EERE measures can be derived from such energy audits. These can be used as a building block for assessing risks and opportunities in environmental finance.[8]

Development Finance Institutions play a prominent role in the overall information-related setup discussed here. For example, development banks can, in their role of government advisor, provide valuable information on best practices with respect to the markets' framework conditions. More importantly, due to their close relationship with the financial market, DFIs can help to directly reduce the information barriers that hamper the development of a self-sustaining environmental finance market. One important instrument is to directly enhance the information

---

7 See for example Capoor and Ambrosi (2007) or Figueres and Philips (2007).

8 WEC (2008).

base of commercial finance institutions through capacity building. Spreading knowledge on the main drivers of environmental markets will directly improve commercial banks' capacity to assess risks accurately and to develop appropriate financing vehicles.

In addition to direct measures for capacity building, DFIs can reduce information barriers by applying instruments of "risk-reduced learning by doing". This class of instruments includes loan guarantees, credit subsides, grants, etc. The general idea is that DFIs directly or indirectly assume part of the credit risk, while commercial banks can build up a credit history under acceptable conditions. These instruments accordingly lay the basis for a more informed risk assessment in the future and increase the expertise of commercial banks in new markets, where they would otherwise not be engaged. However, if such markets are supposed to be self-sustaining, in the future such programmes would need to be of limited duration. In this respect they differ from programmes based on the motives of poverty reduction or other social policy goals.

A successful scale-up through capacity building requires that DFIs build up and spread knowledge on these markets within their own institutional borders. This is an ongoing process, far from being completed, as is shown by the example of the mainstreaming of carbon pricing within those institutions. While development banks were among the first investors in the early years of the Clean Development Mechanism, it is within many of the banks' activities still not taken into account that greenhouse gas emissions are associated with shadow prices. As a recent study by the World Resources Institute points out, the partner country strategies vary widely with respect to the integration of concerns on climate change.[9] The author of this study examines the level of mainstreaming of climate change within four major DFIs. An aggregation of the results of this study is presented in Figure 3, categorizing recent energy-related investments of the World Bank, the International Finance Corporation (IFC), the Asian Development Bank (ADB), and the Inter-American Development Bank (IDB). The total of energy related investments are split up among three different groups defined by the author of the WRI study, namely activities that integrate, mention, and ignore climate change. It is quite obvious that, at least until 2006, mainstreaming of climate change issues was not very advanced within the DFIs. This can be partly explained by the fact that DFIs' strategies were slanted towards supporting few large-scale projects. Investments in renewable energy are often associated with smaller projects and therefore require a lower proportion of DFIs' resources. The most recent development depicted might discern a rethinking in DFI strategies. The 2007 increase in considering climate change might also be a result of the topic's increased media coverage within that year. The years to come will show if the learning process will endure in the longer term.

9 WRI (2008).

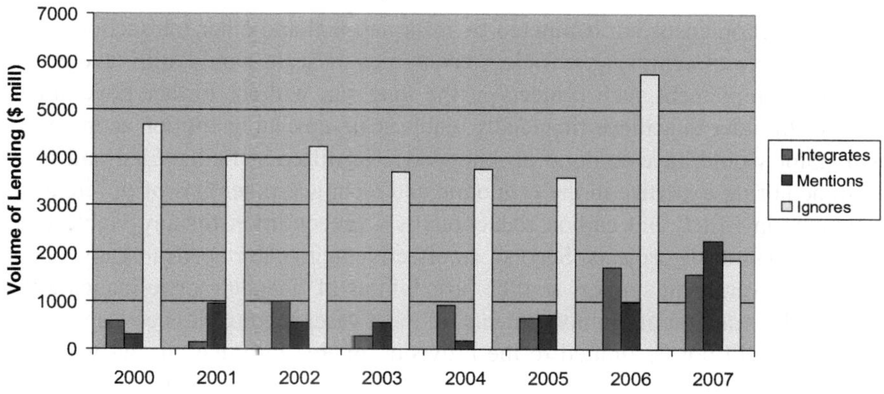

Fig. 3. Shares of Energy Investments by four major DFIs considering Climate Change

Source: Own aggregation based on WRI (2008), Climate Change at the Multilateral Development Banks

As the above-mentioned research by the World Resources Institute showcases, there definitely exists a case for measurement and evaluation with respect to mainstreaming the idea of environmental markets within DFIs. The introduction of a systematic greenhouse gas accounting for DFI-supported projects would provide further insights in future reduction potentials. The calculated project carbon footprints could further be used for a more holistic cost-benefit analysis for such projects, including external costs with respect to climate change. Within such an analysis the associated greenhouse gas emissions could either be valued at the current carbon price, or the value could be constructed based on theoretical considerations on the social cost of carbon, as used, for example, within the Stern Review.

3.4 Information and Technology Brokers on Environmental Markets

While programmes aiming at enhancing the expertise within CFIs are likely to increase the supply side of environmental finance markets, fostering the demand for such financing vehicles would require overcoming the large information and transaction costs associated with this side of the market. One promising approach is to support information and technology brokers, following the business model of pooling small-scale projects into a larger-scale programme in order to participate in the financial gains. Clearly, supporting these aggregators is only one of many strategies that DFIs or governments can apply in order to increase demand in environmental finance. However, given that this approach seems to be promising, it surely deserves to be considered in more detail.

Given the above-exposed logic of environmental markets, when searching for potential project aggregators it is natural to look for actors that pool and implement small-scale projects out of self-interest. If projects were lucrative with respect to their production costs, but hampered by informational and other transaction costs, actors capable of achieving sufficient economies of scale would still have an incentive to implement such projects in the long run without further government support. In order to achieve financially viable scale-ups, an institution acting as an aggregator would have to build up knowledge in different fields. First and foremost, acquiring expertise in the economic and technical potentials of different investments in EERE and carbon reductions is a precondition for any viable bundling of small-scale projects. Second, an effective aggregator needs to know about potential government support and the possibilities of financing or refinancing the front-loaded fraction of the investments. In most cases the business concept of the aggregator will not be limited to the provision of this information, but will also include the actual implementation of the project, including the installation, monitoring and maintenance of the project technology. For this reason we will refer to this class of actors as Information & Technology Brokers.

An effective Information & Technology Broker acting along these lines would not only decrease transaction costs on the demand side of environmental finance: the emergence of such actors can also effectively reduce information problems on the supply side. It can be reasonably assumed that companies procuring I&T brokering have already gathered the information necessary for assessing the risks associated with potential future earnings. This information could easily feed into the decisions of risk capital providers as well as outside creditors. Furthermore, bundling small-scale projects has the interesting side effect that the I&T Broker has already diversified default risks. Furthermore, an Information & Technology Broker is capable of negotiating standardized financing conditions on behalf of the end-users or directly providing them with upfront funding while refinancing his business through more standardized products. In both cases finance-related transactions costs are reduced as well.

Several institutions at least in part assuming the role of an I&T Broker are discussed within other chapters of this publication. Depending on what market is considered, municipalities, Energy Service Companies (ESCOs), CDM project developers, or sometimes even utilities can fulfil the functions of such an aggregator. However, while the idea of an I&T Broker is theoretically appealing, actors that actually take up such a role in the real world still face significant barriers to the financial market. Those barriers are, in principle, not different from those discussed in the context of the financing supply side in general. Owing to a lack of expertise in environmental markets, CFIs have apparent problems in understanding the business model underlying I&T Brokers. This problem is further increased by the lack of a "track record", which is fundamental for a bank's risk assessment. As a consequence, CFIs are very reluctant in providing finance to those I&T Brokers that cannot provide a significant amount of collateral.

While the general overview on information problems attempted within the previous pages is useful for understanding the interrelationships between information and environmental finance, this level of generality lends itself to draw only very rough conclusions. Any detailed discussion of measures to potentially overcome the numerous information problems is beyond the restricted scope of this paper. In order to still be able to discuss the information-financing nexus on a more detailed level, the following analysis concentrates on two classes of actors that could help to overcome informational problems: CDM project developers and ESCOs. This choice is not to be interpreted as being the only field in the nexus that might represent a case for government or DFI intervention. It is rather one of many of such cases. However, given the necessity of scaling up small-scale activities, supporting these actors seems particularly promising.

4 Case 1: CDM and the Project Developer as I&T Broker

As already mentioned, the international climate policy framework includes a sophisticated system of emissions trading for greenhouse gases (GHGs), consisting of several different sub-markets including cap-and-trade as well as project-based mechanisms. This international carbon market has been fully operational since the beginning of the first commitment period of the Kyoto Protocol in 2008. Currently, the only mechanism that links developing countries and their enormous GHG reduction potentials to the worldwide carbon market is the Clean Development Mechanism. The general idea of the CDM is to incentivize GHG reduction or sink projects within developing countries that are financed by parties from industrialized countries by securitizing the offsets achieved within the project, which are then tradable on the carbon market. The GHG offsets achievable within the CDM are considerable. For the first commitment period of the Kyoto Protocol from 2008 to 2012, the estimates of the primary market volume range from 1.5 to 3 billion metric tonnes of CO_2-equivalents.[10] Projections on the long term development of the CDM certificate price are a difficult endeavour, as the price depends also on several political decisions. The spot price on the secondary market for CDM certificates fluctuated in October 2008 between EUR 18 and 20 per tonne CO_2-equivalent.[11]

Initially, the underlying idea of the CDM was that an investor from an industrial country provides the financing (and sometimes the implemented technology) to a project developer situated within a developing country. The latter was to implement and operate the project activity, while the investor was still actively involved in the actual operations by procuring the necessary technical know-how. Within the actual implementation of the mechanism, however, a different organisational structure became predominant, the so-called Emission Reduction Purchase Agreement (ERPA). While the simple buyer-seller structure of the purchase contract provides the market participants with the necessary flexibility that is needed in a newly created market, it has significantly altered the perception of

---

[10] See Fenhann (2008a), PointCarbon (2008a), and UNFCCC (2008).

[11] PointCarbon (2008b).

responsibilities for the actual investments necessary within the CDM. In most implemented CDM projects, the industrialized country party does not represent an investor providing up-front finance for implementing the project, but simply acts as a buyer for the certificates generated by the project. While a purchase contract could, in principle, also include a fixed price component paid up front, including such payments in advance is rather the exception for currently implemented projects involving private sector buyers.[12] Hence, for most CDM projects the financial influx from the buyer's side is reduced to the per unit payment upon delivery of the certificates. As a consequence, if third-party financing vehicles were unavailable the seller would take on all project-related risks. As these risks are particularly important for the availability and type of third-party financing, they are discussed below.

4.1 Risks

Like any other transboundary market, trading in CDM certificates is associated with currency risks, host country risks, off-take risks, and several other risk types. However, the fact that the CDM is a market entirely created through regulation entails several risks specific to that market. For example, there exists genuine uncertainty among market participants about the continuation of the international climate policy regime after 2012. This risk has generally been dealt with by almost exclusively implementing projects which break even within the first commitment period of the Kyoto Protocol. While this regulatory uncertainty hampers the implementation of projects which would be environmentally beneficial in the longer term, resolving this uncertainty is a task for governments and their climate policy negotiators. Market participants have to take this uncertainty as given. Another regulatory risk is that a project might not be recognized as being valid within the CDM and hence fail to be registered. As mentioned in section two, projects have to pass through a complicated and time-consuming regulatory process in order to be accepted within the CDM. Based on the experiences with projects that have been evaluated within this process, Fenhann (2008a) estimates that the probability of project rejection by the regulator is about 5%.[13]

Once the project is registered within the CDM, the associated risks are, in principle, the same as within standard project finance in developing countries. First, there might the standard default risk that the product to be delivered—carbon offsets—cannot be produced.[14] In this respect CDM certificates are not different from

[12] Capoor and Ambrosi (2007), see also Capoor and Ambrosi (2008).

[13] Note that Projects in earlier stages of the CDM cycle face in addition a probability of 18.5% of not being registered. (Fenhann (2008a)).

[14] One specificity here is the fact that CDM credits are only being issued if the emission reductions are verified by a third-party verifier. There exist hence, risks associated with monitoring and verification. (See also section 2).

any other product. Due to any imaginable contingency the project might simply fail to produce the expected amount of deliverables. Furthermore, CDM projects can also suffer from risks which are associated with the uncertainty of future market prices for carbon credits. While such sales risks do, in general, occur on any market, the drivers of these risks might be different within the CDM, as they are mainly of political or regulatory nature. For example, risks might include that regulatory rules determining the scarcity of carbon emission rights change (e.g. the so-called EU ETS risk and Post-Kyoto risk) or that the necessary infrastructure for carbon trading is not yet established within specific buyer countries (ITL risk).[15] It is foreseeable that with the further development of the international climate policy framework both of these risks will diminish or even disappear. Generally, it can be observed that in sum the production and sales risks are quantifiable. As Fenhann (2008b) reports, the probability of a successful issuance is about 96.3% for projects registered within the CDM. The average risk premium for these risks on the forward market ranges—depending on the project type—between EUR 2 and 5 per tonne of CO_2 equivalent.[16]

In summary, as far as the associated risks are concerned, financing CDM projects does, in principle, not differ from standard project finance. However, there exist some particularities to the CDM which require a diligent assessment. Importantly, CDM-specific risks are generally quantifiable and hence manageable, provided the required knowledge base is established.

4.2 The Challenge for Financial Institutions

Given the specificities of the CDM market, there exists not only a large need, but also a lucrative potential, for financial services in this market. There is an urgent need for financial vehicles that allow the future cash flow from certificate sales to be frontloaded and used for project investments. In principle, such vehicles could involve both equity as well as debt finance. A growing number of "carbon funds" provide equity finance for CDM projects, while pooling the risks over a large portfolio of projects. Cochran and Leguet (2007) estimate that in 2007 EUR 7 billion was invested in 58 carbon funds; they project an increase up to EUR 9.4 billion of total fund capitalization in 2008. While in the "trial phase" of the CDM from 2000 to 2005, these funds were mainly operated by development finance institutions and governments, the recent increase in projects financed by carbon funds is to the largest part attributable to private sector engagement (see Figure 4). This development is an example of DFIs' successful pioneering in the field of green finance.

[15] For further reading on the different risks associated with the CDM, see UNEP RISOE (2007).

[16] According to PointCarbon (2008a), in 2007 issued CERs fetched between EUR 14 and 17, while forward prices on CERs from registered projects yielded EUR 12 on average. This is in line with the observations by Capoor and Ambrosi (2008), who present evidence for an issuance risk premium of about EUR 3.

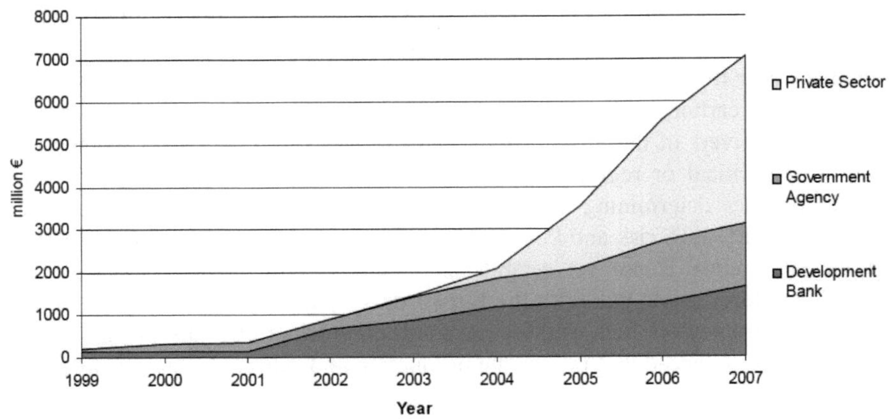

Fig. 4. Evolution of CDM Investment Capital by Vehicle Managing Agent

Source: Cochran and Leguet (2007)

However, in light of the fact that CDM risks are quite manageable, there exists a priori no reason why part of the financing of CDM projects should not be taken over by outside creditors. While there are a few examples of CDM projects partly financed by loans from large international banks, CFIs in developing countries still seem reluctant to enter this market. One of the major reasons for this reluctance is the fact that assessing the risks associated with CDM projects requires a significant amount of knowledge on the project activity as well as a deep understanding of the specificities of the carbon market. Thus, it is likely that with a maturing of the market the amount of debt financing will further increase. However, there may be a case for DFI intervention in this specific market based on the above-depicted reasoning of "risk-reduced learning by doing". In order to generate such an experience base for reluctant CFIs in specific countries, DFIs might intervene by taking over a part of the credit risk through grants or by subsidizing interest over a limited time period. A further reduction of financial market barriers induced by lack of knowledge is likely to significantly foster the CDM's environmental effectiveness while at the same time tapping its potential to contribute to sustainable development.

4.3 Small-Scale Projects and the Potential of Programmatic CDM

The Clean Development Mechanism is often misperceived as being only capable of incentivizing large-scale projects. This is not surprising, as the implementation of large-scale projects, like those involving geo-thermal or tidal power generation, is usually well covered by the media. Furthermore, the CDM accreditation process clearly entails significant transaction costs; therefore, only projects of a certain size become financially viable within the mechanism. However, the Kyoto rules also provide for simpler procedures concerning small-scale projects.[17] A closer look at the CDM project pipeline, which includes all projects currently registered or under review, reveals that implementing such small-scale projects within the CDM is quite popular. As of May 2008, 1462 projects in the pipeline, i.e. 44% of all projects, were small-scale.[18]

To be eligible as a CDM small-scale project, the respective project should not exceed specific thresholds. For example, the reduction in energy consumption attributable to the project activity should not exceed 15 GWh per year.[19] Hence, for energy-intensive SMEs or municipalities, small-scale CDM might be a lucrative option to leverage investments in EERE. Projects on the level of single households would be, however, not financially viable, as the transaction costs associated with the mechanism would far exceed the potential gains from the project. There exists, however, the possibility to pool EERE activities in many different households into one single CDM project. It is in this respect that an ingenious CDM project developer can become an I&T-Broker.

A good example for such a pooling of household activities into a small-scale CDM project is the *Kuyasa low-cost urban housing upgrade project*, in Cape Town, South Africa. This project involves EERE upgrades within a low-income housing settlement in Khayelitsha, a township located on the south-eastern side of the City of Cape Town. The project activity consists of retrofitting 2309 state-subsidised $30m^2$ housing units with three simple EERE measures: the installation of solar water heaters, insulated ceilings and compact fluorescent light bulbs. These measures are generating reductions in CO_2 emissions of about 2.85 tonnes per household per year. The total project reduction is approximately 6,580 tonnes of CO_2 equivalents per annum. As these effects are estimated to accumulate over a 21 year period, the overall impact on emissions is considerable. The savings in energy costs for a single household are estimated to be approximately ZAR 625.84 (USD 63) per year. The measures are further expected to reduce health costs by approximately ZAR 685 (USD 69) per household per annum.[20]

The above example showcases that the pooling of project activities at the household level is already possible under the standard CDM rules for small-scale projects. However, given that the number of household participating must be known before the start of the project, these rules certainly have some limitations to trigger wide-spread EERE measures in developing countries. For this reason, a new set of rules has been added recently to the CDM framework allowing for Programmes of

---

17 See UNFCCC(2002), Decision 17 and Annex.

18 See Fenhann (2008c).

19 Further criteria for eligibility under the CDM small-scale regime are reductions in energy consumption below 15 GWh/year, and emission reductions of less than 15 kilo tonnes of CO_2 equivalents. See UNFCCC(2002), decision 17, §6(c).

20 See CDM PDD (2005) and SouthSouthNorth (2005).

Activities (PoA).[21] These rules open the possibility to register an unlimited number of CDM project activities under a single CDM programme. A Programme of Activities may be coordinated by a public or private entity and, in principle, may include any voluntary sets of measures that result in additional emission reductions. Given the novelty of the instrument, by 1 November 2008, only five PoAs were under CDM validation. These programmes involve: home solar systems in Bangladesh, biodigesters in small pork farms in Brazil, solar water heaters in South Africa, Compact Fluorescent Lights in Mexico, and municipal waste composting in Uganda. The difference in technologies used within these different programmes is an indication of the large potential for triggering small-scale EERE investments that rests within future CDM PoA implementations.[22] Another advantage is that the income from PoAs, which is generated through certificate sales, can be easily channelled back to the end-users, either through consumer credits for individual purchases of household appliances, or for SMEs through microfinancing structures for enterprise development.

Many observers of the CDM have pointed out that the procedural and methodological CDM rules need refinement in order to reduce the hurdles impeding the development of PoAs. In this context, the importance of information generation for scaling-up environmental markets is once again quite obvious. Given that regulators, like market participants, are still in a learning phase, the rules for the mechanisms are sequentially adjusted. These adjustments are based on regular 'calls for input' generating useful feedback by the market participants. As to the further development of the PoA rules, the early lessons will be discussed and incorporated at the next meetings of the parties of the Kyoto Protocol in Posnan, Poland and Copenhagen, Denmark.

Pooling of CDM projects within small-scale rules and PoAs encounter the same barriers to project financing vehicles as CDM projects in general. In many PoAs, the sales of certificates will be the only cash income (e.g. with energy efficiency measures). This exacerbates the above-described problem of front-loaded implementation costs and cash flows occurring only at a later time. As Figueres and Philips (2007) point out, few financial institutions are willing to absorb the corresponding risk, as risk assessment for new instruments which lack a credit history is always difficult. Hence, while CDM project developers in the longer term could well fulfil the role of an I&T Broker, it is likely that in the short-term, they will remain dependent on the build-up of expertise within developing countries' CFIs. Here, there clearly exists a case for intervention either by DFIs or governments.

---

21 See CDM EB (2007), Annexes 28–31.

22 See CDM Project Database, available online at http://cdm.unfccc.int/Projects/index.html.

5 Case 2: Energy Service Companies

Many small-scale EERE investments are already financially viable even without including revenues from the carbon market.[23] Still, informational barriers on the supply and demand side of the environmental finance market hamper the implementation of such measures. Again, supporting actors interested in bundling projects could be an effective instrument to facilitate small-scale EERE investments. In many countries the role of an I&T Broker on this market is assumed by energy service companies, or ESCOs (see the chapter by MacLean in this publication). These companies offer primarily end-user energy efficiency improvement services while receiving a share in the resulting savings in return. Such services generally include the design of energy efficiency projects for specific end-users, consulting on potential financial leverage (like subsidy schemes), the installation and maintenance of the necessary equipment, and monitoring and verification of a project's energy savings. Usually, the remuneration of ESCO is linked to the financial performance of the implemented measures. This fits well into the paradigm of environmental markets, as the financial performance of the measures directly depends on the environmental variable, i.e. the amount of energy saved.

An ESCO's business model also includes either the direct financing of the single project or acting as a mediator between its customers and commercial banks. While this is likely to reduce the transaction costs per project, it also shifts the responsibility to overcome the barriers on the financial market to the ESCO. Whereas ESCOs in industrialized countries can rely on a mature financial sector for project financing, ESCOs in developing countries experience considerable difficulties in securing funding for projects. Survey results presented in the World Energy Council (2008) reveal that ESCOs seeking financing face interest rates of up to 50–70%. The reasons for such high refinancing costs are again mostly of informational nature. As many observers point out, banks and other financial institutions often lack experience in lending to ESCOs. As a consequence, CFIs consider energy services as a risky business, while the financial model involved is not fully understood.[24] In most cases the perception of risks is not based on fundamental market data, as these simply do not yet exist. Hence, the fundamental informational problem which is at the heart of finance supply restrictions for EERE persists, even if ESCOs emerge on the market. As a result, ESCOs themselves tend to lend only to clients that have the highest levels of creditworthiness, and hence preferably engage in projects in the public sector. While in some newly industrializing countries—like for example in Brazil or India—ESCOs also finance industrial sector projects, the residential sector is usually not covered. [25] If ESCOs are

---

[23] In such a case, EERE investments would simply not fulfil the stringent additionality criteria of the CDM.

[24] See for example Painuly et al. (2003), World Bank (2008), and WEC (2008).

[25] See WEC (2008).

to become successful I&T Brokers for smaller-scale projects, reducing financial market barriers will be of primary importance.[26] Since ESCOs in developing countries are often new start-ups and not spin-offs of larger companies, the financial sector is particularly reluctant to provide financing for such companies.

One of the most important instruments for industry start-up is, therefore, co-financing by governments or DFIs, for example through guarantees, start-up loans, loan loss reserve funds, special purpose funds, or interest credits. The most popular of these instruments is the provision of guarantees. The Brazilian government, for example, has created a guarantee facility which is partly aimed at fostering the development of ESCOs, called PROSECO. Within this facility the Brazilian National Development Bank (BNDES) shares up to 80–100% of the ESCO's credit risk, while the remaining risk is taken over by the intermediary bank.[27]

Such grants represent an instrument to foster "risk-reduced learning by doing" for commercial banks, as discussed in section 3. Such instruments provide a controlled-risk environment, within which commercial banks can train to assess the economic potential which lies within the ESCO model. As far as ESCOs in Brazil are concerned, such further training is likely to be welcome. While Brazilian ESCOs generated returns of about BRL 500 million (USD 250 million) in 2006, this represents only 2% of the expected market potential.[28]

Another very successful example for jump-starting an ESCO industry is the World Bank/GEF-supported programme in China. An initial industry development project starting in 1997 included the set-up of three ESCOs, each provided with USD 5 million of GEF grant support and USD 21 million of IBRD loan funds for scaling-up their business. The majority of projects implemented by the three pilot ESCOs were small-sized programmes in the fields of building renovation, boiler/cogeneration, kiln/furnace, and waste heat/gas recovery. The commercial success of the pilot companies was key for other companies' decision to enter the newly created market. These were also provided with technical assistance from the UK's Department for International Development. A second project with USD 26 million of GEF financing through the World Bank was started in October 2002. The objective was to further foster China's ESCO industry up to a national scale. This project includes a major loan guarantee programme and the provision of training, technical assistance, as well as policy development support for emerging ESCOs.[29]

---

[26] As Painuly et al (2003) point out, there exists a plethora of other, mostly institutional barriers for the development of ESCOs, like weak legal frameworks or unfavourable public procurement practices. These are, however, beyond the actual scope of this paper concentrating on information barriers and finance.

[27] See BNDS (2008).

[28] See BfAI (2007).

[29] World Bank (2008).

The example of ESCO development in China is often quoted in the literature as a successful example for leveraging energy efficiency investments in developing countries. Indeed, the program's track record is impressive. In 2006, China's industry had grown to more than 60 ESCOs. Overall project investment volume in this year was about USD 280 million.[30] As most of the new market entrants did not receive large-scale support, the programme can be rightfully considered as a catalyser for a viable and promising new industry that can act as a I&T broker. Given the right framework conditions, the successful model might be replicable within other developing countries as well.

In general, ESCOs are likely to be in need of start-up support in most developing countries before being able to play the role of an aggregator. Instruments for such support should be, however, designed in a way that fosters learning on both sides of the financing market. Successful ESCOs would need to increase their knowledge on tapping the potential of lucrative EERE opportunities in the smaller-scale. As to the supply side of financing, programmes that provide a risk-reduced learning environment with limited duration seem to perform quite well. In the longer-term perspective the acquired expertise is likely to lead to a risk assessment that is rather based on the actual risks rather than unfounded expectations. A direct consequence of this learning process would be an improvement of financing terms for ESCOs. This, in turn, could lead to the development and scale-up of a viable energy service industry which in the longer term does not need further direct support.

6 Conclusion

The logic of market-based instruments in environmental policy is to use the profit motive for environmental improvements. This is usually achieved by privatizing an environmental good in a way that the results of these improvements are made tradable through securitization or by using already existing price mechanisms which are related – at least closely enough – to the environmental variables. The former is the case with emissions trading markets, while the latter applies to EERE. As a consequence, if the market is carefully designed, the achievement of environmental objectives for these markets can be more or less directly deduced from the actual market volume.

Within this paper we have established the case that informational considerations with respect to environmental markets need to go beyond the standard paradigm of simple measurement. It is argued that the major difference between environmental finance and standard project finance is not within the general market setup, but lies rather in the persisting information barriers that characterize the former. It can, for example, be argued that the lack of demand for financing small-

30 Ibid.

scale projects is to a large extent due to rational or irrational ignorance with respect to the potential gains. The supply side on the other hand seems to have a significant lack of knowledge on the principal mechanisms driving these markets and on how to systematically assess the associated risks.

Evidently, the informational problems identified here can only explain a part of the underprovision of environmental project finance. However, instruments that reduce these information barriers are very likely to lead to an increase in market volume. One measure that seems to be promising for fostering small-scale investments is the bundling of such projects by an I&T Broker. In principle, such brokers are capable of yielding economies of scale and scope by pooling small- and medium-scale projects. While the development of such aggregators is clearly not a magic bullet solving all inefficiencies on the environmental markets, there is promising anecdotal evidence suggesting that this can effectively reduce the information barriers on the demand side. These examples show that project pooling can significantly increase the amount of implemented projects. We have examined two actors that could assume such a role more closely: the CDM project developer and energy service companies. As it turns out, while these actors could be quite effective in bundling projects and hence scaling-up the demand side, they still encounter significant problems for interim financing for the respective investments. In fact, the informational problem on the supply side of environmental finance seems to persist. While there is growing evidence that the risks associated with CDM and EERE projects are manageable, commercial finance institutions still seem reluctant to procure finance for these endeavours. Many observers of these markets point to the fact that this reluctance is rather based on a general lack of expertise with respect to the newly created markets, rather than a rational assessment of project risks. In light of these observations, it is important to improve CFIs' capacity to collect and process information on technical and economic potentials in all considered fields, i.e. GHG emissions mitigation measures, measures to increase energy efficiency, and projects using renewable energy resources. In this context there exists a case for government or DFI intervention. The approach of several development banks in particular – to provide risk-reduced environments for learning by doing – yielded promising results in both markets. As several of the quoted examples have shown, guarantee programs of limited duration can help to jump-start an I&T Broker industry which would be viable in the long run. In the field of the CDM, where DFIs were among the first to provide start-up equity, they provided valuable first-mover experience to the market, generating information on the actual risks for the private sector. In the field of carbon funds, private sector engagement has recently overtaken the volumes provided by DFIs. A similar effort would be needed for starting up successful programmatic CDM projects where governments could also play a significant role.

References

Benzion, U., Rapoport, A., Yagil, J. (1989) Discount Rates Inferred From Decisions: An Experimental Study. Management Science 35:270–284.

BNDES (Brazilian National Development Bank) (2008) Support to Energetic Efficiency Projects (PROSECO). Available online at http://www.bndes.gov.br/english/proesco_in.asp.

BfAI (Deutsche Bundesagentur für Außenwirtschaft) (2007) Brasilien bietet Potential bei Energieeffizienz. Article, Database: Länder und Märkte, 31.10.2007, Available online at: https://www.bfai.de/DE/Content/__SharedDocs/Links-Einzeldokumente-Datenbanken/fachdokument.html?fIdent=MKT200710308000.

Capoor, K., Ambrosi, P. (2007) State and Trends of the Carbon Market 2007. Washington, DC: World Bank and IETA.

Capoor, K., Ambrosi, P. (2008) State and Trends of the Carbon Market 2008. Washington, DC: World Bank.

Cochran, I.T., Leguet, B. (2007) Carbon Investment Funds: The Influx of Private Capital, Note d'etude 12. Paris: Mission Climat Caisse des Depots.

CDM EB (2007) Report of the 36th Meeting of the CDM Executive Board, 26–30 November 2007, Bali, Indonesia, Official Document, available at: http://cdm.unfccc.int/EB/036/eb36rep.pdf.

CDM PDD (2005) Project ID: 0079, Simplified Project Design Document for Small-Scale CDM: Kuyasa Low-Cost Urban Housing Energy Upgrade Project, Khayelitsha (Cape Town, South Africa), available at: http://cdm.unfccc.int/Projects/DB/DNV-CUK1121165382.34.

Epper, T., Fehr-Duda, H., Bruhin, A. (2008) Uncertainty Breeds Decreasing Impatiance: The Role of Risk Preferences in Time Discounting. Institute for Environmental Decisions, ETH Zurich, mimeo.

Fenhann, J. (2008a) UNEP Risoe CDM/JI Pipeline Analysis and Database. Version November 1st 2008, Available at: http://cdmpipeline.org.

Fenhann, J. (2008b) The CDM Pipeline Is Getting Longer …, Carbon Finance, February 08th, available online at: http://www.carbon-financeonline.com.

Fenhann, J. (2008c) Why Are There So Many Small-Scale CDM Projects? Carbon Finance May 19th available online at: http://www.carbon-financeonline.com.

Figueres, C., Philips, M. (2007) Scaling Up Demand-Side Energy Efficiency Improvements Through Programmatic CDM. ESMAP Technical Paper 120/07, Washington, DC: Energy Sector Management Assistance Program and The World Bank Carbon Finance Unit.

IEA (2008) International Energy Agency, Mind the Gap, Quantifying Principal-Agent Problems in Energy Efficiency. Paris: IEA.

Nakhooda, S. (2008) Correcting The World's Greatest Market Failure: Climate Change and the Multilateral Development Banks. Washington, DC: World Resources Institute Issue Brief.

Painuly, J., Park, H., Lee, M.K., Noh, J. (2003) Promoting Energy Efficiency Financing and ESCOs in Developing Countries: Mechanisms and Barriers. Journal of Cleaner Production 11:659–665.

PointCarbon (2008) Trading Carbon, Graphs and Charts, Data. Vol. 2(9):42–43, November.

Roine, K., Tvinnreim, E., Hasselknippe, H. (eds.) (2008) Carbon 2008 – Post-2012 Is Now. Oslo: PointCarbon Report.

SouthSouthNorth (2005) Profile of CDM Project Activity, Kuyasa Low-Cost Urban Housing Energy Upgrade Project, Khayelitsha (Cape Town, South Africa), Project Documentation, available at: http://www.southsouthnorth.org/default.asp?/country_home.asp?country_id=11.

Taylor, R., Govindarajalu, C., Levin, J., Meyer, A., Ward, W. (2008) Financing Energy Efficiency: Lessons from Brazil, China, India, and Beyond. Washington, DC: World Bank.

UNEP RISOE (2007) Guidebook to Financing CDM Projects. Capacity Development for CDM (CD4CDM) Project. Roskilde, Denmark: UNEP RISOE Centre.

UNFCCC (2002) Report of the 7th Conference of the Parties, held at Marrakesh. Official Document. Bonn: United Framework Convention on Climate Change.

WEC (World Energy Council) (2008) Energy Efficiency Policies Around the World: Review and Evaluation. London, UK: World Energy Council.

CHAPTER 6

UNEP Perspectives

Paul Clements-Hunt[*]

1 Introduction

This chapter describes how, since the mid-1980s, a slow-burning, push-and-pull dynamic between public policy and public sentiment regarding environment and sustainability is succeeding in changing the basis upon which our capital markets and financial institutions view the financial materiality of environmental, social and governance (ESG) issues. It shows that the manner in which the financial services sector and the broader investment chain integrate natural and social value at risk into their risk considerations is changing, albeit slowly, across the mainstream. In time, these changes mean that the risks and market opportunities associated with, amongst others, climate change, resource depletion, the destruction of ecosystems, social challenges and human rights issues, may be more fully integrated into financial, investment and capital market considerations.

The "maybe" is an important element. After several years of intense activity concerning ESG issues across different facets of the financial services sector, the financial crisis of 2007–2009 has created a fork in the road. The destruction of value, cost cutting and job losses across the financial services sector may prompt a demotion of ESG issues to a marginal add-on, as the thinkers within sustainability and business units are squeezed into a short term "results, results, results" focus. Alternatively, the sector has the opportunity to take the "road less travelled" and embed ESG considerations into their policy-making, their business practice and, critically, the culture of finance and investment, in a manner that delivers results which are aligned with shifting public policy and public sentiment. Notably, the "G" of ESG, given the systemic and institutional governance debacles of the financial and economic collapse, demands attention. Despite the "green-tech, clean-tech, low- carbon" thrust of the over USD 3 trillion global public stimulus packages, there is no guarantee that mainstream finance and investment will opt for this path ahead of the next asset bubble forming.

Finally, this chapter shows how the unfolding financial and economic crisis of 2007–2009 has posed some fundamental questions for the concepts of sustainable finance and responsible investment (SFRI). Given the near-breakdown of our fi-

* Head, UNEP Finance Initiative.

D. Köhn (ed.), *Greening the Financial Sector: How to Mainstream Environmental Finance in Developing Countries*, DOI 10.1007/978-3-642-05087-9_6,

nancial system in the final quarter of 2008 and the loss of some "too big to fail" institutions, the reality of SFRI, quite rightly, should come under intense forensic examination. To date, this examination has not been undertaken to a sufficient degree by the SFRI community.

2 The Friday Before Doomsday 2008

On 12 September, 2008, the Friday before Lehman Brothers collapsed and at least one money market fund "broke the buck" for the first time in 14 years, a group of financial executives, climate change campaigners and lawyers met in a HSBC meeting room 28 floors above Canary Wharf in the revamped heart of London's Old Docklands. Despite the gathering gloom associated with the unfolding financial meltdown that had been gaining pace since August 2007, the energy and focus on next steps for finance and investment in the climate change arena remained robust. The meeting at HSBC had been called to foster stronger links between the different facets of financial services on the road to the United Nation's annual climate change summits, held in Poznan, Poland, in December 2008, and then a year later in Copenhagen, Denmark.

At the heart of the discussions in Canary Wharf was the idea that climate change has the potential to bring devastating economic and financial losses while offering the prospect of new markets for financial services. In June 2007, a group of 23 CEOs of financial institutions brought together by UNEP Finance Initiative (FI) warned the Heads of State at the G8 meeting that "Unless action is taken now to set in motion a worldwide transition to a low carbon economy, some scenarios suggest that by 2040, the world could experience annual economic losses as high as USD 1 trillion; and grave social and environmental harm from climate-related disasters."[1]

Earlier in 2002, a landmark UNEP FI study predicted that economic losses from climate change and natural disasters would reach USD 150 billion a year by 2012. The figure was reached seven years early in 2005 and, once again, in 2008 the economic loss figure according to UNEP FI member company Munich Reinsurance Group has topped USD 200 billion, with insured losses rising to USD 45 billion. Announcing the 2008 figures, the Munich Re Group stated: "Driven by high losses from weather-related natural catastrophes, 2008 was – on the basis of figures adjusted for inflation – the third most expensive year on record … Climate change has already started and is very probably contributing to increasingly frequent weather extremes and ensuing natural catastrophes." The scale of the economic and financial risks associated with climate change, which are capable of impacting whole economies and global industries, cannot be ignored by forward-looking institutions that take their fiduciary responsibility seriously and seek to

---

[1] Extract from the "Declaration on Climate Change by the Financial Services Sector", 5 June, 2007, UNEP FI Statement for the G8 Heads of State meeting in Germany.

grow and protect their clients' assets over the long-term. The participants at the 12 September meeting in London clearly recognized this fact.

How have we come to the point where the CEOs of the world's largest financial institutions are warning policymakers, in clear economic and financial terms, of the coming environmentally- triggered threat to our communities, ecosystems, markets and institutions? Is this merely a blip driven by the spotlight focused on climate change in recent years or is there something deeper?

To understand these changes we have to cast our attention back to 1987 and remember the hope and optimism that came with the vision in the report "Our Common Future" presented by the Brundtland Commission. That report, which captured the work of the United Nations World Commission on Environment and Development, set in place the political context that has enabled environment and development to be discussed as one issue. This global discussion over the past twenty years, while complex and at times glacial and often infuriating, has yielded a way of thinking and a set of disciplines that are now infecting markets like a virus. The most forward-thinking segments of mainstream finance and investment are responding. The end result of this way of thinking fuses the ethical and ESG dimensions of business with the business case. It does this in a manner that can help bridge the gap between those who demand an ethical and ESG foundation to underpin all business activity with those who demand a business case based on financial materiality.

What do I mean? The Brundtland Commission emboldened governments to undertake the 1992 Rio Earth Summit, which itself delivered international agreements – frameworks in fact – dealing with climate change, biodiversity and desertification. The landmark gathering of world leaders in Brazil also yielded Agenda 21 and the Rio Declaration, and saw the creation of the UN Commission for Sustainable Development. In 2000, the Millennium Development Goals were unveiled by former UN Secretary General Kofi Annan and the UN Global Compact was established. In 2002, when the World Summit for Sustainable Development gathered in Johannesburg and in December 2007 – on the mystical isle of Bali – the global community finally seemed to jointly "get it" on global warming. The people and bodies involved in this 20-year process were, to say the very least, often a long way removed from the worlds of high finance and capital markets.

However, the community that has delivered the concept, mechanisms and tools to foster sustainable development has now captured both the attention and creative imagination of the finance and investment community. If one were to fast forward the tape from Brundtland in 1987 to today, one would trace a period when – quite rightly – the role and responsibilities of the markets and business have been forensically dissected as never before. That dissection continues anew today as amid the wreckage of the latest market implosion. Through a twenty two-year period of unimaginable political, social and economic change, the issues around the ethical, environmental, governance and social responsibilities of business have remained a constant, nagging and unresolved series of complex questions. The context set by "Our Common Future" and carried on through Rio de Janeiro, Johannesburg and

Bali drove a process that demanded new thinking from business and, more recently, has demanded new thinking from the mainstream finance and investment community.

The responses by the business and financial services community have yielded a myriad of initiatives and activities – at the global, national and sectoral levels – that have set the stage for a fundamental change in the way we do business, secure finance and make investments in the decades to come. Whether through the World Business Council for Sustainable Development (WBCSD) in the early 1990s, the emergence of UNEP Finance Initiative in 1992, the evolution of the United Nations Global Compact (UNGC) since 1999, or the Principles for Responsible Investment in 2006, the business community and, latterly, the financial services and investment community, have been encouraged to focus on the financial materiality of the questions raised by the Brundtland Commission. Greater granularity was added to these questions through subsequent international, regional and national agreements covering climate, biodiversity, water, waste and chemicals management, amongst other issues.

3 ESG and Risk as It Really Is

For our capital markets, for the financial services sector and for the businesses and companies they invest in, the ESG threats identified and classified over these 20 plus years of public policy debate, discussion and implementation need to be understood and, ideally, they need to be quantified as risks understandable to the full range of market actors. The ability to understand and quantify risks sets modern developed society apart from the past and, only now – in a faltering and imperfect manner – is this thinking to the planet itself and the systems and resources that underpin all human development. Ironically, the past two years have seen the markets' financial risk management rule book – built on the altars of efficient market theory, modern portfolio theory and sophisticated financial modelling – thrown out of the window.

Up until August 2007, it appeared that the global financial services sector had managed, finally, to tame the gene of risk as finance traditionally had seen it, through the evolution of complex financial models, the deployment of structured finance and the emergence of derivatives to spread risk more effectively across the system. The concepts of Value at Risk and financial materiality appeared to have anchored a system that enabled more adventurous financial engineering that freed up credit markets. Post crisis, the different actors in the financial services system – asset owners, asset managers, banks and insurers – will have to work hard to reconfigure their understanding of the best way to assess, manage, transfer and contain risk at both the institutional and financial system levels This will take place as the political, policy and regulatory disciplines that govern our financial and capital market systems and institutions are themselves fundamentally overhauled.

At the same time, and as the economic perils of climate change, resource depletion and ecosystems destruction become more apparent, there is an accelerating need for our capital markets and financial institutions to understand how natural and social value at risk will impact their business within both short- and long-term horizons. This need and its implications for our economies give rise to a series of complex questions for the broader business community and, most notably, for the financial services sector. These questions are crucial for those parts of the system, such as the pensions and investment sector, which need to protect and grow assets over the long-term. The questions under consideration include:

- How do we value and price systems that support life and enable economic and social development?
- How do we place a future value and price on these planetary support systems?
- In effect, how do we value our options for a secure economic, social and environmental future?

These are questions of great complexity and, most certainly, our economists will at a global level play a role in addressing them. However, it is essential that our financial institutions, lead by the investment community, ask these questions and seek answers if they are to deepen their understanding of the impacts of natural and social value at risk. This is also crucial to enable financial institutions to identify early those new vibrant global markets and investment opportunities associated with sustainable development.

At a global level, what are these emerging risks to our planet and the economies and societies it supports? In October 2007, the United Nations Environment Programme released its fourth Global Environment Outlook report, known as GEO-4. Every four years this planetary assessment is updated as UNEP explores the state of the world. GEO-4 made for disturbing reading; it is worth highlighting a number of its key findings that are particularly relevant for the global investment community:

- First, environmental exposures now cause almost 25% of all diseases, including respiratory diseases, cancers and emerging animal-to-human disease transfers;
- Second, around the globe more than two million people die prematurely because of air pollution;
- Third, two billion people are likely to suffer absolute water scarcity by 2025;
- Fourth, only one in ten of the world's major rivers reaches the sea all year round;
- Fifth, all species, including animals and plants, are becoming extinct at rates 100 times faster than those derived from fossil records;
- Finally, fish stocks, a key protein source for several billion people, are in crisis. Some 30% of global fish stocks are classed as collapsed and 40% as over exploited.

In summary, the GEO-4 report warned that the world's current population of 6.75 billion people has reached a stage where "the amount of resources needed to sustain it exceeds what is available." Indeed, GEO-4 was a haunting wake up call for all of the earth's inhabitants, and it outlines clear dangers for future generations. Yet within this detailing of threats and risks there exists for the financial services sector the seeds of future opportunity. For each economic, social and environmental risk highlighted above there exists investment opportunities, potential innovative insurance products and bankable projects. The markets that will provide the most explosive commercial opportunities and the index-beating returns of coming decades are already emerging. The brightest and most forward-thinking investors are preparing to benefit from the markets, asset classes and investments that will define the 21st century. I would like to highlight a few of these new opportunities:

- First, global carbon markets stood at USD 126 billion[2] in 2008 and clean energy markets are expected to approach or surpass USD one trillion by 2020 given a supportive policy environment. Whatever questions of political uncertainty exist around the future of carbon markets post 2012, it is clear that the most forward-thinking business leaders understand that the future is carbon-constrained. These leaders are working to re-engineer their products and services to serve and profit from this new economic context. The world's largest investors are also looking at a whole new range of opportunities associated with the emergence of the "green, carbon-proofed" economy. In the seven months from September 2006 to March 2007, carbon funds jumped to USD 11.8 billion, an increase in value of approximately 50%, or USD 4.7 billion. Investment capital flowing into renewable energy jumped from USD 80 billion in 2005 to USD 100 billion in 2006 – and then to USD 148 billion in 2007.[3] Despite the severe economic downturn, the capital flowing into renewable energy in 2008 was close to the 2007 figure. In February 2008, a group of nearly 50 institutional investors, building on the work of the Investor Network on Climate Risk and managing over USD 1.75 trillion in assets, backed a climate change action plan, "… that will boost investments in energy efficiency and clean energy technologies and require tougher scrutiny of carbon-intensive investments that may pose long-term financial risks."
- Second, for the first time in 2006 more than 50% of humanity lived in cities. Many of these are mega cities in developing countries, where life for the poorest citizens – often for environmental reasons – is brutally hard. The markets for environmental utilities and new integrated approaches to old urban challenges – such as water supply, flood control, urban and in-

[2] "State and Trends of the Carbon Markets," World Bank, 2009.

[3] New Energy Finance/ UNEP, 2008.

dustrial wastewater, municipal solid waste management, emission and pollution control, mass rapid transit systems and clean energy – will be some of the most dynamic markets of coming decades. Innovative investment approaches and financial engineering around environmental utilities which align public needs and private capabilities will become an attractive asset class in its own right;

- Third, markets for biodiversity and ecosystems services will become, in time, buoyant areas of commercial and investment activity. The scale of the coming opportunities is captured by the fact that the value of carbon locked in the boreal forests of Canada alone at USD 3.7 trillion falls just short of the annual premiums collected in 2007 by the world's largest industry, namely insurance.

4 Changes in Finance and Investment – Real or Illusionary?

Digging deeper into how these developments at the international level have affected, over more than 20 years, the thinking and working of the capital markets and financial institutions, one is struck by the slow, smouldering and almost unobservable nature of the change. In short, twenty plus years of debate, policy discussions, imperfect policy innovation and an embedding of ESG disciplines in the working of the markets have seen finance and investment wake, not only to the risk management aspects of ESG integration, but more recently to the upside market opportunities that ESG has to offer. This is not to say that finance and investment have been transformed into a paragon of sustainability, but rather that the global financial services community is beginning to see the "value in the business case of values". A quick look at the key developments in various sub-sectors of financial services confirms this.

Whether the investment, banking, or insurance fields, the period 2003–2009 has witnessed a staggering range of new initiatives as institutions, individually and collectively, have focused on their role in SFRI.

5 Investment

In April 2006, the launch of the Principles for Responsible Investment (PRI), now backed by more than 500 institutions representing assets of USD 18 trillion, heralded a significant change for the world's largest institutional investors. This change has profound implications for the way capital markets work, for the financial service organizations that compete in those markets, and for the companies that raise capital on those markets. A month ahead of the July 2009 PRI annual meeting in Sydney, the gathering was already oversubscribed with a sound global representation – despite the travel restrictions and cost-cutting reality so many investment institutions face.

Despite the dynamic nature of the PRI and associated responsible investment initiatives, some observers allege that the work underway is little more than a public relations exercise, at a time when the public, clients and politicians have become increasingly sensitised to environmental issues, notably climate change, and also to scandals in the marketplace as a result of the high profile corporate debacles in the early years of this century. Those sceptical about the upsurge in ESG-focused activities within financial services and capital markets often question the real impact of voluntary initiatives such as UNEP FI, the UNGC and the PRI. Others see that forward-looking financial institutions are re-casting their policies and operations to finance the entrepreneurs, technologies and companies of the future, rather than being seen as institutions and investors associated with the grime of the industrial past. In effect, they are embedding a new ESG-supporting DNA, which plays a role in determining corporate identity, values and activity. Leading institutions are beginning to understand the public policy changes around ESG that have taken place over the past twenty years and the shift in public sentiment: they are adjusting to the dawning of a new reality that resonates at a deeper level than the credit crisis.

Importantly, the emergence of the PRI reflects a growing understanding and appetite amongst the world's largest institutional investors – pension funds, special government reserves and foundations – that a fuller integration of ESG in their investment policy-making and decisions can provide a more effective tool to manage new risks and builds a better understanding of new market opportunities. In time, dynamic implementation of the commitments created by the PRI has the power to align more effectively the entire investment chain with ESG thinking and values. The PRI came about, in part, because the timing in the marketplace was right. That is reconfirmed by the fact that just three years after the former UN Secretary General Kofi Annan launched the PRI at the New York Stock Exchange, nearly USD 18 trillion in assets now backs this voluntary set of principles. The sheer size and influence of the asset-owning institutions backing the PRI, in many cases the largest universal investors owning chunks of entire markets, is driving change within the asset management community: an increasing number of fund managers realize that their biggest clients want to work with money managers that understand ESG. In the marketplace there is growing evidence of how fund managers are reacting to serve this growing ESG demand from the institutional investment community.

6 Banking

Few of the world's leading global banks do not now understand the need to set in place policies and procedures that set out their position with respect to sustainable finance. The challenge of driving this thinking and approach through the core business lines of massive institutions, often with tens if not hundreds of thousands of employees, is a formidable one that will continue into the next decade. In many instances, there remains significant internal resistance to change amongst banking business units, where the mantra of "results, results, results" has often undervalued or ignored ESG issues. What is changing rapidly amongst an influential group of the most senior banking executives, however, is the understanding that good ESG practice often helps deliver sustainable results for the institution. A notable example is governance: the early lessons of the sub-prime experience and the credit crisis are confirming the importance of honest risk assessment that takes into account a full range of risks, traditional and otherwise. At the same time, and as the "war for talent" intensifies, it is becoming apparent that valued professionals coming into the financial services labour market increasingly want to work for institutions where responsibility is part of the fabric of the organization, rather than just part of the public relations department. The crisis of 2008–9 has intensified this sentiment as markets pick up and financial institutions start to hire the next crop of bankers to serve the post-crisis markets. A combination of this evolving top-down philosophy of the most senior management and the bottom-up desire from bank staff to work for organisations that understand both value and values will drive and accelerate change within the largest of the institutions.

Ranging from climate change, water and ecosystems services to human rights issues, as well as the responsibility of financial service organisations in regions of conflict, the sustainability and responsibility agendas for the banking sector have grown exponentially since 2003. At the same time, the basic tools for analysing, reporting and measuring the impact of the various policy and practice approaches have evolved. For example, the Global Reporting Initiative (GRI) initiated a process during 2004–6 that saw a group of major banks, cooperating with insurers, asset managers and a multi-stakeholder group, develop a financial services sector reporting protocol. The GRI Financial Services Sector Supplement was piloted by a group of banks during the 2006–7 sustainability and Corporate Social Responsibility reporting cycle, and it was then launched in October of that year. Critically, the GRI reporting protocol was based on the need to report indirect impacts of financial service organisation operations, thereby extending the reporting requirement to the impact of the institutions' products and services

Taking examples from two contrasting areas of activity, project finance and private banking, gives a sense of how very different arms of banking are striving to understand complex issues and build them into their operations, products and services.

For banks involved in project finance, the emergence in 2003 of the Equator Principles, based on International Finance Corporation (IFC) guidelines, has been a revelation. By June 2009, nearly 70 banks and financial institutions representing more than 85% of global project finance volume had signed the ten principles that cover environmental and social issues related to projects with a total capital cost above USD 10 million. The original principles were revised and strengthened in 2006. A 2007 memo from the law firm LeBoeuf, Lamb and Greene & MacRae, co-authored by international environmental law expert, Paul Q. Watchman, states: "Though the EP are non-binding, they have become an extremely important factor in the project finance market. There are no sanctions for breach of the EP but given their prevalence, the importance attached to compliance with the EP by leading bankers and the ever-increasing scrutiny of projects by civil society, it can be said that there is strong pressure to adopt the EP."

Separately, the private banking community that serves the rich and super rich, as well as institutional clients, are waking to the growing demand for responsible investment products from their clients. By 2012, the expectation is that global assets of High Net Worth Individuals (HNWI) will reach close to USD 60 trillion. By the end of 2008, some 10 million people worldwide were considered to have high net worth, with the average wealth of this category surpassing USD 4 million for the first time and total assets reaching USD 40.7 trillion. In 2007–8 the Middle East, Eastern Europe and Latin America advanced more rapidly than the other regions. Market analysis indicates that 32% of the HNWI community finds ESG investment concepts attractive, yet to date just 4–5% of HNWI assets integrate ESG factors in any way. Increasingly, innovative private banking institutions are seeing ESG-inclusive investment as a business opportunity and source of competitive advantage.

7 Insurance

The insurance industry is a strong lever for implementing sustainability due to its size, the extent of its reach into communities and the significant role it plays in the global economy. In 2007, the worldwide premium volume exceeded USD 4 trillion, making insurance the largest industry in the global economy, while its global assets under management stood at USD 19.9 trillion.

The insurance and reinsurance community were amongst the first financial service organisations to engage and explain the long-term economic risks posed by climate change. A group of the largest financial companies now agree that a USD 1 trillion loss in a given year by 2040 is a viable scenario. The Stern Report, commissioned by the UK Government, underpinned work undertaken in recent years by insurers and re-insurers highlighting the potentially catastrophic global economic costs of no or low climate action.

Apart from climate change, the insurance industry is now starting to explore the commercial viability of conceiving, developing and rolling out new products and services that address global sustainability issues. The industry is beginning to realize the macro potential of microinsurance – insurance for the poor – as both a prime business opportunity and a powerful tool for sustainable development. Products and services that address environmental impairment liability, aging populations and lifelong income, modern day health risks, and weather insurance for farmers are coming to the fore. Potential new markets include insurance for emerging man-made risks and the protection of natural resources, in particular, biodiversity, ecosystems and water. The insurance industry is also awakening to the fact that acting sustainably, as in the cases of internal resource efficiency and the recycling of damaged assets, save money and are concrete ways of leading by example. Beyond their raison d'être of managing and carrying risks, insurers are major institutional investors and increasingly recognise that responsible investment is a critical component of the overall sustainable insurance agenda. A group of insurers convened by UNEP FI is developing the Principles for Sustainable Insurance (PSI) for the global industry. This effort will provide a responsibility framework that mirrors the PRI conceived for the investment community. As part of UNEP FI's efforts to support the evolution of PSI, a global survey of insurers and re-insurers has been undertaken during late 2008–9. The survey obtained more than 250 respondents across the insurance value chain and other stakeholders from over 50 countries representing the regions Africa, Asia-Pacific, Europe, Latin America and the Caribbean, and North America. The results of the survey and a comprehensive analytical report were released at UNEP FI's 2009 Global Roundtable, "Financing change, Changing finance" that took place in Cape Town, South Africa from 22–23 October 2009.

8 The United Nations Promoting ESG

During this time, different arms of the United Nations were actively pushing the ESG agenda amongst the global finance and investment communities in order to prompt sustainability and ESG-focused initiatives at the sectoral and institutional levels. Uniting these efforts was the underlying question: how do financial institutions, investors and the capital markets deal with ESG issues? These activities gave real momentum to the emergence of the PRI. Within weeks of the publication of the first UNGC and UNEP FI reports focused on responsible investment in June 2004, the UN launched an initiative to create a responsible investment framework for pension funds and other large institutional investors. In time, this framework would become the PRI. On 16 July 2004, The Financial Times reported: "The United Nations has launched a campaign with leading pension funds and other large asset managers to develop a set of guiding principles for responsible investing."[4] Three of the United Nation's key efforts in this area are outlined below.

9 The UNGC Who Cares Wins Series and Stock Exchange Engagement

The "Who Cares Wins" report series was a joint initiative of leading financial institutions invited by then UN Secretary-General Kofi Annan. The research process leading to the first Who Cares Wins report, which was initiated in late 2003, involved some of the investment world's most innovative thinkers in the field of responsible investment. The research, forged through a collaboration of leading

4 Extra-Financial Concerns: "UN to develop responsible investing guideline", Financial Times, 16 July, 2008.

asset management companies, enhanced clarity on the respective roles of different actors in the financial market – from companies, regulators, stock exchanges and investors, to asset managers, brokers, analysts, accountants, financial advisers and consultants – and outlined recommendations on how ESG issues can be better integrated into financial analysis, asset management and securities brokerage. The UN Global Compact launched the first report, "Who Cares Wins – Connecting Financial Markets to a Changing World" at the UNGC Business Leaders Summit, which was held at the UN Headquarters in New York in June 2004. The report, endorsed by the CEOs of more than twenty leading firms in the financial industry, articulated the growing consensus, supported by an increasing body of evidence, that good management of ESG issues enhance company value. It provided a critical impetus to embed ESG issues in mainstream investment practices to achieve the long-term goals of stronger and more resilient financial markets and, accordingly, more sustainable societies. The report also provided one of the cornerstones that supported the process leading to the PRI. The meeting of the minds that generated the in-depth report underscored that collaborative action among stakeholders is imperative in order to realize significant progress. In June 2004, the UN Global Compact also established a bridge to an integral component of the capital markets – stock exchanges. The UN Global compact issued a statement, endorsed by ten of the world's stock exchanges, that these exchanges would explore collaborative initiatives to advance the tenets of good corporate citizenship and trust-building in society. This laid the foundation for the UN Global Compact's work with the World Federation of Exchanges, the international umbrella organisation comprising the world's leading markets. This has propelled an even broader engagement with public companies to which the unequivocal message of responsible investment is fundamental.

10 The UNEP FI Materiality Series

In late 2003, UNEP FI's Asset Management working group, at the time a group of 14 asset managers collectively representing USD 1.7 trillion in assets under management, asked whether the materiality of a range of ESG issues traditionally overlooked or undervalued by many investment approaches should be reconsidered. To move the exercise forward, the UNEP FI Asset Management working group invited a group of the world's leading investment research companies to explore the financial materiality of ESG issues in a range of business and industry sectors. At the heart of the exercise stood the challenge of understanding how different ESG issues in various sectors impacted the value of securities. The resulting studies yielded more than 1,000 pages of research contained in 11 analytical reports undertaken by 10 research companies. Participating institutions included Deutsche Bank, Dresdner Kleinwort Wasserstein, Goldman Sachs, HSBC and UBS. The research was synthesized into a 52-page UNEP FI summary report entitled "The Materiality of Social, Environmental and Governance Issues to Equity

Pricing". The report was published in June 2004. The robust conclusions of the "Mat 1" project, as it became known, UNEP FI launched a meeting of Europe's largest pension funds in Paris in June 2004, during which the results of the research were presented. The Paris meeting heard, for the first time, the suggestion that there should be a responsible investment framework for institutional investors that in time would be realized through the PRI. The success of UNEP FI's Mat I exercise persuaded the UNEP FI Asset Management working group to launch a second call to sell-side researchers to produce further ESG-inclusive research. The resulting "Mat II" study broadened the work on financial materiality to look at additional sectors and methodologies. Institutions participating in the Mat II research included ABN AMRO, Deutsche Bank, Goldman Sachs, JPMorgan, Merrill Lynch, Morgan Stanley and UBS. The resulting summary report, entitled "Show Me The Money: Linking Environmental, Social and Governance Issues to Company Value", found a striking increased sophistication of the work undertaken by analysts compared with the original work. In short, the sell-side's ability to integrate and analyse ESG issues had improved a great deal in a very short time. The reports submitted for the Mat II process describe an emerging taxonomy of ESG risk categories. While not all the reports use the same language, many acknowledge similar factors. Additionally, there are issues that are uniquely important to certain industries or sectors. The findings of Mat II reconfirmed that company valuation is not complete unless it includes a consideration of ESG issues. Regarding the UNEP FI materiality series, the UNEP FI partnership will launch the "Mat III" report, which will explicitly examine the materiality of climate change issues across various business and industry sectors.

11 The UNEP FI Freshfields Report and Fiduciary II – The Legal Underpinning

In parallel to the work undertaken to conceive, frame and launch the PRI, a discussion was started in late 2004 between members of UNEP FI's Asset Management working group with one of the largest law firms in the world, Freshfields Bruckhaus Deringer. The asset managers wanted to understand the legal implications and realities of integrating ESG issues into investment processes within the major capital market jurisdictions worldwide. Paul Q. Watchman, at the time a partner of Freshfields and lead author of the legal interpretation that became known as the Freshfields Report, wrote: "Despite the evidence that ESG issues often have a material impact on the financial performance of investments, many institutional investors still insist that their legal duties prevent them from taking such issues into account. In short, institutional investors who hide behind profit maximisation and the limits supposedly placed by their legal duties do so at their own peril. There is no legal bar to the integration of ESG considerations into decision making (provided the focus is always on the beneficiaries)."

Clearly, much progress has been made since the publication of the original Freshfields Report, but more can and must be done. In July 2009, UNEP FI has launched a follow on to the original Freshfields report, with the working title "Fiduciary II". This report will serve as a sequel to the original report in both scope and spirit. The purpose of the report is to provide a roadmap for fiduciaries looking for concrete steps to operationalise their commitment to responsible investment.

Specifically, the report offers guidance on the following areas:

- Legal commentary on fiduciary duty and the implementation of ESG in investment mandates, including sample ESG language for investment management contracts to legally require asset managers to provide ESG integration services;
- Best practices being developed by investment consultants on ESG integration, including the assessment of asset managers' competencies in providing ESG-inclusive investment strategies and approaches;
- Practical developments on ESG integration, which provide insights into the extent to which institutional investors have adopted, and can adopt, longer-term and more sustainable investment approaches; and a review of legal developments on fiduciary duty and ESG issues since and including the Freshfields Report.

12 The Good News and the Bad News

Despite the intense SFRI activity since 2003 across the banking, investment and insurance sectors, where does the financial and investment community stand today? Clearly, the developments in SFRI must be set within the context: once again, capitalism has teetered on the brink through one of its episodic crises. A combination of experimentation in financial engineering, greed and misdeeds in our financial markets has endangered the real economy. From 2007 through 2009, the sub-prime credit crunch wiped trillions of dollars from the market; and this has been followed by a severe global economic downturn. The market's memory is indeed a short one. From the Mexican crises of 1995, through the Asian collapse in 1997, the 1998 demise of Long-term Capital Management that was linked to turbulence in Russian markets, followed by the dot com boom and bust and the governance meltdowns that plagued the markets at the turn of the century, we have become accustomed to these all-too-frequent shivers and shifts in the tectonic plates of the markets. Some would say that such volatility is simply part of the destructive creation that comes with our powerful and increasingly interlinked markets.

The nine months following the 12 September climate meeting at Canary Wharf saw hundreds of thousands of job cuts globally across the financial sector and intense pressure levied inside institutions to cut costs to the bone. There is no question that sustainability units within banks, insurers and asset management companies have suffered losses; nascent teams carefully assembled during the boom years to service emerging environmental markets (climate, water, biodiversity, infrastructure, microfinance) have been emasculated.

In these crises, which atomise value and jeopardize the economic well-being of communities and families worldwide, ethical and governance issues are often unearthed as causes and drivers of value destruction. As public policy shifts to reflect deepening concern for our planetary challenges, resource constraints, and social tensions based on inequality and environmental threats, the liabilities associated with environmental and social factors will contribute increasingly to these intermittent processes of value destruction. Must the investment community, ranging from the world's largest institutional investors to the "mom and pop" retail savers seeking a reasonable return on their retirement investments,, accept the occasional ethical, environmental, social or governance landmine, as they invest in the future? In a worst case scenario, these create unimaginable systemic risk for the global financial system. The jury is still out as the financial system and markets seek to remake themselves, and as they are remade by policy-makers and regulators who understand now how close the system came to collapse after the doomsday of Monday, 15 September 2008.

Those involved in promoting SFRI thinking and approaches must also ensure a deep examination to understand how SFRI approaches can be deployed more effectively in years to come. Without an honest and urgent assessment of SFRI's contribution to date, the opportunity presented by the crisis of 2007–9 to accelerate and further embed an SFRI approach in mainstream finance and investment will be lost. This approach should include the integration of ESG issues into the entire investment chain. Broad guiding questions that should be asked include:

- At worst, is SFRI as practiced a public relations fig leaf for financial institutions that, in reality, threw honest risk management to the wind? Institutions that signed up to a range of SFRI-focused codes and disciplines were, over the past decade, driving and benefiting from new exotic markets; the outstanding notional value of over-the-counter (OTC) derivatives contracts approached the staggering figure of USD 600 trillion by the end of 2008.[5] Some 975 commercial banks, a significant number of these professing adherence to various sustainability and corporate social responsibility codes, were holding derivatives by 2008. Is a financial institution's adherence to SFRI incompatible with reckless excesses in the marketplace? What needs to change to see SFRI rolled out cohesively across institutions policies, practices and cultures?

- How have the world's seemingly most conservative institutional investors, which bear serious fiduciary duties that affect the well-being of future generations, faired in the aftermath of the financial crisis? These institutions,

5 "Let Battle Commence," Financial Times, Wednesday, 20 May 2009.

whether pension funds, sovereign wealth funds, special government reserves or foundations, woke up in 2009 with a titanic credit crisis hangover after having asked very few pertinent governance questions – the "G" of ESG – about the financial institutions whose rising stocks they were investing in during the boom years. Many of these institutions had recently converted to the concept of respsonsible investment. How can SFRI ensure that the institutional investors ask the right questions —ahead of time – next time?

- Were SFRI disciplines and advocacy a simple "nice to have" add-on during the boom years, while the main business units of many financial institutions conceived, developed and rolled out products suited to the Goldilocks economy? Such financial products were in reality built on global imbalances and a tidal wave of cheap money and easy credit that duped regulators and swamped western consumers. How can SFRI be integrated in a pervasive, holistic way in financial institutions?

Developments at the international level over the past twenty years have changed – in ways not yet fully apparent – the political and economic context to the way that our societies, ecosystems, markets and finance interact. The finance and investment community has reached a fundamental fork in the road; the path littered with ethical and environmental, social and governance (ESG) landmines does not have to be followed. The finance and investment community – by better understanding the ethical and ESG dimensions of the market while, importantly, appreciating the need to build the investment business case around the ideas, entrepreneurs, technologies and companies that will define the future – can play a leading role in determining a positive, inclusive future development path.

CHAPTER 7

Trading of Emission Certificates for Climate Protection: Using Markets and Private Capital for Development

*Rainer Durth**

The realisation that climate change is caused and can also be stopped by humankind gained increasing recognition in 2007. The magic threshold up to which an increase in the average global temperature is considered to be still tolerable is between 2° and 3° Celsius. If this threshold is exceeded, the consequences are significant and almost impossible to control. In order to avoid this, greenhouse gas emissions will have to be cut in half against 1990 emission levels over the next 40 years around the globe. To achieve this, the European Union set itself ambitious goals in early 2007.

It has resolved

- to reduce its carbon dioxide emissions by 20% against 1990 levels. If a successor to the Kyoto Protocol can be agreed upon, it even considers a reduction by 30%;
- to improve energy efficiency in Europe by 20% percent by the year 2020; and
- to meet 20% of end-energy consumption in the EU with renewable energies by the year 2020.

1 Kyoto and the Consequences for Carbon Emissions

What efforts are required to achieve this becomes clear when we look at the Kyoto Protocol of 1997 – though it did not enter force until 2005 – which for the first time called for a limitation and reduction of greenhouse gas emissions. Under the Protocol, the European Union had aimed for a reduction of 8% in 15 years, and it achieved this objective primarily because the carbon dioxide emissions in many EU accession countries in Eastern Europe were declining anyway after the collapse of socialism. Now, another 12% reduction of the carbon dioxide emissions of 1990 is being aimed for in only eight years. Again, the reduction may increase

* Head of Division, KfW Carbon Fund.

D. Köhn (ed.), *Greening the Financial Sector: How to Mainstream Environmental Finance in Developing Countries*, DOI 10.1007/978-3-642-05087-9_7,

up to 22% if a successor to the Kyoto Protocol materialises. This time, however, these reductions must be achieved without the "coincidental benefits". And after these cuts, further similar reductions must be achieved before 2050.

These goals are set to be achieved in a twofold manner: first, via promotional programmes of the German Federal Government and legislation consistently targeted at reducing carbon dioxide emissions (established in the Meseberg decisions of the Federal Government); and second, through the revision and expansion of the European Emission Trading System (ETS) for carbon emissions.

What does the carbon dioxide emission trading scheme look like? The fundamental idea behind the market for certificates is relatively simple: climate change is said to be caused by the emission of specific gases. The most well-known of these gases, carbon dioxide (CO_2), is a product of all combustion processes. The impact of carbon dioxide on the Earth's climate is completely independent of who emits the CO_2 and where it is emitted. In order to contain climate change, the emission of these gases must be reduced. The reduction requirements under the Kyoto Protocol, however, currently apply only to industrialised countries.

2 Advantages of Trading in Certificates

In order to keep the costs of reducing CO_2 emissions as low as possible, the Kyoto Protocol permits a country to purchase carbon dioxide emission reductions in another country. To enable trading, a title of ownership of CO_2 emission allowances was created in 1997. Purchasing a certificate allows the newly-entitled owner to emit an additional tonne of carbon dioxide, while selling a certificate obliges the seller to reduce emissions by one tonne. The ownership rights can be traded so that CO_2 emissions are reduced where it is least expensive for all parties involved. Many countries break down the restrictions among their enterprises. In Europe, this is done for roughly half of European enterprises within the framework of the Emission Trading System.

Carbon dioxide emission reductions are usually least expensive where the relevant facilities do not just have to be converted but actually need to be erected. This is usually the case in developing and emerging countries, for which no cap on CO_2 emissions has yet been set. However, the participation of these countries in the international market for certificates is highly desirable for two reasons: first, they can reduce carbon dioxide emissions at a particularly low cost; and second, they accrue development benefits from the quite significant international capital inflows. This is why the so-called "Clean Development Mechanism" (CDM) was created. Individual projects or programmes which advance a country's industrial and ecological development are evaluated to determine the quantity of CO_2 reductions they will bring about. Certificates are issued for these reductions which the project owner can then sell.

An example of a typical project is a wind farm in India which generates urgently needed electricity using renewable energy, that is, without any emissions. The project owner can sell the certificates to a German energy provider and invest the proceeds in the next wind farm, which might then operate with even more advanced technology. Through this process, climate protection and development can be mutually reinforcing.

2.1 How Are Ownership Rights Awarded?

Ownership rights describe the possibilities for using scarce resources. The ownership rights which are the object of the market for certificates are pollution rights. They are an entitlement to emit carbon dioxide into the atmosphere and were only created under the Kyoto Protocol in 1997. The initiator at the time was the USA, which has been working with similar environmental concepts since the 1980s in order to reduce sulphur dioxide emissions at as low a cost as possible. In 2005, the Kyoto Protocol entered into force. For European enterprises, it went into effect with the introduction of the ETS, which also began operating in 2005. From an economic perspective, an unprecedented experiment has taken place over the past roughly ten years: an entirely new, rather abstract right of ownership was created in international negotiations, and it is now being traded in a novel, global market.

The new ownership title raises many exciting questions. How are the emissions capped in the industrialised countries? Under which rules are the ownership rights actually awarded to project owners in developing countries? Does emissions trading really promote the development of these countries? Another interesting aspect is the emerging market for trading the ownership rights. How is a price for carbon dioxide set? To what extent does the market function on its own; where does the market fail? Today, international financial markets are highly differentiated. How are the risks spread in the nascent market for certificates? Which of the otherwise customary financial derivatives are usable in this market? And what parallels are there to the commodity markets and their instruments?

2.2 A Staggering Development – Annual Average Growth of 120% Since 2005

The new market for CO_2 certificates is very dynamic. Since the ETS was introduced in the European Union in 2005, it has grown by an average of some 120% annually (until 2009 and on US dollar basis). In 2008 it had a worldwide volume of USD 118 billion, nearly doubling its volume over the previous year. In only five years, the global carbon market has reached the volume of worldwide development assistance payments, which also posted a record year in 2008 (official development assistance in 2008 stood at USD 119 billion). Despite the current crisis, experts anticipate that the carbon markets will continue growing in 2009: an annual volume of USD 150 billion could be achieved within a few months.

Projects in emerging and developing countries currently account for roughly one-fifth of the new market. Revenue generated from the certificates, in turn, partly finances projects whose volume of investment is already roughly equal to

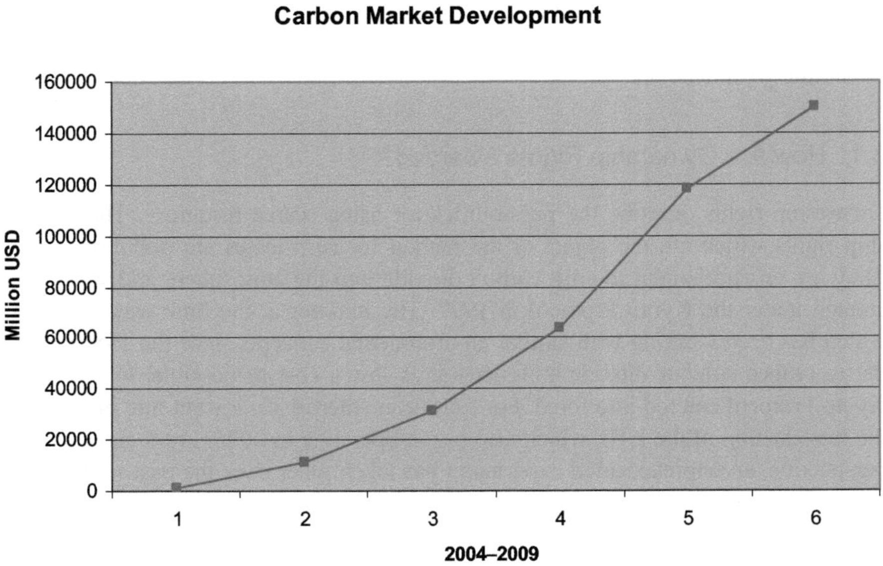

Fig. 1. Staggering growth of market volume – from 2004 to 2009 the global market for carbon emission certificates developed with great dynamism.

the official development assistance provided worldwide. According to expert estimates, by the year 2020 the market for climate protection projects in developing countries may have again increased tenfold. What is particularly intriguing from an economic point of view is the fact that the market can be used as an allocation mechanism, that is, as a mechanism for the large-scale allocation of financial resources, productive forces and materials, to set development processes in motion. The more successfully this can be done, the faster the market for certificates will grow and the more additional resources for development will be available.

Climate change is one of the greatest present-day challenges. By launching the international trade in emission certificates just over ten years ago, a worldwide economic-policy experiment was initiated – with an impressive history of success. Some qualifications also need to be made, however. This emerging market is not yet a perfectly competitive one: efficiency can be increased, thereby reducing the cost of climate protection policy. On the buyer side in particular, there are mostly small numbers of large buyers, such as states and energy supply companies. Information about the market is incomplete, uncertain and usually distributed unevenly among the individual market participants, and adjustments are always slow to be implemented. Moreover, given the uncertain future of the traded ownership rights after 2012, it is important to finalise a so-called "Post-Kyoto Agreement".

Although growth is also expected for 2009, the current economic and financial crisis is having a crippling effect on the market for certificates. The uncertainty over how it will continue after 2012 and the reduced economic activity in industrialised countries are negatively impacting demand for CERs. At the same time, the supply of CERs is pre-established by the projects that were set up years ago and can only partially be adjusted in the short term. This leads to declining prices for CERs and, hence, less incentive to implement a climate protection project. Moreover, in the current environment of economic uncertainty, investors are perceivably more averse to risk. Financing a climate protection project today is much more difficult than just a year ago, particularly in developing countries, where risks are high. Combined, these factors have led to a reduction in the number of new climate protection projects than was originally expected; and there will be a reduced offer of certificates in the future than was originally expected.

3 An Appropriately Engineered Emissions Trading Supports Development Policy

Although the CDM was developed with a view to the developing countries, it must be said that it currently benefits primarily large emerging countries. Roughly 75% of the CER market is in China, India and Brazil, countries whose megacities benefit through their vast energy demand. This means that capital inflows under the CDM are highly concentrated, even more so than those generated by foreign direct investment. And it is precisely the smaller and poorer developing countries that have had little access to this market. Suitable project forms for these countries must urgently be developed; they should also reward improvements made in rural energy demand by issuing certificates. So-called programme-based approaches that enable a large number of small activities covering a large area hold promise for success in these countries.

From the point of view of development policy, the existing market inadequacies should be addressed in such a manner as to effectively facilitate developing countries' access to the rapidly growing market for certificates. The focus should lie on two aspects:

- Uncertainty and risk. Project investors need to have certainty about the expected capital inflows and possible financings. Down payments and guarantees of acceptance for developmentally desirable projects can be helpful in this regard.

- Transaction costs. Using the market for certificates requires extensive expertise and methods tailored to the needs of developing countries. In both cases, development cooperation can achieve much at a low cost.

4 Carbon Funds: Promoting Climate Protection Projects in Developing Countries and Access for Small and Medium-Sized Enterprises from Europe

Investments in CO_2 reductions must be made today. The market for certificates cannot fully unfold its potential unless the existing market inadequacies are effectively addressed. This is an objective pursued by the Carbon Fund of KfW Bankengruppe. The principle of the KfW Carbon Fund is simple. The Fund purchases internationally-recognised certificates from projects that improve energy efficiency or convert energy from renewable sources. In comparison with other funds, the share of certificates from projects in African or Latin American countries is particularly high. In order to enable small and medium-sized European enterprises in particular to access the market for certificates as buyers, KfW acts as a trustee of a buyers' pool in the international market.

In 2004 the KfW Carbon Fund started by focusing on developing the market for emission rights. Since then, the market has developed quite dynamically but, as described above, parts of the market are not yet functional. Now, important individual market segments in which market mechanisms fail must be effectively developed. This may be accomplished, for instance, by:

- developing specific project approaches which benefit the developing countries in particular;
- employing innovative financial products; or
- generating demand for "post-Kyoto certificates" which cannot be generated until after 2012 and for which no legally binding rules are yet in place.

As a promotional bank, KfW assumes a pioneer role, wherever possible together with other European promotional banks.

5 Lessons from Financial and Commodity Markets for Development and Climate Protection Policy

Market mechanisms still need to be harnessed more consistently for development policy measures and for an economically efficient climate protection policy. Here, the young market for certificates can learn much from the international financial and commodity markets. In the market for certificates, there will be an increasing number of new products which will be fraught with risks of their own and will require new hedging mechanisms, for instance hedges against price or climate risks. A wide range of services will therefore emerge around the market for certificates, ranging from specialised certificate brokers and consulting services for monitoring and reporting on avoided CO_2 emissions, for example, to law firms specialising in contractual relations, usually based on common law, involved in the purchase of certificates. Soon the market for certificates will have shed its exotic character and will increasingly reach banks, project developers and development policymakers.

In the future, a particular task for development economists will be to structure the markets and rights of disposal in such a way that they meet the specific needs of the frequently small and poor developing countries better than today. The main issue in the short term will revolve around how developing countries can guard against the consequences of climate change ("adaptation"). In the long term, the question will be: how can they integrate their economic potential with their support of international climate protection policy while pursuing their own development goals ("avoidance")? All along this path, new technologies will be developed and tested on a large scale, and they will have to be made available to developing countries and disseminated there ("technology transfer").

Fig. 2. Landfill in São João, São Paulo, Brazil. The fermenting of waste releases methane which is captured to protect the atmosphere. This facility was partly financed through emission certificates.

CHAPTER 8

Microfinance and Climate Change: Threats and Opportunities

Paul Rippey[*]

Changes to the world's climate that were once imperceptibly slow are now clearly visible and happening quickly. Dying coral reefs, the disappearing arctic ice sheet, and proliferating invasive insects in temperate zone forests are among the most visible signs, but countless less dramatic phenomena show that climate change is real. The changing climate is part of a new global environment that impacts all countries, economies, sectors, and people. Microfinance, like everything else, will not be spared.

Climatologists say that the impact of climate change will fall disproportionately on tropical and semitropical regions. Poor countries, and the poorest people in these countries, will likely be hardest hit. Climate change is an immediate threat to economic development in poor countries, which have the least resources to cope with these changes. Development priorities, such as public health, that had been on a path to resolution are suffering from serious setbacks. Meanwhile, new challenges, including migrations of poor people displaced by drought, heat, flooding, and storms, are appearing (see Box 1).

Box 1: The Effects of Climate Change

The predicted impact of climate change goes way beyond the comfortable warmth suggested by the popular term *global warming*.

Water. Many of the most severe effects of climate change will be related in one way or another to water, fresh and salt, liquid and frozen.

Disappearing Glaciers. With very few exceptions, mountain glaciers are receding rapidly. Glaciers feed rivers that are used for irrigation and drinking water. Forty percent of the world's population gets at least half its water from runoff from the Himalayan glaciers. Runoff from melting glaciers will initially increase flood risk. Later, as glaciers disappear, water supplies will decrease, and people who depend on glacier-fed rivers will suffer.

* Consultant, Climate Change and Microfinance.

D. Köhn (ed.), *Greening the Financial Sector: How to Mainstream Environmental Finance in Developing Countries*, DOI 10.1007/978-3-642-05087-9_8,

Rainfall. The amount and the timing of rainfall are changing around the world. As a broad generalization, temperate areas will initially get more rain, subtropics will get less, and the tropics will have changes that vary widely from region to region. The percentage of land area experiencing extreme drought at any one time could increase from one percent to 30 percent by the end of this century.

Flooding. Two hundred million people, mostly in the developing world, live on coastal flood plains. A temperature increase of three to four degrees could lead to tens or hundreds of millions of people being affected by floods. Sea level rise continuing for centuries or millennia is now inevitable because of the stock of greenhouse gasses already in the atmosphere. But it is not too late for us to influence its extent and speed of change from these gasses.

Ocean Warming and Acidification. Ocean temperatures are increasing, and oceans are becoming more acidic as they absorb CO_2. The effect of warming on fisheries is poorly understood and is probably mixed, depending on the species and the location. Acidification is having unambiguous negative impacts, because acidity affects the ability of ocean creatures to form shells and skeletons. These changes, combined with systematic overfishing, mean that nearly all commercial marine species are declining. According to some projections, essentially all commercial fishing will end within the next 50 years with terrible repercussions: one billion people rely on fish as their principal source of animal protein. FAO estimates that 38 million people earn their living fishing or fish farming.

Heat. The earth is getting hotter, and this trend is accelerating. Temperatures will increase worldwide, though more so in higher latitudes. By cruel irony, many of the areas that will be most negatively affected are in the developing world. Some of the areas that will be least negatively affected, or have net short-term positive effects, are in the colder north, where some of the worst polluters are.

Some parts of the Sahel and other very hot regions may become uninhabitable. Some airports will have to limit flights because of thinner air. But the greatest effects from increased temperature will be on agriculture, because the climate in some areas will become increasingly inhospitable to common plant species.

Ecosystems, Disease Vectors, and Pests. With a 2° C increase in global temperature, 15 to 40 percent of existing species of plants and animals will be at risk of extinction. Unfortunately some harmful species will expand unchecked into new ecological niches that open up as the climate changes. At present levels of heating, the World Health Organization predicts 300,000 additional deaths a year from climate-related diseases (diarrhea, malaria, and malnutrition). A 3° C increase could lead to 1 million to 3 million deaths from malnutrition, and a 4° C increase could lead to 80 million additional people being exposed to malaria. In some cases, the higher levels of CO_2 in the atmosphere may help plant growth through a phenomenon known as carbon fertilization. Unfortunately, carbon fertilization is limited in effect and only partially offsets other climate-related impacts.

Three factors keep insects and other pests in check: vibrant ecosystems with lots of competition; cold nights; and cold winters. All three are diminishing, and there are numerous documented cases of pests moving into new areas.

Extreme Weather Events. With higher temperatures, the frequency, duration, and severity of extreme weather events—flooding rains, high winds, hail storms, and others—are all expected to increase. The amount of damage caused by extreme events is being compounded by increased building on flood plains and other vulnerable areas.

Within the microfinance sector, the word *sustainable* has tended to be used in a very narrow way, mainly referring to institutions that are *financially viable*. In the past few years, the term has broadened to include social performance. Today, the increasing emphasis on responsible finance has added environmental impact to the factors considered as measures of success for a microfinance institution (MFI).

Proponents of responsible finance sometimes speak of the triple bottom line of "profits, people, and planet"—that is, maintaining financial viability while advancing the social interests of stakeholders and protecting the environment. Among many others, Calvert Funds specializes in socially responsible investments, and Triodos assesses social and environmental benefits as criteria for financing institutions and projects. Several MFIs, such as Grameen and BASIX, have begun to address specific aspects of climate change, including the need to reduce emissions. Other MFIs, including ACLEDA in Cambodia, Findesa in Nicaragua, FIE FFP in Bolivia, and Banco Solidario in Ecuador, report on social and environmental, as well as economic performance.

This evolution within microfinance around the understanding of what sustainability really means is positive (see Box 2). Microfinance that is sustainable in this sense meets the definition of sustainable development offered by the Bruntland Commission (1987): meeting the needs of today, without compromising the ability of future generations to meet their needs. The Commission was appointed by the United Nations to examine the "accelerating deterioration of the human environment"—by improving the lives of poor people today and their children's lives in the future.

Box 2: Key Advantages of MFIs in Clean Energy and Forestry

Large, well-managed MFIs are potentially key players in forestry and clean energy projects. In fact, they have the distribution channels, clientele, linkages, credibility, and efficiency that can enable them to reach millions of poor people.

Distribution channels. Financial institutions targeting the poor have an existing client base in the tens of millions of people worldwide.

Clientele and organizational resources. MFIs frequently already include small suppliers of renewable energy equipment and reforestation inputs among their clients and are eager to expand their client base.

Management information systems. Some MFIs have the experience and competence with information systems that will be necessary to track the thousands of small transactions necessary under large tree-planting or household clean energy schemes.

Linkages. Strong MFIs have good relationships with local governments, and they already understand the performance and reporting requirements of international partners.

Credibility and transparency. Financial institutions are necessarily held to high standards of transparency. All credible MFIs have annual audits, and many have been rated or evaluated by international firms.

Efficiency and standardization. At present, prices paid for offsetting carbon emissions are low, which puts a high premium on scale, efficiency, and product standardization. MFIs have already demonstrated, sometimes in the face of skepticism, that they are able to conduct large numbers of small transactions profitably.

This paper proposes ideas for what we can do to combat climate change at the household, microbusiness, MFI, and systemic levels. We hope that MFI managers will be inspired by some of the examples provided. However, each MFI should find its own way of addresing climate change, weighing the risks of inaction against the cost and risks involved in institutional change.

1 Climate Change and Economic Development

Economic development has been possible in large part thanks to the burning of huge quantities of fossil fuels—coal, petroleum, and natural gas. Over the past 50 years, there has been growing realization, first among scientists and now among the broader public and policy makers, that the atmospheric residue of burning fossil fuels, primarily carbon dioxide (CO_2), has created a big problem.

CO_2 and other greenhouse gasses trap the earth's heat and inexorably make the planet hotter and stormier, change rainfall patterns, facilitate invasive pests and diseases, raise sea levels, and generally make life more difficult and less predictable for wealthy people and more precarious for poor people (see Box 3).

Box 3: A Quick Overview of the Science of Climate Change

Anyone who has stood outside on a sunny day has directly experienced the way sunlight heats the earth. It is less obvious that the earth also gives off heat in the form of infrared radiation. This is the heat one can feel radiating up from, say, a paved road in the sun at midday. Most of the heat that is radiated up escapes into space, but a bit is trapped by heavy molecules in the atmosphere, a process called the **greenhouse effect**. Although it is sometimes thought of as a bad thing, the greenhouse effect keeps the world warm enough for plants and animals to live. If all the infrared heat were allowed to escape into space, the earth would be 30° to 50° C cooler, and there would be no life as we know it.

The gasses that trap outgoing infrared radiation are called **greenhouse gasses**. Although there are many such gasses, most efforts to mitigate climate change concentrate on two of them: carbon dioxide (CO_2) and methane. The heat-trapping effect of other greenhouse gasses is often expressed as **carbon dioxide equivalents** (CO_2e), that is, the amount of CO_2 alone that would be required to trap the same amount of heat.

Around the middle of the 19th century, new technologies and industries began to make life easier by enabling us to heat and cool buildings, generate electricity, fuel vehicles, and power machines by burning **fossil fuels**—coal, petroleum, and natural gas. The steady spread of industrialization, the expansion of technology into more and more human activities, and a five-fold increase in the world's population since the beginning of the Industrial Age have meant that the use of fossil fuels has grown rapidly, with a corresponding increase of greenhouse gas emissions into the atmosphere. About half of these gasses are absorbed by the oceans or by growing plants or are broken down by natural processes, while the other half stay in the atmosphere and constitute the stock of greenhouse gasses that is heating the planet today and will do so in the future.

We know from the study of ice cores and other sources that the concentration of CO_2 in the atmosphere never exceeded 300 parts per million (ppm) for a period of at least a million years up to the beginning of the Industrial Age. Since then, the concentration of CO_2 has risen to about 380 ppm. This increase is enough to be the principal cause of the changes we have already seen in the earth's climate; the stock of greenhouse gasses in the atmosphere will continue to cause changes for many years, under any scenario. In fact, there is a time lag between the emissions of climate change and their effects on climate: by the time negative effects begin to be apparent, it is too late to take steps to reverse them.

The amount of CO_2 and the increase in global temperature are related in complex ways. While increases in CO_2 in the atmosphere lead to increases in temperature, the reverse is also true: as temperature increases, the amount of CO_2 in the atmosphere also tends to increase. This surprisingly vicious circle is due to three things: (*i*) as the oceans and soils get hotter, they lose their ability to capture CO_2 from the atmosphere;(*ii*) the frozen soils of northern Asia and North America hold huge amounts of CO_2 and methane, which are released as the soils melt; (*iii*) an increase in temperature may lead to massive destruction of tropical forests, which will release enormous amounts of stored greenhouse gasses.

There is a real danger that the climate is moving out of our control and into a state at which the amount of greenhouse gasses in the atmosphere will continue to increase, independent of our actions. This will happen when **sinks**, or areas that absorb carbon from the atmosphere, turn into **sources**, or areas that release carbon.

While the concentration of CO_2 has increased to about 380 ppm since the beginning of the Industrial Age, the earth's mean temperature has increased about 0.8° C. Scenarios developed by the Intergovernmental Panel on Climate Change (IPCC) predict temperature increases of between 1.8° C and 4.0° C by the end of this century. To put this in perspective, the difference between present temperatures and the last Ice Age, when sheets of ice a kilometer thick covered large parts of North America and Europe, is only about 5° C. There is a developing consensus that the least increase in temperature this century that it is realistic to hope for is 2° C, a large increase, but one we will have to live with. Scientists fear that beyond 2° C, it will be impossible to prevent further increases of a greater magnitude, because of the problem of sinks turning into sources and other natural processes. For instance, the reflectivity of parts of the earth is already decreasing as the glaciers and ice sheets, particularly the Arctic Ocean ice cap, disappear, and instead of millions of square kilometers of ice reflecting most of the sunlight that hits it, dark ocean water or rocky mountain tops are absorbing most of the sunlight that falls on them.

Rising temperatures lead to rising sea levels for two reasons: (*i*) water expands as it gets hotter, and (*ii*) the amount of water in the oceans is increasing as glaciers and ice sheets melt. Since the beginning of the Industrial Age, the oceans have risen about 200 millimeters. IPCC projects sea level increases in the rest of this century to be between 0.18 and 0.59 meters, although IPCC specifically excludes from its projections the possibility of "rapid dynamical changes in ice flow," by which is meant the possibility that significant amounts of the ice sheets in Greenland or Antarctica might slip into the sea. Because some semi-permanent increase in global temperature is inevitable, ice is expected to continue to melt for millennia, which means that sea levels will rise indefinitely. The rate and degree of melting, however, are still under our control.

No one knows the exact point of no return at which sinks become sources and catastrophic changes begin. Some, like the British futurist James Lovelock, think we have already passed the point of no return, while a handful of optimists are more sanguine about the future. A majority of climatologists think that there is still time to avert the worst aspects of climate change, but very little time—IPCC's Fourth Assessment Report (see Box 6) said that we have perhaps 4–8 years to stabilize emissions, while Nicholas Stern said in late 2006 that we had 10–20 years.

Recent news is more bad than good:

- The rapid industrialization of some developing countries and the accelerating clearing of tropical rainforests have helped increase emissions to near the top of the range of projections.
- Recalcitrance and political inertia have slowed progress toward international agreements to limit emissions.
- For reasons not fully understood, the rate of absorption of CO_2 by the oceans seems to have decreased faster than predicted.

What is certain is that rapid reductions in emissions are extremely urgent.

Industrial development can still proceed, and life can continue to become better for most people, but we have to rethink the ways we power industrialization and reexamine some of our basic concepts of what development means. Climate change and poverty reduction may well be the two greatest challenges of the century. We need to address both. But poor countries should not pay disproportionately for the price of climate change. Finding innovative solutions and long-term responses require that we think of climate change and poverty reduction as intricately linked and mutually reinforcing. Poor countries have a right to develop, and to do so will require energy; rich countries can help them use energy wisely, but should not try to stop their legitimate aspirations of offering a better life to their citizens.

2 Mitigation and Adaptation

Responses to climate change fall into two broad categories: mitigation and adaptation. Mitigation focuses on reducing the severity of climate change by limiting greenhouse gas emissions. Adaptation focuses on taking measures that help people adjust to changed conditions. Many actions, like promoting clean energy products and agricultural innovation, support both mitigation and adaptation.

In selecting and prioritizing responses—whether for mitigation or adaptation—both intended and unintended consequences must be taken into account. Some actions are clearly benign and have few negative impacts. Other actions have impacts that are complex or subject to debate. For instance, using agricultural land to grow biofuel crops instead of food crops might seem to be a good way to reduce carbon emissions while increasing revenue in poor countries. However, as discussed

Table 1. Areas Where MFIs Can Respond to Climate Change

Customer Level (actions that affect microfinance clients directly at the household and microbusiness levels)	Clean energy products – Lighting – Cooking Forestation, avoided deforestation Biofuels Low-carbon agriculture Community-level projects Crop choices and farming practices Financial products to help clients manage risk
Institutional Level (actions that affect the function and finance of MFIs)	Reduced emissions Carbon finance and aggregation
Systemic (actions at national and international levels)	Monitoring and using information about climate change Smart subsidies Advocacy and contribution to policy debate

later in this paper, biofuel production often fails to reduce net emissions significantly and is likely to reduce food security for poor people.

Table 1 indicates areas in which MFIs can work in response to climate change. The sections that follow will describe possible activities in each area.Most of this paper addresses customer-level interventions (customers include both households and microbusinesses), because this is where MFIs are likely to have the greatest impact and the most varied activities. However, the customer level is also where MFIs face the greatest risk in addressing climate change. There is little risk for an MFI in such institutional actions as in-house energy savings and customer and staff education or in an advocacy role, but customer-level actions often involve changes in products that can put pressure on the competencies of the institution and put its loan portfolio at risk.

Although all MFIs can find some role to play in responding to climate change, management needs to think carefully about their ability to take on the different customer-level activities presented in this paper. In many cases, MFIs' contributions to protecting the environment will take shape through partnerships with other organizations.

3 Promoting Clean-Energy Products

Financial services can help customers reduce their carbon emissions by enabling them to switch to energy sources that emit less greenhouse gas. At present, by far the greatest amount of energy used by most microfinance customers around the world is for home cooking and lighting. There are 200 million households in Africa alone that could switch from kerosene to solar/LED lighting. Clean energy products present an opportunity for developing countries to leapfrog over some of the intermediate technologies that the developed world has passed through. Just as millions of people in developing countries are using mobile phones and may never see a wired telephone, perhaps in some cases, they will never use electricity from coal or oil, but can jump directly to clean sources like solar and wind.

There are two main entry points for microfinance for clean energy, whereby MFIs can acquire large numbers of new customers and grow their portfolio. MFIs can lend directly to households so that they can purchase household-sized, proven energy savings devices. MFIs can also provide financing to microbusinesses. MFIs could provide financing to microenterpreneurs who supply the energy savings devices to households as a business. The appropriateness of either entry point will depend on several variables, including average loans sizes, availability and cost of equipment, etc. A third option, discussed only briefly in this paper, is for MFIs to support community-level mitigation efforts.

Lending to Households. Working together with the suppliers of household-sized proven energy savings devices, such as small solar panels or biogas digesters, MFIs can provide credit to households to buy the equipment. Financing can be an incentive for households to switch to these cleaner, cheaper sources of energy, since it may take several years for the energy cost savings to equal the upfront investment.

A recent study (Morris, Winiecki, Chowdhary, and Cortiglia 2007) on the use of microfinance for energy found that end-user finance can work for home products, if repayments are matched to existing energy expenditure patterns. The study identifies mutually beneficial partnerships between MFIs and suppliers of clean energy products as the key to determining success. Most success stories linked to end-user finance for clean energy successes come from South Asia, with thousands of households switching from dirty energy sources like wood, dung, or coal to cleaner ones like improved cock stoves or biogas digesters and wind generators.

However, in many cases, financing end-users to purchase clean energy products may not be appropriate. This is often because the products are in a price range too low for MFIs to lend, and many purchases can be covered by personal savings or informal sector credit (IFC 2007). This appears particularly true across Africa, where loan sizes are on average much higher than in South Asia.

Lending to Microbusinesses. There are many opportunities beyond end-user finance, and MFIs should think of financing other parts of the production and distribution chain. Suppliers and in some cases importers and manufacturers will need working capital in amounts MFIs may be able to supply. Where loans are relatively high and products are relatively inexpensive, it may make much more sense to fund existing or start-up retailers.

Lending to Communities. Most discussion in the rest of this section is directed toward working with household-level activities or small entrepreneurial businesses providing clean energy to households. These are most important from the perspective of many MFIs. However, MFIs have options to support community-level mitigation efforts as well. BASIX, a prominent livelihood promotion organization in India, offers a wide variety of services through a group of linked firms, including financial institutions serving the poor. Among its many interventions, BASIX promotes off-grid decentralized community-level power projects that not only bring energy to off-grid villages, but also enable the creation of small enterprises. Small-scale hydropower projects are particularly promising and have a relatively low cost per ton of reduced greenhouse gas emissions.

MFIs that have the scale and management ability and can mobilize the technical competence necessary to work at the community level will likely find gains in efficiency and scale, and advance social objectives of decentralization and local control.

Partnering Is Key. Grameen Shakti, a nonprofit company that is part of the Grameen family, is distributing clean energy products in remote areas of Bangladesh. As of December 2007, it had installed over 130,000 solar home systems, 5,000 improved cook stoves, and 2,000 biogas plants. Grameen Shakti attributes its success to linking solar installations to income-generating activities and to fostering a network of local energy entrepreneurs to ensure installation and service. Also in Bangladesh, BRAC has a similar program run through the BRAC Foundation in which it links its customers to a supplier of solar energy systems, Infrastructure Development Company Limited. And Sewa Bank in India has formed a close partnership with SELCO, a supplier of solar panels. SELCO, Sewa, and other financial institutions have brought solar electricity to over 100,000 households, while creating new enterprises and employment. In all three cases, there is a three-way partnership among the supplier of the energy-saving device that also provides installation and servicing, the MFI that provides financing and identifies customers, and the household acquiring the new device.

Lighting. Electric grids often fail to reach rural areas, especially in Africa, and even when they do, hook-up costs and minimum monthly charges are too expensive for many people. About 2 billion people around the world use kerosene (paraffin) for household lighting; they often rely on locally produced lanterns with an open flame. Globally, household kerosene lighting consumes the equivalent of 1.7 million barrels of petroleum a day, more than the petroleum production of Libya (Mills 2002). Kerosene lanterns, particularly locally produced ones, are unsafe, smelly, and dirty and give mediocre light. People use household kerosene lighting because they lack affordable alternatives.

Until recently, solar lighting has been too expensive for poor people, with solar lamps costing USD 100 or more and solar installations with fixed panels costing even more. However, new technologies, in particular inexpensive, reliable solar/light-emitting diode (LED) systems,[1] have opened up the possibility of consumer lighting products that are cost-competitive with kerosene lighting, even for very poor people. Replacing kerosene with solar/LED lamps has been identified as the most effective way to reduce greenhouse gas emissions from lighting (Mills 2002).

Prices for the least expensive solar/LED lamps—perhaps the only way to reach large numbers of rural poor in some regions—have become so low that most MFIs will not want or need to finance end-user purchases. Rather, these purchases can be covered by personal savings or informal sector credit.

In such cases, MFIs may consider making loans to entrepreneurs who purchase solar arrays to charge battery-powered home lighting systems. This approach, which can run in parallel to solar home systems, is useful because fixed-panel systems that need to be installed by skilled technicians are too expensive for many poor people; solar lamps with small panels that require no installation may be preferable. A promising initial market for solar/LED lamps is street vendors, who need lighting to sell their goods in the evenings and usually have the cash necessary to purchase small systems without needing credit. (See Box 4 for a short case study.)

Box 4: Lighting Africa Initiative

The Lighting Africa initiative is designed to promote clean lighting solutions in Africa through deepening market intelligence, working with partners to establish quality assurance criteria, administering a competitive small grants program, and developing a streamlined carbon finance approach. Its web site (www.lightingafrica.org) features lists of suppliers looking for partners, including financial partners.

MFIs should insist that recycling systems be put in place before promoting solar/LED solutions. Specifically, lead and nickel cadmium (NiCad) batteries must be recycled, to prevent their heavy metals from entering the local environment. Nickel metal hydride (NiMH) batteries are less toxic, but should be recycled if they are distributed in large numbers. There will be a market for recycled lead batteries that will cover some or all of the cost of recycling in most countries. This recycling market probably won't exist for other types of batteries, however, and MFIs should ask how NiCad and NiMH batteries are being disposed. Including a small deposit in the purchase price of the lamp is a straightforward way to motivate consumers to return batteries for recycling.

1 As this is written, LEDs seem to have compelling advantages over their technological rivals, compact florescent bulbs. However, technologies are evolving rapidly, and it goes without saying that we are not endorsing any particular product or approach.

Cooking. Kirk R. Smith, professor of Global Environmental Health at the University of California at Berkeley, describes typical stoves as toxic waste factories, because they involve incomplete combustion of fuel and convert from 6 to 30 percent of carbon into methane, a potent greenhouse gas, or a wide variety of toxic substances.[2] Smith describes the use of traditional fuels in developing countries as "the most wasteful, unhealthy and [greenhouse gas] intensive fuel cycle in the world."[3]

New cooking approaches include cookers that use bottled gas, solar cookers, biomass digesters, improved cook stoves, and biomass briquettes.[4] Improved cook stoves vary in design and are known by different names around the world. In all cases, the stoves are designed to control the rate of fuel burning; retain the heat from combustion in a small, insulated space; and concentrate the heat on the cooking pot. The typical result is a 50 percent decrease in the fuel needed for cooking, although consumer education in proper stove use may be necessary to attain this theoretical level of fuel savings. In some cases, the stoves are manufactured and movable, like jiko ceramic stoves in Kenya and many other countries. In other cases, they are fixed installations that must be constructed in the customer's cooking area. Beyond mitigation of climate change and financial savings to users, replacing traditional biomass stoves that use wood, charcoal, grass, or dung with cleaner cooking sources also has enormous public health benefits.

Using cookers that run on bottled gas reduces emissions of greenhouse gases and toxic byproducts and provides a better cooking experience. Of course, relying on a nonrenewable fuel source cannot be a definitive solution, and the price of all fossil fuels is destined to rise substantially in coming decades. Nonetheless, using bottled gas can be a good interim solution. Solar cookers, which use reflecting surfaces to concentrate sunlight onto a cooking pot, are inexpensive and rely on sunlight, a nonpolluting free resource that is plentiful in most parts of the world. However, solar cookers are fragile, take a long time to heat food, stop functioning

---

2 The list of toxic substances produced by traditional stoves is intimidating to chemists and nonchemists alike, and includes n-hexane; 1,3 butadiene; benzene; styrene; benzo(α) pyrene; oxygenated organics; formaldehyde; acrolein; alcohols and acids, such as methanol; phenols, such as catechol and cresol; many quinones, such as hydroquinone, semiquinone-type and other radicals, and chlorinated organics, such as methylene chloride and dioxin.

3 Presentation at Sustainable Development Network Conference, World Bank, February 2008.

4 MFIs should be wary of products that require the use of charcoal, which uses four or five times the quantity of wood to produce the same amount of heat as simple firewood. Douglas Barnes, Priti Kumar and Keith Openshaw have produced a series of detailed country reports on improved stoves available on the World Bank web site. The most up-to-date of these will be published later this year in: "Cleaner Hearths, Better Homes: Improved Stoves for India and the Developing World" (Oxford University Press, forthcoming).

at a time of day when many women are traditionally still cooking, and require frequent attention (to refocus the reflective panels). They are accepted in some areas where there are few alternatives, but they face market resistance in most cases.

Home- or village-level biomass digesters have become an affordable, reliable technology. Biomass digesters convert dung and other waste into methane, which is piped to the kitchen for cooking. They also produce solid digested waste that can be used in fields as fertilizer. (Because they use dung as an input, they are an especially good way to add value to chicken farms). Methane is an acceptable cooking fuel, although one barrier to consumer acceptance is the low amount of heat it generates relative to bottled gas or wood, and thus the longer time needed for cooking or boiling water.

The Biogas Support Programme (BSP) in Nepal is a model for massive rollout of biogas digesters. Between 1992 and 2007, BSP worked with 145 MFIs and 70 construction firms to finance the installation of 172,858 village or household biogas plants. BSP estimates the total potential market in Nepal to be as much as 1.5 million units. Over 95 percent of the plants are functional; 65 percent use waste from the household toilet as well as animal waste. BSP has been able to access funding of as much as USD 1 million annually through the Clean Development Mechanism (see Box 5), which will help the project to confront one of the major hurdles to more widespread acceptance—the high initial cost.

Box 5: Carbon Markets

Carbon markets exist because of the desire to set a limit, or a cap, on the amount of greenhouse gasses companies or other entities are allowed to emit. Carbon markets are a way of financially rewarding those that emit less than they are allowed and penalizing those that emit more.

There are two types of carbon markets, compulsory and voluntary. The compulsory market is funded by businesses that are required by international agreements to keep their greenhouse gas emissions below a certain cap or, failing that, to offset additional emissions by paying to reduce emissions elsewhere. The principal compulsory market was established under the UN Framework Convention on Climate Change, under which the Kyoto Protocol was signed in 1997. Under the Kyoto Protocol, there are three mechanisms for capping carbon emissions. The most relevant one for microfinance is the Clean Development Mechanism (CDM), which allows businesses to offset emissions above their caps by investing in projects that will reduce emissions in developing countries (called *nonannex 1 countries* in the language of the Protocol). About 1,000 CDM projects worth over USD 5 billion had been funded by the end of 2007, but a large majority of them were in just a handful of countries, including China, Brazil, and India.

CDM funding has become more accessible to MFIs and their partners because of the decision to allow a group of separate activities to be treated as a

Programme of Activities (popularly, Programmatic CDM). Under Programmatic CDM, activities can be in multiple locations, even multiple countries, and not all of them need to be analyzed or even identified before the funding mechanism is approved. Thus, an MFI carrying out several activities in, say, clean energy could be approved for Programmatic CDM funding.

The compulsory market requires that any investments to offset carbon emissions have extensive independent certification of baseline emissions, the amounts of reductions, additionality (evidence that the reduction would not have happened anyway), registration of offsets to avoid double counting, indication that the benefits will be persistent, and an analysis of leakage or increases in emissions elsewhere caused by the project. Such certification is expensive, typically costing tens of thousands of dollars per case and requiring skills that very few MFIs possess. To date, few MFIs have received carbon payments under any compulsory carbon cap and trade scheme, with Grameen Shakti being an important exception. Institutions that are confident of their ability to deal with complexity might want to consult the useful guide to CDM funding at www.cdmrulebook.org. Others will want to use the services of a specialized intermediary, such as the MicroEnergy Credits Corporation (www.microenergy-credits.com).

In addition to the compulsory carbon market, there are hundreds of voluntary mechanisms that allow people or firms who choose to do so to make voluntary contributions to offset emissions. The amount of money that flows through the voluntary market, around a USD 100 million a year, is tiny compared to the amounts in the compulsory markets. The rigor of the voluntary schemes in terms of independent evaluation, efficiency, and transparency varies quite a bit. The best voluntary traders subscribe to rigorous standards, such as the Gold VER Standard, the CCB Standard, and the Voluntary Carbon Standard (now in draft).

Two voluntary schemes will soon begin functioning in North America: the Regional Greenhouse Gas Initiative unites nine northeastern U.S. states, and the Western Climate Initiative involves five states and one Canadian province, led by California. Also, the Chicago Climate Exchange is a scheme through which participants voluntarily sign legally binding agreements to reduce their net emissions with rigorous verification.

The cost of carbon offsets under any of these schemes is usually expressed in terms of the value of a ton of emitted carbon. This price varies according to the supply of offsets and the demand by industries that are over their cap; it is much less under voluntary than under compulsory schemes. The cost, typically about USD 20 per ton, is widely considered much less than the damage done by greenhouse gasses emissions and too low to force needed changes in the way energy is used in Europe and North America.

To give a rough example of what carbon credits could mean in practice, a single kerosene lantern typically emits about 100 kg, or 0.1 ton, of CO_2 a year. If the lantern were replaced by a solar lamp, the savings would be worth about

USD 2 a year, if carbon credits were going for USD 20 per ton. However, the substantial cost of applying for credits and administering the program would need to be subtracted from the carbon income, and a program would be profitable to an MFI supporting the distribution of solar lamps only if it were able to reach large numbers of people.

There is strong pressure to require more rigorous caps, which will increase the cost of a ton of carbon, thus leading to larger flows of carbon funds toward developing nations.

Digesters cost USD 400–800 to construct, and even with various subsidies, each end-user household must pay USD 300 or more—a large expense for rural homes, but within the range of typical MFI financing.

In Uganda, the Ugandan Ministry of Energy and Mineral Development and GTZ are supporting a network of entrepreneurs who have installed 350,000 stoves, mostly Rocket Lorena fixed stoves. Entrepreneurs are trained to build the stoves. Homeowners provide the bricks and other materials needed for construction and make a small payment to the entrepreneurs. This is an example of how MFIs might finance the entrepreneurs who construct and sell the stoves. MFIs could promote a similar program and make small loans to the entrepreneurs to get them started. Barnes, Openshaw, Smith, and van der Plas (1994) report that the factors leading to massive acceptance and sustained use of improved cook stoves include awareness-raising campaigns, training in correct use, and stoves that are distinguishable from traditional stoves through shape, color, or brand.

Finally, almost any form of organic material, from agricultural waste, to newspapers, to sawdust, can be turned into a firewood substitute through the production of biomass briquettes. Organic material is shredded, made into slurry, compacted in a hand-operated press, and then dried in the sun. A biomass briquette production unit typically employs about six people and requires an investment of a few hundred dollars. This could be a good loan for an MFI, provided that the cost of labor, the price of alternative fuels, and the availability of raw materials are favorable. Practical documentation on briquette economics and manufacturing is available at www.legacyfound.org.

As with lighting, MFIs should also look beyond simple end-user consumer financing to find the points at which their funds will be most useful in the manufacturing and distribution chains for clean cooking products. It may make more sense to finance people who sell or install improved cooking products, rather than end users.

Forestry. The amount of carbon locked up in trees and other parts of forest ecosystems is greater than that in the atmosphere, and the preservation of forests is one of the most cost-efficient strategies for reducing worldwide emissions. Emissions from the destruction of forests constitute one-fifth of global emissions of greenhouse gases (Stern et al. 2007). Clearing land always involves great amounts of emissions because of brush fires, greenhouse gases from disturbed soils, and accelerated decomposition of forest waste. Planting new trees (*reforestation*, if trees are planted in areas that had previously been forested, *aforestation* otherwise) helps to reduce greenhouse gases in the atmosphere and possibly to create cooler and wetter microclimates. However, far greater carbon savings come from preserving existing forests.

People who cook with wood, build wooden houses, or live where there is a market for firewood or lumber, as well as farmers who see the value in windbreaks or tree crops, likely already have a predisposition to plant trees. Whether woodlots can make for a viable loan in the absence of subsidies depends on local conditions and interest rates. It would be difficult for MFIs with their short loan periods and high interest rates to finance forestry projects. However, carbon credits are likely to become increasingly available for forestry projects, as awareness of how incentives can work to address preserve forests and increase planting grows. Small holders who plant trees are possible recipients of payments through both the voluntary and compulsory carbon markets. This approach, however, poses particular challenges because of the need to aggregate many small actions and to keep accurate records over the long periods needed for trees to capture enough carbon to justify receiving payments. (See boxes 2 and 5.)

MFIs that support work in forestry often do so in partnership with specialized institutions, such as the Nature Conservancy and Conservation International. In those cases, the MFI's role is usually limited to the support of income-generating alternatives to deforestation.

Biofuels. Biofuels are made from recently living plants or animals, in contrast to fossil fuels, which come from long dead plants or animals. Where organic wastes are already collected for some other purpose, such as from domestic animals, breweries, chicken farms, sugar mills, or coffee processing, biofuel production is likely both to be profitable and to lead to the mitigation of climate change. This is because the costs (both financial and in terms of emissions) of growing the plants or animals, harvesting, and transporting the waste to one place have already been incurred; the additional cost of processing the waste is low.

However, growing plants specifically for biofuel is questionable financially and from the point of view of net greenhouse gas emissions. Biofuel production in the developing world is already leading to the destruction of forests, conversion of farmland away from food crops, and exclusion of local communities from participating in decisions that affect their livelihoods and environment. Nonetheless, biofuels are being widely grown in the developing world, in part because of government subsidies and mandates and in part because of the widespread, but false, belief that they are a benign way to keep automobiles supplied with fuel. The impact on the world's food supply is extremely damaging: recent worldwide food shortages are blamed in part on the conversion of farm land to biofuel production.[5]

---

5 Jatropha, a genus that includes small plants, shrubs, and trees, may be an exception to this rule. It grows around the world in tropical and semitropical areas and is resistant to drought and pests. Its seeds are crushed and transformed into biodiesel. Small farmers can intercrop jatropha so that its production does not compete with food crops. However, even jatropha schemes should be examined carefully to evaluate their nonfinancial impacts.

Low-Carbon Agriculture. Agriculture emits greenhouse gasses through the decay of farm wastes, the reduction in the amount of organic matter in tilled soils, the emission of gases by farm animals, and indirectly through the production of chemical fertilizers, whose manufacture is particularly energy intensive.[6] The green revolution was made possible in large part by the widespread adoption of chemical fertilizers and other chemicals, as well as farm mechanization and irrigation. Any large reversal in the use of these inputs is both unlikely and undesirable unless other ways can be found to feed a growing world population.

Agriculture presents some of the most delicate tradeoffs between economic development in poor countries and climate change mitigation. Active campaigns in Europe and North America urging consumers to buy local produce to reduce carbon emissions from transporting the food actually work against the immediate interests of small farmers from Africa, Asia, and Latin America. Climate-conscious MFIs in rural areas of developing nations will feel contradictory pulls.

The challenge in much of the developing world lies in helping farmers who are modernizing their traditional agriculture to adopt low-carbon paths to increased production. Depending on the region, this might mean no-till agriculture rather than tractor plowing, integrated pest management instead of insecticides, intercropping and crop rotation to reduce the need for fertilizer, and drip irrigation rather than other methods. These low-energy options will become steadily more competitive as the cost of fuel drives up the cost of chemical fertilizer and of operating farm machinery. Norman Uphoff of Cornell University argues that farmers can double their rice production with no increase in inputs, simply through adopting improved cultivation practices: planting times, irrigation, and plant spacing.[7]

MFIs working in agricultural finance could look for opportunities to partner with institutions that are promoting low-carbon agriculture. Some innovations, such as vaccinations to reduce methane emissions from animals or drip irrigation equipment, help to mitigate climate change but are costly to poor farmers and may offer them little or no financial benefit in return. New farming technologies have little chance of being adopted, and less chance of being used correctly, unless they are accompanied by agricultural extension. Sometimes subsidies will be necessary. In situations where education in the use of sustainable agricultural techniques is available from other sources, MFIs should consider partnering.

We now turn from farming choices that lead to lower emissions to choices that enable farmers to adapt to changing climate conditions.

---

6 Also, although it seems laughable, burps from livestock consist of methane, a greenhouse gas that is 20 times more potent than CO_2. Cattle emit about 1 kg of methane for every 2 kg of meat they give. Results from experimental work suggest that vaccination or changes in diet, including adding yeast and garlic to feed, can reduce the emission of methane from farm animals by up to 50 percent.

7 An accessible presentation of Uphoff's ideas is at http://www.nytimes.com/2008/06/17/science/17rice.html or http://tinyurl.com/5yokyp.

Adaptive Agriculture. Sometimes, farmers can adapt to small changes in rainfall and temperature by choosing either more resilient varieties of existing crops or different crops. In other cases, more difficult changes will be required for survival. In many cases these changes will lead to loss of culture and social identity, and will likely meet initial resistance from MFI clients.

For example, for people from the Bolivian and Peruvian altiplano, adaptation may mean that they will need to raise cows instead of llamas, alpacas, and vicuñas. Similarly, in Uganda, it is estimated that 90 percent of land on which Arabica coffee, the chief export crop, is now grown will soon become unsuitable for coffee production because of an increase in temperature. Ugandan coffee is grown on the lower slopes of mountains, and as the temperature increases, coffee cultivation is expected to become possible at higher elevations on the same mountains, leaving lower slopes of the mountains available for other crops. These changes will involve complicated issues of property and land-use management, but they will be less painful than the alternative of lost livelihood.

In some countries, areas that have traditionally supported rain-fed agriculture will find that changing weather conditions require introducing irrigation. Again, this type of change is unlikely to succeed without some sort of extension service, because introducing irrigation involves risks and a steep learning curve for farmers.

An MFI that wants to help its clients stay ahead of changes in the climate should realize the uncertainties in climate predictions and urge clients toward gradual diversification and incremental introduction of new approaches, rather than risky wholesale adoption of new technologies.

4 Institutional Level

Financial Products to Help Clients Manage Risk. The climate crisis provides another reason, if one were needed, for MFIs to diversify the financial services they offer and to stop relying exclusively on loan products. Whatever the merits or drawbacks of credit, this product becomes riskier the more borrowers undergo economic stresses, including those due to a less hospitable climate. Savings are a critical buffer against losses and stress, and institutions that can offer secure deposit services to their customers should do so. There is evidence from MFIs all over the world that when the poor are offered a safe and convenient way to save money outside the household, they will use it. In many, perhaps even most, cases savings are a preferred financing means when compared to borrowing.

For rural customers, another valuable risk management instrument can be insurance. A lot of work is being done on crop and weather insurance. Crop insurance carries the risk that farmers whose crops are insured may let a dubious crop fail rather than take extraordinary measures to protect it. Weather insurance does not offer the same perverse incentive, and it can protect against the risk of unusual intense weather events, which are increasingly likely, according to climate change projections. However, it is important to note that while insurance is useful in helping smooth out highs and lows, it is not relevant in the face of a trend. Climate change is certainly a trend, and so while weather insurance can be useful to farmers, it is not a viable, long-term response to climate change.

Since an MFI's sophistication, financial resources, mission, market, management information systems, and the regulatory environment will influence its ability to develop and offer new products, especially savings products, product diversification will not be practical or relevant for all institutions.

Reducing an MFI's Emissions. Many MFIs want to reduce their carbon footprint—the net emissions coming from their business operations—simply because it is the right thing to do and is consistent with their mission. There are additional reasons, of course: reducing emissions can improve their image or brand, and it can serve as a way to urge staff to be more efficient.

Many actions that reduce the carbon footprint of businesses are simply good business practices that save money in the long run. Not all rich country solutions will apply to poor country MFIs, but many will, including switching to low-energy light bulbs or reducing paper waste and trips in vehicles.[8] Investments that lead to more efficient energy use will save more money as the cost of fossil fuels rises. In light of the magnitude of global climate change, companies may want to develop a top-to-bottom corporate commitment to responding to climate change, touching all areas of operations, in the same way that some companies have embraced customer service or total quality management as cross-cutting values. Having a green brand—that is, being thought of as a company committed to environmental concerns—is now widely recognized as an important business consideration.

Strategic Thinking for MFIs on Climate Change. Climate change should be part of MFIs' strategic planning, and those plans should include concrete steps for both mitigation and adaptation. If the strategic plan of a financial institution does not address climate change, it is time to revisit the plan. A simple way to ensure that climate change is included is through a climate SWOT analysis, looking at the institution's strengths, weaknesses, opportunities, and threats in the face of the changing climate.

MFIs need to think through the sequence of their actions in response to climate change. There are many steps institutions can take quickly, before tackling the demanding tasks of developing new financial products or approaching carbon markets:

- Starting with simple energy-saving measures like using low-energy lighting and taking other measures to reduce waste. Many of these measures can be easily implemented, can save money, and can help to sensitize staff.
- Organizing awareness campaigns aimed at customers about the availability of renewable sources of energy (or cleaner sources) for cooking and lighting.

---

8 For an example of one microfinance bank's approach to this issue, see ACLEDA Bank's Sustainability Report: http://www.acledabank.com.kh/EN/BP_sustainabilityReport.asp.

- Seeking information about other local climate initiatives whether by donors, government, or the private sector. Looking for win–win ways to collaborate is good business and may lead to unanticipated benefits through discovering new markets and sources of finance.
- Conducting on-going research to understand the economic activities and other realities of clients. Market research has long been considered a microfinance best practice, and this activity can be broadened to gain a better understanding of client energy use and environmental risks.
- Holding meetings to sensitize staff and boards about current science and economics of climate change. These can be included as part of on-going training and information management.

Once these and other easy steps have been taken, MFIs can move progressively to more challenging tasks.

An MFI's scale and outreach, the regulations to which it must adhere, and the depth and skills of its staff will all affect its ability to diversify product offerings and take on new risks. MFIs that are able to diversify the products they offer should begin with accepted good practices in product development, including the important steps of market research, careful planning, pilot testing, and meticulous implementation.

Carbon Finance and Aggregators. Funding designed to address issues around climate change flows through the compulsory and voluntary carbon trading markets—that is, payments that are contingent on, and proportional to, specific reductions in greenhouse gasses. With increased concern about climate change, there will be substantial funding available to companies, including MFIs, that take measures to address the issue. At present, carbon markets provide USD 60 billion for mitigation and nothing for adaptation, but increasingly donors have identified adaptation as an important funding need.

Qualifying for carbon funding is complex and requires extensive documentation and specialized knowledge that MFIs are unlikely to possess. Specialized firms are being created to aggregate reductions from multiple interventions or to help develop proposals for carbon finance. One interesting start-up in this area is MicroEnergy Credits (www.microenergycredits.com). This complex subject is addressed in more detail in Box 6.

Box 6: Implications for Donors and Investors: Smart Subsidies

The use of fossil fuels has inflicted an enormous cost on our planet. Yet, rather than make people pay the real cost of using fossil fuels, many governments have done the opposite, subsidizing the use of fossil fuels through public subsidies for roads and airports, energy companies, carbon-intensive agriculture, and other drivers of greenhouse gasses. Nicholas Stern (2007) famously summarized this situation by saying that "climate change is the greatest market failure the world has ever seen."

The International Energy Agency estimates that world subsidies on energy (net of taxes) are in the order of USD 250 billion to 300 billion per year, equal to 0.6 percent to 0.7 percent of world gross domestic product. Fossil fuels are the most heavily subsidized energy sources, totaling an estimated USD 180 billion to 200 billion per year. But support for the deployment of low-carbon energy sources amounts to only USD 33 billion a year, with a mere USD 10 billion going to renewable energies. The smart use of subsidies would mean reversing the subsidy balance in favor of sustainable energy solutions.

So what role can microfinance subsidies play in protecting the environment, and what can donors and investors do?

Donors and investors that want to work with MFIs in combating climate change might consider these broad ideas:

1. Providing support through technical assistance or an equity investment to help strengthen MFIs' systems and management is perhaps one of the most important contributions donors and investors can make. Only the strongest and best managed institutions will be able to fully integrate climate change into their strategic and business planning, and remain flexible and creative enough to meet new challenges.

2. MFIs may need help developing new products or adapting existing ones so that clients can meet their evolving needs and adapt to changing climatic and economic realities. Examples of new products are found throughout this paper.

3. MFIs may also require support to look beyond traditional microfinance models, and to create linkages with suppliers of clean energy devices. Figuring out the supplier, distribution, and finance chain may require investments in new technologies or other innovations to create more efficient delivery channels. Donors can also underwrite the costs of linking to extension workers and others who provide farmers with market information and advice on alternative agricultural products and methodologies.

4. Donors and investors can help fill the information gap on: what works in environmental finance and where microfinance can fit in; impacts of climate change on the end-client and scenario planning to help prepare for the future; new energy-efficient products and technologies that work; and successful cases of MFIs that have incorporated adaptation responses as part of their business.

5. Donors and investors can combine forces with MFIs to raise a strong policy voice. Many MFIs are well known and well respected, and combined advocacy efforts may have a greater impact.

6. Development finance institutions and other investors can offer appropriate financial instruments, such as credit lines and debt facilities, to support the strongest MFIs to lend to small and medium enterprises innovating with renewable energy. Guarantees and other risk-sharing facilities also can play a role in facilitating commercial money for environmental projects.
7. Obtaining carbon credits and carbon credit aggregation are outside the scope of most MFIs, but these could be important ways to bring funds from the carbon markets closer to the people who will be most affected by climate change. Carbon credit aggregators and consultants are usually independent businesses, but a competent MFI apex organization could take on that job. Donor assistance might be necessary to help these meso-level firms get established.

5 Reinforcing Institutions' Actions to Combat Climate Change or Systemic Level

Monitoring and Using Information about Climate Change. Observable impacts of climate change are happening fast, and the strategies and resources to mitigate and adapt to those changes are developing quickly. Box 7 presents some resources for readers who want to learn more about climate change; even these sources of good information are changing rapidly.

Box 7: More Information on Climate Change

The following sources are starting points for those wishing to learn more about climate change.

Fourth Assessment Report of the Intergovernmental Panel on Climate Change. IPCC is a scientific intergovernmental body set up by the World Meteorological Organization and the United Nations Environment Programme. It is the most authoritative voice on climate change, representing the consensus view of the participating governments. About every five years, IPCC has released an assessment report with sections documenting the physical science basis of climate change; impacts, adaptation, and vulnerability; the mitigation of climate change; and a synthesis report. The Fourth Assessment Report (AR4) was released in 2007. AR4 represents a consensus of 130 participating countries, reflecting the work of 2,500 scientists over six years. No other source of information on climate change has the broad circulation and general acceptance of AR4. IPCC was awarded the Nobel Peace Prize in 2007. The reports are necessarily technical, reflecting the nature of the subject matter, but they are written for knowledgeable generalists. Available at www.ipcc.ch.

IPCC's assessments of *regional impacts and vulnerability* can be found at http://www.grida.no/climate/ipcc/regional/index.htm.

The *Stern Review of the Economics of Climate Change* was commissioned by the U.K. Government to assess the costs and economic implications of climate change. Nicholas Stern, the principal author, is a former World Bank chief economist and a lecturer at the London School of Economics. The document is clear and persuasive. Stern argues that the cost of doing nothing about climate change is higher than the economic cost of taking urgent strong actions to mitigate it. The report is available in three versions, ranging from the full report of almost 600 pages to a short executive summary of four pages. The executive summary is available in a dozen languages at http://xrl.us/Stern or http://www.hm-treasury.gov.uk/independent_reviews/stern_review_economics_climate_change/sternreview_index.cfm.

The 2007–2008 Human Development Report of UNDP, *Fighting Climate Change: Human Solidarity in a Divided World*, stresses that climate change threatens to reverse much of what has been achieved in human development and exhorts governments and people to take effective action quickly. The information is very current and very alarming. It is available at http://hdr.undp.org/en.

World Resources Institute has an informative web site that tends toward policy and scientific analysis. www.wri.org.

www.realclimate.org offers a great deal of information about climate science, much of it technical but written to be as accessible as possible.

The World Environmental Organization gives its opinion of the 100 top climate change sites at www.world.org/weo/climate. It lists the Pew Center on Global Climate Change as the number one site: www.pewclimate.org

Former U.S. Vice President Al Gore's film *An Inconvenient Truth* is an alarming presentation that makes the complicated science of climate change accessible to lay people.

ACCION International's Center for Financial Inclusion is producing a series of podcasts called Energy Links, available on Apple's iTunes—search for *Energy Links* under podcasts.

The World Bank has a lot of useful resources at http://web.worldbank.org/WBSITE/EXTERNAL/TOPICS/ENVIRONMENT/EXTCC/0,,menuPK:407870~pagePK:149018~piPK:149093~theSitePK:407864,00.html
The April 2008 issue of the World Bank Institute's *Development Outreach*, available at www.worldbank.org/wbi, also has interesting, accessible, and relevant articles on climate change and development.

The *United Nations Framework Convention on Climate Change* (UNFCCC) is the agreement formalizing the intentions of UN member countries to collaborate on climate change. Each participating country has a designated national authority, which represents the country on climate issues (http://cdm.unfccc.int/DNA/index.html). Less developed countries have also written *National Adaptation Programmes of Action* (NAPAs). The country representatives and NAPAs are useful resources for understanding the particular challenges in a country and the adaptation responses that have been recommended by technical experts. NAPAs are available through UNFCCC's Web site: http://unfccc.int.

On the impact of climate change on the oceans, see *The End of the Line* by Rupert Murray, Daily Telegraph: http://www.endofthelinemovie.co.uk/facts.htm and http://www.washingtonpost.com/wp-dyn/content/article/2006/11/02/AR2006110200913.html.

A discussion of subsidies, important for donors and investors, can be found in Morgan, Trevor, *Energy Subsidies: Their Magnitude, How They Affect Energy Investment and Greenhouse Gas Emissions, and Prospects for Reform*, UNFCCC Secretariat/Financial and Technical Support Programme, June 2007. Available at http://unfccc.int/files/cooperation_and_support/financial_mechanism/application/pdf/morgan_pdf.pdf.

Agriculture and Climate Change by William Cline, predicts changes in temperature and rainfall on a country or subcountry basis. Available at http://www.cgdev.org/content/publications/detail/14090/.

Although predictions of the future can help guide today's actions, inevitably there will be changes over the next few years and decades that are now largely unimagined. In any case, MFIs need to stay informed about the repercussions of a changing climate so that they can make wise strategic choices. At a time when some commentators argue that the future of our civilization as we know it is at risk, it is not an exaggeration to say that the future of the microfinance industry as we know also may be at risk.

6 Advocacy and Contribution to Policy Debate

MFIs are widely perceived as representing large numbers of the world's poor. As such, they can have a prominent role in raising awareness around climate change, adding their voices to those who are demanding prompt, effective action. Some MFIs may want to play a direct role in national and international policy debates, education, and activism; in other cases, a national or regional association, if one exists, might be an appropriate interlocutor. Large and stable MFIs—sometimes significant employers in their countries as well as providers of financial services—may be well placed to contribute to policy debates on issues such as land use, flood plain management, energy, transportation, water infrastructure, forest use, family planning, and pro-poor carbon markets. To make the best decisions in any of these areas, it is important that all voices be heard, and MFIs can play a role in making sure that the interests of their clients are considered.

MFIs cannot and should not be expected to be the world's environmental police.

But the world's response to climate change does not yet measure up to the size of the problem. Advocacy and contribution to the policy debate is one of the ways that almost all MFIs can contribute to its solution.

References

Barnes, D.F., Openshaw, K., Smith, K.R., van der Plas, R. (1994) What Makes People Cook with Improved Biomass Stoves? World Bank Technical Paper No. 242, Energy Series. Washington, D.C.: World Bank.

Barnes, D.F., Kumar, P., Openshaw, K. (forthcoming) Cleaner Hearths, Better Homes: Improved Stoves for India and the Developing World. Oxford: Oxford University Press.

International Finance Corporation (2007) Selling Solar: Lessons from More than a Decade of IFC's Experiences. Washington, D.C.: IFC, September, http://www.ifc.org/ifcext/sustainability.nsf/AttachmentsByTitle/p_CatalyzingPrivateInvestment_SellingSolar/$FILE/SellingSolar.pdf.

Mills, E. (2002) Global Lighting Energy Savings Potential. Light & Engineering 10(4).

Morris, E., Winiecki, J., Chowdhary, S., Cortiglia, K. (2007) Using Microfinance to Expand Access to Energy Services. Washington, D.C.: SEEP Network. http://www.seepnetwork.org/content/library/detail/5875.

Stern, N., et al. (2007) Stern Review: The Economics of Climate Change. Cambridge, United Kingdom: Cambridge University Press, pp. 216. http://www.cambridge.org/catalogue/catalogue.asp?isbn=9780521700801 or http://www.hm-treasury.gov.uk/sternreview_index.htm.

Morgan, T. (2007) Energy Subsidies: Their Magnitude, How They Affect Energy Investment and Greenhouse Gas Emissions, and Prospects for Reform. UNFCCC Secretariat/Financial and Technical Support Programme, June.

De la Torre, A. (2008) Low Carbon, High Growth: Latin American Responses to Climate Change. Washington, D.C.: World Bank, December.

United Nations (1987) Report of the World Commission on Environment and Development: Our Common Future. New York: United Nations, http://www.un-documents.net/wced-ocf.htm.

CHAPTER 9

Environmental Finance Through the Financial Sector – An Approach with Growing Potential – Experiences of KfW Entwicklungsbank

Klaus Pfeiffer, Matthias Adler, and Constanze Kreiss[*]

During the last two decades, it has been widely acknowledged that financial sector promotion is an instrument that is well-suited to help achieve the Millennium Development Goals, particularly by increasing poor people's income, by fostering the economic growth necessary to fight poverty and by contributing more directly to gender equality. However, the financial sector also has a huge potential to help protect the environment (MDGs 7 and 8).

The potential of the financial sector lies in its capability to reach out to a broad parts of the population, particularly through Micro-, Small and Medium Sized Enterprises. This outreach can be ensured by the leverage effect of refinancing means of financial institutions.

From this perspective, building inclusive financial systems clearly includes the protection of the environment and addressing the challenges of climate change, because the consequences of environmental problems hit poor people more severely than other parts of the population in developing countries.

Furthermore, damages caused by ecological challenges require enormous investments in the future. Public sector financing source will by far not be sufficient to meet the financing needs for these investments. Therefore a smart combination of private and public funds is needed. Development Finance Institutions together with private Investors are therefore increasingly called to help to develop broad scale approaches for local financial sectors and to mobilise international and local sources of financing.

However, entrepreneurs and private households in the developing world are facing a number of environmental challenges, including

- continuously increasing energy demand – and hence increasing energy tariffs – due to high growth rates and high energy intensity in major middle-income countries;

[*] Financial Sector Experts, KfW Development Bank.

D. Köhn (ed.), *Greening the Financial Sector: How to Mainstream Environmental Finance in Developing Countries*, DOI 10.1007/978-3-642-05087-9_9,

- the fact that despite high world market energy prices, in many developing countries energy tariffs have been – and continue to be – highly subsidised. This policy is a challenge for any efforts to promote financial products, e.g. to invest both in production technologies and housing improvements that have a higher degree of energy efficiency and fewer negative environmental consequences, such as CO_2 emissions.

So an enhanced effort to help mitigate and adapt to the effects of climate change is needed. Climate change as such cannot be reversed. However, there are ways to contribute to slowing down climate change processes and to develop, in a relatively short period of time, innovative financial products that reduce the vulnerability of shocks resulting from climate change, such as natural disasters of all kinds, and to adapt to the consequences of those shocks.

More specifically, the financial sector has a huge potential to help achieve environmental goals such as saving energy and reducing emissions relevant to climate change by promoting financial products tailored to finance environmentally beneficial investments. This potential needs to be tapped effectively and efficiently. The central challenge for development finance in the area of financial systems development therefore is how to involve financial institutions in emerging environmental finance markets on a sustainable basis. Particularly, financial institutions should develop environmental finance products as part of their own strategies. There is a business case for environmental finance if the products offered by the local financial institution in line with the clients needs as well as its own commercial requirements and constraints.

Environmental finance includes saving energy and reducing greenhouse gas emissions. Typical products include environmental credit lines to small and medium-sized industries, energy efficiency programmes (for micro, small and medium sized enterprises – MSMEs – as well as housing improvement). It also provides new approaches, especially to help rural people use appropriate financial services to cope with the effects of climate change via weather insurance schemes.

Against this background, the programmes for "Environmental Finance through the financial sector" focus on two core topics which already make up more than 10% of the financial sector portfolio of KfW Entwicklungsbank: On the one hand, refinancing the portfolios of financial institutions to increase energy efficiency, and investments in renewable energies, on the other. Both fields are well suitable for broad-scale promotion through local financial institutions in transition and developing countries. The essential precondition of involving local financial institutions is that customers can turn to "their" local bank for financing corresponding investment measures. In order to meet with clients needs, the loan officer of the bank has an opportunity to inform clients about the advantages of investments in renewable energies or energy efficiency and is hereby increasing the clients' awareness of that topic.

Furthermore, the infrastructure of a local financial institution makes it possible to finance small-scale measures in an efficient way. This enables loans for energy efficiency/renewable energies (EERE) to be standardised, an important pre-requisite for efficient provision of services. In this regard, the credit lines provided by KfW Entwicklungsbank in South-Eastern Europe – the "pioneer region" of KfW Entwicklungsbank for EERE promotion – usually have sub loan sizes of around EUR 2,000 for private customers (housing loans) and on average EUR 69,000 for small and medium-sized enterprises. The sub loans thus are characterized by volumes which are not attractive for large international financial institutions. Nevertheless, the financing of a large number of smaller individual investments can make an important contribution to reducing greenhouse gases and increasing energy efficiency in transition and developing countries. That's why financial institutions with a good track record in serving the needs of SME clients and private households are at the cutting edge of implementing these innovative products. The provision of adapted loan products creates an incentive for small and medium-sized enterprises or private households in these countries to make investments in modern, energy-efficient equipment. It supports the countries in achieving economic growth and expanding their production capacities based on energy-efficient technologies with a more sustainable use of resources. In addition, providing corresponding financing products locally will create markets for environmental technologies and promote a CO_2 efficient economic development.

In order to address these issues, KfW has embarked on financing energy efficiency and renewable energy investments through the financial sector. It is now a global player in environmental finance. KfW is working with financial partner institutions in Asia, Latin America and the Caribbean, the MENA Region and Southeast/Eastern Europe. The total active portfolio in environmental finance sums up to EUR 789.1 million, of which EUR 651 million have been committed in 17 countries and EUR 138.1 million in regional and global funds devoted to environmental finance.

At bilateral level, KfW is supporting more than 38 partner institutions projects in 17 countries globally. The largest part (33%) of these credit lines has been committed to projects in Europe and Central Asia, with a total volume of EUR 337.4 million (45 projects in 8 countries). Latin America and the Caribbean follows with a volume of EUR 192.9 million (7 projects in 2 countries and several other countires through two regional partners). 8 projects have been supported in Asia with credit lines totalling EUR 134.2 million. and the MENA region with a volume of EUR 17.2 million (3 North African countries).

In South-Eastern Europe, KfW Entwicklungsbank has been refinancing environmental credit lines now for more than two years. The refinancing is carried out on a bilateral level at near-market conditions.

KfW also invests in two funds for renewable energy and energy efficiency (see Box 2 below). On behalf of the German Government, KfW holds a EUR 33 million equity participation in the *Green for Growth Fund Southeast Europe* financed out of Government funds as well as KfW's own funds. Its mission is to contribute to enhancing energy efficiency and fostering renewable energies in the Southeast Europe region including Turkey.

KfW committed to invest on behalf of the German Government another EUR 57.3 million of its own funds as well as funds form the German Government in the *Global Climate Partnership Fund.* The fund provides financial support to small and medium sized enterprises (SMEs) as well as private households in developing countries and emerging markets for investments in energy efficiency and renewable energies.

The context in which the local financial institutions operate in this regard is different from country to country. Some countries, such as Serbia and Turkey, have requirements and regulations that offer a legal incentive for investments in renewable energies and energy efficiency for small and medium-sized enterprises as well as private households. In this case it is easier for the financial institutions to provide their customers adequate financial products to support in fulfilling legal requirements.

Box 1: Project Example Yumis, Nis (Republic of Serbia)

The company Yumis has been active in food processing since 1991. Located near Nis (250 km northeast of Belgrade) the medium-sized enterprise produces instant soups, ice cream and roasted peanuts, among other products. In 2009 the company decided to upgrade the production line for producing the peanuts. A new, energy-efficient machine replaced a 16 year-old machine with a lower production capacity.

The production process requires two energy sources: electricity and diesel. While the energy consumption of the old and new machine is the same, the production volume has increased considerably, from 1,752,000 kg to 3,942,000 kg of peanuts. Thus the specific energy consumption – i.e. related to one kilogramme – dropped from 0.61 kWh/kg to 0.27 kWh/kg. This results in energy savings of 55.6% compared to the old machine, which alternatively could have been expanded to a larger production capacity. For the company this translates into a cost savings of EUR 121,791 per year, whereby the investment is amortised within a short period of time. The company's competitiveness has improved considerably due to the significantly lower energy costs.

The owner of Yumi became interested in energy efficiency for cost reasons. Based on the positive experiences gained from upgrading the peanut roasting machine and the resulting cost savings, the company now has built up a cooperation with the university in Nis to improve the energy management of the company. At the end of 2010 the company planned to convert the heating system from electricity to gas and install a new efficient boiler.

Other countries still lack the appropriate legal framework and incentive systems. In these markets, local financial institutions can act as a spearhead to promote investments in energy efficiency and renewable investments because they have a broad clients base and can create awareness for using energy efficient and resource-conserving technologies. By making their customers sensitive to the potential of energy efficiency and renewable energy, loan officers can contribute to generating demand for this kind of investments. These institutions know their region well and have contacts to local producers or importers of energy efficient technology or renewable energy products. In this regard the direct client relationship is key. But it is also important not to overburden the loan officers and thereby the financial institutions. This means that the loan officers can and should not be a replacement for a trained energy adviser or engineer. However, financial institutions should train their internal staff as well as those employees who are in direct contact with clients and work to anchor the principle of energy efficiency and the use of renewable energies in their businesses.

Local financial institutions are thereby enabled to establish themselves as "green", "eco-sensitive" financial institutions – which is often still rather a niche in those local markets than a mainstream pattern.

At the end of 2009, KfW Entwicklungsbank started on a new course of refinancing of financial institutions that is oriented towards promotion of investments in renewable energies and energy efficiency. The Green for Growth Fund Southeast Europe was founded in December 2009 with support of the European Union. Its global counterpart, the Global Climate Partnership Fund, was founded in the same year with support of the German Federal Ministry for the Environment. Both funds are structured funds for refinancing financial institutions.

Both funds have an advisory facility. This facility is a special account into which the fund posts a portion of its earnings, thus financing technical assistance for financial institutions in partner countries. Apart from start-up financing for establishment of the facility, it is self-sufficient and is not dependent on the constant supply of grant funding from public donors. The measures typically financed by this facility serve to support local financial institutions in the partner countries when introducing a EERE loan product. This also includes training employees to recognise the potential of corresponding investments and to assess the climate effects. Additionally, financial institutions are enabled to provide the funds with information on saved energy and reduced greenhouse gas emissions as a consequence of the financed investments. This information from the financial institution is naturally based on simplified assumptions and models in order to avoid prohibitive costs and enable the product to be used to finance small-scale measures. After a certain period of time impact analyses using representative samples will be conducted to increase the accuracy and informative value of the information provided. The first investments have started at the end of 2010. Combined, both funds will be supporting projects in over 22 countries worldwide.

Box 2: The Fund Approach – Intelligent Use of Public Funds

The Green for Growth Fund Southeast Europe (GGF) and the Global Climate Partnership Fund (GCP) are both structured in several tranches with different risk/return ratios. This allows investors to make investments based on their capacity and willingness to bear risk. The "junior tranche" usually consists of public donor grants which are available to the funds for unlimited duration. In addition, it is subordinate in relation to the other tranches (mezzanine and senior tranche), thereby serving as a risk cushion for these other tranches. This enables bilateral and multilateral development banks as well as private investors to invest in the fund. Bilateral and multilateral development banks mainly invest in the mezzanine tranche, which usually has a term of 10 – 15 years. If the funds of the junior tranche are depleted, further losses will initially be offset by the mezzanine tranche. Only after depletion of both the junior and mezzanine tranche, the investors of A-tranche (shares and notes held by international financial institutions and private investors would be affected.

This so-called waterfall structure allows scarce public funds to be intelligently used and leveraged with additional funds from public and private investors. In this way public funds and funds of international financial institutions help facilitate the involvement of private investors in promoting the private sector in developing countries. Depending on the region and the design of the funds, scarce public funds can be supplemented many times over with the funds of other investors.

The experiences gathered so far for broad-based refinancing of measures for energy efficiency and renewable energies show that it is important to convince the financial institutions of this concept. On the other hand, it is also important to convince individual customers of the economic advantages of such investments. These customers then serve as multipliers and examples for attracting further customers and as a focal point of a broader awareness raising. By the same token advantages of investments in renewable energies and energy efficiency for customers can be demonstrated, and existing technologies in the respective countries can be promoted. The use of innovative financial concepts such as structured funds not only help to bundle the resources of international donors, international development financial institutions and private investors, but also to harmonise their promotional approaches. By providing adapted loans through local financial institutions it is possible to support the promotion of energy efficiency and renewable energies in transition and developing countries with significant broad-scale effects, while also contributing to environmental financing and greenhouse gas emission reduction.

Index of Regions, Countries and Organisations

D. Köhn (ed.), *Greening the Financial Sector: How to Mainstream Environmental Finance in Developing Countries*, DOI 10 1007/978-3-642-05087-9,

V

W

MIX
Papier aus verantwortungsvollen Quellen
Paper from responsible sources
FSC® C105338
FSC
www.fsc.org

If you have any concerns about our products,
you can contact us on
ProductSafety@springernature.com

In case Publisher is established outside the EU,
the EU authorized representative is:
Springer Nature Customer Service Center GmbH
Europaplatz 3, 69115 Heidelberg, Germany

Printed by Libri Plureos GmbH
in Hamburg, Germany